insight

Intermediate Student's Book

OXFORD

Jayne Wildman

Cathy Myers   Claire Thacker

Unit	A Reading and vocabulary	B Grammar and listening
1 The way we are	**p4 The art of beauty** Reading Ideal beauty Strategy Guessing the meaning of unknown words Vocabulary Describing appearance Vocabulary insight Compound adjectives: appearance	**p6 Appearance and survival** Grammar Present simple and present continuous Listening Humans and survival
Vocabulary insight 1 p14 Recording vocabulary **Review 1 p15**		
2 Travellers' tales	**p16 The power of tourism** Reading A road less travelled Vocabulary insight Compound nouns: travel Vocabulary Travel	**p18 Memorable journeys** Grammar Narrative tenses Listening Alternative holidays
Vocabulary insight 2 p26 Using a dictionary: compound nouns **Review 2 p27** **Cumulative review units 1–2 p28**		
3 Feeling good	**p30 Happiness** Reading Is chocolate the answer? Strategy Identifying main ideas of paragraphs Vocabulary insight Idioms: happiness and sadness Vocabulary insight Noun suffixes: -ness, -ity	**p32 Healthy bodies, healthy minds?** Grammar Past simple and present perfect Listening Physical activity in school
Vocabulary insight 3 p40 Building word families through suffixes **Review 3 p41**		
4 A right to fight	**p42 Disappearing worlds** Reading Island story Vocabulary The environment Vocabulary insight Prefixes: semi-, under-, over-, re-, co-, inter-	**p44 Action!** Grammar Expressing the future Listening A Critical Mass bike ride
Vocabulary insight 4 p52 Word-building: the meaning of prefixes **Review 4 p53** **Cumulative review units 1–4 p54**		
5 Rights and wrongs	**p56 Teenage gangs** Reading The choice Strategy Using referencing to understand a text Vocabulary Crime Vocabulary insight Noun prefixes: mis-, dis-	**p58 Natural born liars** Grammar First and second conditionals Listening Moral dilemmas
Vocabulary insight 5 p66 Using a dictionary: phrasal verbs **Review 5 p67**		
6 Paying the price	**p68 Word on the street** Reading The influencers Vocabulary Advertising Vocabulary insight Collocations: advertising	**p70 Fair trade** Grammar The passive Listening A fair-trade fashion show
Vocabulary insight 6 p78 Using a dictionary: collocations **Review 6 p79** **Cumulative review units 1–6 p80**		
7 The senses	**p82 Taste** Reading A question of taste Strategy Understanding the purpose of a paragraph Vocabulary insight Perception and observation Vocabulary insight Adverb–adjective collocations	**p84 Beyond human senses** Grammar Reported speech Listening Dogs to the rescue
Vocabulary insight 7 p92 Using a dictionary: homonyms and homophones **Review 7 p93**		
8 Decisions	**p94 Think differently** Reading The big question Vocabulary Describing jobs Vocabulary insight Idioms: work	**p96 If they hadn't …** Grammar Third conditional; I wish and If only Listening Help from Heifer Listening Regrets
Vocabulary insight 8 p104 Using a dictionary: idioms **Review 8 p105** **Cumulative review units 1–8 p106**		
9 Digital humans	**p108 A day in the life** Reading A day in the life of a digital human Vocabulary insight Phrasal verbs: relationships Vocabulary insight Words often confused	**p110 Friendships now and then** Grammar Defining relative clauses Listening Online friendships
Vocabulary insight 9 p118 New words **Review 9 p119**		
10 Creativity	**p120 Art is everywhere** Reading The stories behind the names Strategy Summarizing what you read Vocabulary Abstract nouns: talent Vocabulary insight Phrases with and	**p122 Around the world in one dance** Grammar Participle clauses Listening Singing in the Rain
Vocabulary insight 10 p130 Fixed phrases with two key words **Review 10 p131** **Cumulative review units 1–10 p132**		

C Listening, speaking and vocabulary	D Culture, vocabulary and grammar	E Writing
p8 First impressions Listening First impressions Vocabulary insight Words often confused: personality adjectives Everyday English Speculating Grammar Speculating; *looks like, looks as if*	**p10 British fashion** Reading Fashion never forgotten Vocabulary Clothes and fashion Grammar Verb patterns	**p12 An informal email** Strategy Checking your writing Vocabulary Position
	Vocabulary bank 1 p134 Describing hair; Clothes	
p20 One journey, different travellers Listening Tourist or traveller? Strategy Identifying purpose Vocabulary Types of journey Everyday English Persuading and negotiating	**p22 America on the move** Reading The Mother Road Vocabulary insight Verbs + prepositions: travel Grammar *used to* and *would*	**p24 A story** Strategy Writing opening paragraphs Ordering events in a story
	Vocabulary bank 2 p135 Types of holiday; Travel and transport	
p34 Be a good sport! Listening Individual and team sports Vocabulary Values Everyday English Giving and reacting to news	**p36 Fat America** Reading Fat America Vocabulary insight Adverbs Grammar Present perfect simple and present perfect continuous	**p38 A personal letter** Strategy Showing your attitude Expressing reason and purpose
	Vocabulary bank 3 p136 Feelings: intensity; Health problems	
p46 Making our voices heard Listening An inspiring campaign Strategy Identifying facts, opinions and speculation Vocabulary insight Verbs + prepositions Everyday English Asking for and expressing opinions	**p48 Make a difference** Reading Go the Extra Mile Vocabulary insight Collocations: charities Grammar Future perfect and future continuous	**p50 An opinion essay** Strategy Organizing an opinion paragraph Introducing arguments and giving opinions
	Vocabulary bank 4 p137 Global issues; Charities	
p60 Sorry is the hardest word Listening Why we don't like to apologize Vocabulary insight Three-part phrasal verbs with *to* and *with* Everyday English Apologizing and accepting apologies	**p62 Young people's rights** Reading Coming of age Vocabulary insight Synonyms: the law Grammar Modals of obligation, prohibition and permission	**p64 A letter to a newspaper** Strategy Making suggestions and expressing results Grammar *should* and *ought to*
	Vocabulary bank 5 p138 Crime and punishment; Law and order	
p72 How to spend it? Listening Teenagers' spending habits Strategy Listening for specific information Vocabulary Describing amounts Everyday English Talking about photos	**p74 Traditional festivals** Reading Traditions for sale Vocabulary Trade Grammar *have / get something done*	**p76 A formal letter of complaint** Strategy Deciding on register: formal and informal Vocabulary Addition and contrast
	Vocabulary bank 6 p139 Types of advertising; Consumerism	
p86 Don't shout, I can see! Listening Teenagers with sensory impairments Vocabulary insight Noun suffixes: -ion, -sion Everyday English Complaining and asking people to do things	**p88 A Walk in the Woods (Bill Bryson)** Reading An extract from *A Walk in the Woods* Vocabulary Sight and sound Grammar Reported questions and commands	**p90 A report on survey findings** Strategy Making your writing flow Vocabulary Approximations and fractions
	Vocabulary bank 7 p140 Food texture; Ways of speaking	
p98 Important decisions Listening Decisions that made a difference Strategy Dealing with unknown words while listening Vocabulary Decisions and ideas Everyday English Giving presentations	**p100 Do the right thing** Reading A bus ride to freedom Vocabulary Conflict Grammar Speculating about the past	**p102 A covering letter** Strategy Avoiding general statements Vocabulary Action verbs
	Vocabulary bank 8 p141 Gender-neutral job titles; Conflict	
p112 Can't live without … Listening Favourite gadgets Vocabulary Describing gadgets Everyday English Asking for instructions, explanations and clarification	**P114 iPeople** Reading *Touchscreen* by Marshall Soulful Jones Strategy Understanding poetry Vocabulary insight Words with more than one meaning Grammar Non-defining relative clauses	**p116 A for and against essay** Grammar Introductory *It* Strategy Making your writing neutral
	Vocabulary bank 9 p142 Technology; Poetry	
p124 What's the point of art? Listening Art therapists Vocabulary Describing art Everyday English Debating	**p126 On stage** Reading Famous festivals Vocabulary insight Compound adjectives: describing events Grammar Determiners	**p128 A review of an event** Vocabulary insight Synonyms: evaluative adjectives Strategy Creating emphasis
	Vocabulary bank 10 p143 The arts; Organizing a festival	

1 SPEAKING Read the things that people do to change their appearance. Why do they do them? What other things do they do?

- put on weight ■ wear make-up ■ get a tattoo
- pierce lips, tongues, eyebrows ■ shave their heads
- stretch their necks with metal rings ■ go on a diet
- have cosmetic surgery ■ spray themselves with fake tan

2 Read the article about beauty in different cultures. Which things in exercise 1 are mentioned? Why do people do them?

STRATEGY

Guessing the meaning of unknown words

When you come across a new word, there are several things that you can do to help you guess the meaning:

1 Use the context. Looking at words before and after the unknown word and identifying the part of speech (noun, verb, etc.) of the word can help you to understand the meaning.

2 Understand a word through its different parts. You may already know one or more parts of the word.
sun + shine = sunshine

3 Use your own language. Sometimes the English word or part of the word is similar in your own language.
English = *norm* Dutch = *norm* Czech = *norma*
Polish = *norma*

3 Read the strategy. Then guess the meaning of the underlined words in the text. What helped you to guess: the context, understanding the different parts or your own language?

4 Read the text again and answer the questions.

1 What did Happiness Edem want to do?
2 What kind of images of beauty do we see in the media?
3 What is the traditional image of Egyptian women in paintings?
4 What significance do tattoos have in Borneo and New Zealand?
5 What do the people of Myanmar consider elegant?
6 Would you ever consider doing any of the things in the text?
7 Which things would you never do? Why?
8 What is the ideal of beauty in your culture?

V Describing appearance

5 Study the highlighted adjectives in the text. Which ones have a positive meaning, which a negative one and which can have both meanings?

Ideal beauty

Nigerian teenager Happiness Edem had just one aim in life: to put on weight. So she spent six months in a 'fattening room' where her daily routine was to sleep, eat and grow fat. She went in a trim 60 kg, but came out weighing
5 twice that. In some parts of Africa, being fat is desirable because it symbolizes attractiveness in women and power and prosperity in men. However, in magazines and in the media we are bombarded with images of slim, blonde-haired and sun-tanned women or handsome, blue-eyed and
10 broad-shouldered young men. Where are the short-sighted, middle-aged models? Is one idea of physical beauty really more attractive than another?

Ideas about physical beauty change over time and different periods of history reveal different views of beauty,
15 particularly of women. Egyptian paintings often show slender dark-haired women as the norm, while one of the earliest representations of women in art in Europe is a carving of an overweight female. This is the *Venus of Hohle Fels* and it is more than 35,000 years old. In the early 1600s,
20 artists like Peter Paul Rubens also painted plump, pale-skinned women who were thought to be the most stunning examples of female beauty at that time. In Elizabethan England, pale skin was still fashionable, but in this period it was because it was a sign of wealth: the make-up to achieve
25 this look was expensive, so only rich people could afford it.

Vocabulary: describing appearance, personality, fashion and style; position
Grammar: present simple and present continuous; speculating; verb patterns

Speaking: discussing ideals of beauty; speculating; discussing fashion
Writing: an informal email

1A

Within different cultures around the world, there is a huge <u>variation</u> in what is considered beautiful. Traditional customs, like tattooing, head-shaving, piercing or other kinds of body modification can express status, identity or beliefs. In Borneo, for instance, tattoos are like a diary 30 because they are a written record of all the important events and places a man has experienced in his life. For New Zealand's Maoris they reflect the person's position in society. In western society, where tattoos used to be considered a sign of rebellion, the culture is changing and they are now a 35 very popular form of body art.

For Europeans, the tradition of using metal rings to stretch a girl's neck may be shocking, but the Myanmar people consider women with long, thin necks more elegant. In Indonesia, the custom of sharpening girls' teeth to points 40 might seem strange to other cultures, but it is perfectly acceptable elsewhere to straighten children's teeth with <u>braces</u>. Body piercing, dieting, cosmetic surgery or the use of fake tan might be seen as ugly and unattractive by some cultures, but they are commonplace in many others. 45

It appears that through the ages and across different cultures, people have always changed their bodies and faces for a wide variety of reasons. Does this mean that underneath the tattoos, rings and piercings, we're all beautiful in our own way? 50

6 **Choose one word that you <u>cannot</u> use to complete each sentence.**

1 Most of my female friends go to the gym and keep fit to look **trim / slim / handsome**.
2 Happiness Edem went to a 'fattening room' because she wanted to be **plump / slender / overweight**.
3 There aren't many photos of **stunning / unattractive / fat** models in magazines.
4 Some cultures may find different forms of body modification **ugly / slender / unattractive**.
5 Women tend to spend more money than men on their general appearance in order to look **overweight / beautiful / attractive**.
6 Men usually wear suits because they want to look **elegant / handsome / ugly**.

V **insight** **Compound adjectives: appearance**

7 **Match the words in the circles to make compound adjectives. Check your answers in the text.**

blonde
blue short
pale middle
broad sun

+

-shouldered
-aged -haired
-tanned
-eyed -sighted
-skinned

8 **How many compound adjectives can you make with the words below?**

dark fair
straight long
blue green far

+

-sighted -skinned
-haired -eyed

9 **SPEAKING** **Work in pairs. Use the adjectives in exercises 5, 7 and 8 to make sentences about people you know.**

10 **SPEAKING** **Work in groups. Discuss the statements.**

1 The Western ideal of beauty is not beautiful.
2 Our society puts too much emphasis on appearance.

Vocabulary bank | Describing hair page 134

Hide-and-seek

Today, in the last in our series on wildlife, [1]we're looking at animals and their appearance. Why are polar bears white? Why do leopards have spots? Why do zebras have stripes? [2]It's all about survival.

Wild animals spend half their life looking for something to eat and the other half trying not to get eaten! Life is just one long game of hide-and-seek. Luckily for them, the way they look usually helps them. The zebra is a very good example.

[3]Zebras usually travel in large groups. Imagine [4]a hundred zebras are moving together across the savannah. [5]The herd is getting bigger and bigger. A lioness is lying under a tree, watching and waiting. The zebras are getting nearer, but they're running very close together. [6]The lioness sees a big mass of black and white stripes, so it's impossible for her to attack a single zebra. She's very annoyed, but what can she do? [7]The animals on the savannah are always trying to hide from her. Breakfast must wait.

But do zebras' stripes confuse other zebras like they confuse lions? No, they don't. Actually, they often help zebras to recognize each other. Every zebra has a different pattern of stripes and zoologists believe this is how zebras know who is who in the group. A mother zebra always recognizes her foal among the crowd because its stripes are just a little different from the others.

Present simple and present continuous

1 **SPEAKING Look at the photos and describe the animals. How can their appearance help them to survive?**

2 **Read the text and answer the questions.**
   1 How do zebras travel?
   2 Why can't the lioness attack an individual zebra?
   3 How does a mother zebra recognize her foal?

3 **Study sentences 1–7 in the text. Which ones are in the present simple and which are in the present continuous? Match sentences 1–7 to rules a–g. Then find more examples in the text.**

We use the present simple:
a to talk about routines or habits.
b to talk about facts and general truths.
c with verbs that describe states: *believe, have, know, like, need, think, see, seem, want, understand,* etc.

We use the present continuous:
d to talk about actions happening now.
e to talk about temporary situations.
f to talk about changing or developing situations.
g to describe an irritating habit, usually with *always.*

Time expressions:
Present simple: *always, every day, often, regularly, usually, sometimes, hardly ever, never, …*
Present continuous: *right now, at the moment, this week, …*

We often use the present continuous tense when we describe photos.

Reference and practice 1.1 | Workbook page 104

4 Use the prompts to make questions in the present simple or present continuous tense. Then match questions 1–7 to answers a–g.

1 Why / leopards / have / spots
2 What / the leopard in the photo / hunt for
3 How / a zebra's stripes / help it to survive
4 Why / polar bears / become / an endangered species
5 Why / a tree frog / bright blue
6 How / peacocks / attract / a mate
7 Why / stick insects / look like / sticks

a Because the ice where they live is melting.
b It's hunting for its dinner.
c So that their enemies can't see them.
d So that the animals they are hunting can't see them coming.
e They help to confuse its enemies.
f It's warning its enemies that it's dangerous.
g They usually show off their feathers.

5 Complete the text with the correct form of the verbs in brackets.

Mimicry

Animal survival is a fascinating and complex subject. As these photos [1]................................ (show), nature usually [2]................................ (play) tricks on us. Two insects [3]................................ (sit) on a flower. They both [4]................................ (look) like bees, but one of them [5]................................ (not be) a real bee. It [6]................................ (imitate) a bee in order to protect itself from possible predators. The real bee on the left [7]................................ (have) a sting, which it uses as a weapon to attack its enemies. However, the hover fly on the right [8]................................ (not be) dangerous. It's completely harmless. This imitation of one species by another often [9]................................ (happen) in nature and is called mimicry. Animals [10]................................ (copy) the appearance, actions or sounds of another animal and this [11]................................ (help) them to survive.

6 🔊 **1.01** Listen to an interview about humans and survival and answer the questions.

1 How does Dr Walker describe the boy's appearance and personality?
2 How does Dr Walker describe the girl's appearance and personality?

7 🔊 **1.01** Listen again and answer the questions.

1 What is the boy doing while he's walking?
2 How is the girl walking?
3 What is she doing while she's walking?
4 How do 'streetwise' people usually act?
5 What does the girl need to be careful about?
6 What does the boy do which people might find aggressive?

8 **SPEAKING** Work in pairs. Look at the photo and use the questions below to describe one person to your partner. Can your partner identify the person you are describing?

1 What does the person look like?
2 What are they doing?
3 What do you think their personality is like?
4 Are they streetwise? Why / why not?

1 SPEAKING Work in pairs. How important are these things when you form a first impression?

■ height ■ clothes ■ personality ■ eyes ■ body language
■ facial expressions ■ age ■ hair colour and style
■ tone of voice ■ attractiveness

A

2 ◉ 1.02 Listen to an interview with a psychologist. Which of the things in exercise 1 does she say influence our first impression of someone?

3 ◉ 1.02 Listen to the interview again. Are the sentences true (T) or false (F)? Correct the false ones.

1 It takes a long time for the human brain to process a first impression.
2 In the past, humans needed to form first impressions quickly in order to escape from dangerous situations.
3 What a person says has more impact than a friendly expression or gesture.
4 We make assumptions about a person's personality based on their physical appearance.
5 Handsome or attractive people always make a good first impression.
6 If you are happy and relaxed, you will usually create a positive first impression.
7 If you look happy, the negative parts of your character are not so important.
8 People with tattoos and piercings always create a negative impression.
9 A negative first impression is not difficult to change.
10 You need to get to know a person better to change your first impression.

V | insight Words often confused: personality adjectives

4 Study the adjectives from the interview and match them to the definitions. Which adjective in each pair has a negative meaning?

1 lazy / easy-going
   a relaxed and happy to do whatever people want
   b not liking to work or use energy
2 determined / stubborn
   a not letting anything stop you doing what you've decided to do
   b not willing to change your decision or consider anyone else's opinion
3 modest / shy
   a not feeling confident in the company of people you don't know
   b not wanting to talk about the things you do well
4 sensitive / emotional
   a having intense feelings about things and showing them
   b being aware of your own feelings and other people's
5 arrogant / assertive
   a thinking you are better and more important than others
   b expressing your opinions and feelings in a confident way

5 Complete the sentences with an adjective in exercise 4.

1 Sarah is very .... She's achieved a lot in her life, but not many people know about it.
2 I like getting up late at the weekend, but that doesn't mean that I'm ....
3 Zack is so .... – he never listens to anyone's advice.
4 Harriet is very relaxed with people she knows, but in a new situation she's very ....
5 Jenny always knows if you're not happy. She's very .... to others.
6 Frank has a very superior attitude to everyone around him. He's really ....
7 Carl finds academic work quite difficult, but he wants to succeed. He's very ....
8 Jed is very easy to get on with and he never worries about anything. He's so ....

6 SPEAKING Work in groups. Prepare four tips on how to make a good first impression. Then compare your tips with another group and agree on the best three tips.

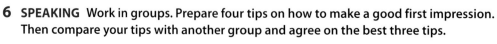

B   C   D   E

Speculating

7 **SPEAKING** Work in pairs. Look at the photos. Which words in exercise 4 would you use to describe the people? Why?

8 🔊 **1.03** Listen to two dialogues about two of the people in the photos in exercise 7. Which two people are they talking about?

9 🔊 **1.03** Complete the phrases from the dialogues. Then listen and check.

Speculating	
Modal verbs	***look / look like / look as if***
He [1] .... be in his thirties.	He [6] .... younger than I expected.
He [2] .... understand us better.	
She [3] .... be nearly two metres tall.	He [7] .... a typical head teacher.
seem	She [8] .... she's an Olympic athlete.
[4] .... nice?	
[5] .... easy-going.	

10 🔊 **1.04** Listen to the two people talking about themselves. Which words do they use to describe themselves?

11 🔊 **1.05** Complete the dialogue about another person with the phrases below. Then listen and check. Which person in the photos are they talking about? Underline two more phrases for speculating.

■ he could be the new school secretary then ■ looks nothing like him ■ this one looks much older than that ■ But he seems nice ■ He must be our new science teacher then ■ That might be his dad ■ they both look happy ■ No, he can't be ■ He looks as if he's a manager of a big company

Amber	Who's that guy in the suit talking to Craig?
Samuel	[1] ....
Amber	No, I know Craig's dad. This guy [2] ....
Samuel	[3] .... It's the only teacher we haven't met yet.
Amber	[4] .... The new science teacher is in his thirties and [5] ....
Samuel	Well, [6] ....
Amber	No way. [7] ....
Samuel	I know what you mean. [8] .... He's been chatting to Craig for quite some time now and [9] ....

12 **SPEAKING** Work in pairs. Discuss your first impressions of the other people in the photos.

1 SPEAKING Work in pairs. Discuss the questions.

1 What influences the way you dress?
   ■ friends ■ brothers and sisters ■ music
   ■ fashion magazines ■ the weather ■ parents

2 Where do you buy your clothes? Do you ever make changes to the things you buy?

3 What's your favourite item of clothing? Why do you like it?

2 What do you know about these fashion styles: mod, hippie, punk, goth? Read the text and compare your ideas. Then complete the text with sentences A–F. There is one sentence that you do not need.

A I bought ordinary T-shirts, cut holes in them, fastened them with safety pins and then wrote things on them using a marker pen.

B And although it's dark, it's a very pretty look, with lots of lace for the girls.

C We were the first generation that didn't <u>need to do</u> that, so we had money to spend on stylish clothes.

D It was important that the clothes were very comfortable to dance in.

E That's what happened before the 1960s brought the age of teenage rebellion and young people started their own innovative and original fashion styles.

F And it wasn't just the girls – the boys <u>liked wearing</u> pink and purple flowery designs, too!

V Clothes and fashion

3 Study the highlighted words in the text and in exercise 2. Then match them to definitions 1–6.

1 used by someone before ....

2 using a style from the recent past ....

3 completely new and different ...., ...

4 fashionable in a way that looks expensive ...., ...

5 with a famous name ....

6 a high quality example of something made in the past ....

4 SPEAKING Work in pairs. Use the adjectives in exercise 3 to describe the clothes and style of people you know.

5 SPEAKING Work in pairs. Answer the questions.

1 How did teenagers change in the 1960s?

2 Why did mods have money to spend on clothes in the 1960s?

3 Which of the fashions mentioned in the text do you think is the: cheapest? most expensive? most modern? most old-fashioned?

4 Which of these fashions is your favourite? Are any of them popular in your country?

5 What fashions have there been since 2000, in your country, and around the world? Are they connected with styles of music?

DVD extra Junky Styling

Fashion never forgotten

Can you <u>imagine dressing</u> in exactly the same way as your parents? ¹ .... The different 'looks' were started by the new rock and pop bands, who often came from the UK. Four British people remember the excitement of being part of these fashion movements, which they still see alive in retro fashion today.

Mod fashion started in the early 1960s. Most mods were fans of the rock band The Who. They often fought with 'rockers', who were traditional rock and roll fans with leather jackets and motorbikes.

'In the difficult economic times before the 60s, parents <u>expected teenagers with jobs to pay</u> rent. ² .... The mod look wasn't cheap – the classic outfit was a slim-fitting suit with a shirt and thin tie, and pointy leather shoes. There was a more casual mod look, too. Although it borrowed a lot from Italian and French style, we <u>liked to give</u> it a very British character, with Union Jacks and RAF emblems. It's a fashion that'll always be popular with people who like to dress smartly.' **Alan, the mod**

Hippie fashion started in the USA, but in the London of the late 60s, the designer boutiques of Carnaby Street and the King's Road made it more chic. It was popular with fans of the Rolling Stones and The Beatles.

'I sometimes spent a lot on hippie-style clothes – I had a fabulous purple dress that cost a fortune! But for the real hippie look, I bought things in second-hand shops. Long skirts and flared trousers <u>seemed to be</u> everywhere, in all kinds of bright colours. ³ .... I can see a return to the hippie look in the 'festival style' young people wear to music festivals today.' **Carol, the hippie**

Punk fashion became popular with the British punk bands of the late 1970s, the Sex Pistols being the most famous. Punks were anti-pop music, anti-government, and … anti-everything, even fashion!

'You <u>might think</u> all punks were angry and aggressive, but a lot of us were just having fun and <u>enjoyed dressing</u> in ways that would shock people. We <u>wanted to have</u> a kind of fashion that was cheap and 'do-it-yourself', so we <u>avoided buying</u> things from fashion shops. ⁴
Piercings became fashionable with punk and the hair was an important part of the look. You still often see people with a Mohican haircut today.'   **Jack, the punk**

The goth look started with the 'gothic' rock bands of the 80s and 90s, which came out of the British punk scene. Much of the style comes from the Victorian period in Britain.

'It's easy to say what the most important thing about goth fashion is – black! It <u>can be</u> leather trousers, long dresses, boots or gloves, but black is the first choice of colour. ⁵
You can find some great goth clothes in vintage shops. I loved goth culture as a teenager – it's perfect for those times when life seems sad and serious. The goth style seems to be more and more popular these days, especially with all the interest in vampire books and movies.'   **Gemma, the goth**

Verb patterns

6 **Study the rules below. Then add the underlined verbs in the text and in exercise 2 to 1–4.**

1 Verbs + infinitive with *to*: decide, promise, choose, ... , ... , ... , ...

2 Verb + infinitive without *to*: shall, must, could, will, ... , ...

3 Verb + *-ing*: suggest, consider, admit, ... , ... , ...

4 Verbs + infinitive or *-ing*: love, ...

Reference and practice 1.2   Workbook page 105

7 **Complete the second sentence so that it has a similar meaning to the first sentence. Use the correct form of the verbs in brackets.**

1 a I never thought I would see so many punks in Japan!
   b I never .... so many punks in Japan! (expect)
2 a 'Let's go to the festival in Reading,' said Mike.
   b Mike .... to the festival in Reading. (suggest)
3 a I'm thinking of buying that black leather coat.
   b I .... that black leather coat. (consider)
4 a Looking for vintage clothes is something we enjoy.
   b We .... for vintage clothes. (love)
5 a My mum said she'll buy me some new boots for my birthday.
   b My mum .... me some new boots for my birthday. (promise)
6 a It looks like 1980s fashion is popular again.
   b 1980s fashion .... popular again. (seem)

8 **Study sentences 1–5. What is the difference in meaning between sentences a and b?**

1 a I remember wearing flared trousers when I was young.
   b I remembered to wear flared trousers to the sixties party last Saturday.
2 a I'll never forget seeing that photo of your dad dressed as a punk!
   b Don't forget to bring that photo of your dad dressed as a punk – I want to show it to Mark.
3 a They stopped to look in the shop window.
   b They stopped looking in the shop window.
4 a I tried changing my clothes before I went out, but I still wasn't happy.
   b I tried to change my clothes before I went out, but I didn't have enough time.
5 a I regret spending all your money.
   b I regret to tell you that I spent all your money.

9 **SPEAKING Complete the questions with the correct forms of the verbs in brackets. Then work in pairs and answer the questions.**

1 Why do you think people want .... (be) fashionable?
2 Have you ever chosen .... (wear) something in order to shock people?
3 Can you imagine ever .... (dress) like your parents?
4 Do you think you'll need .... (change) the way you dress when you start work?
5 Are there any colours you avoid .... (wear)?
6 Have you ever tried .... (have) your hair longer or shorter?
7 Where do you most enjoy .... (shop) for clothes?
8 Which item of clothing do you most regret .... (buy)?

1 **SPEAKING** Read the advert and answer the questions.

1 Does your school have a partner school? Where is this school?

2 Do you or your friends email students in other countries? What do you write about?

Link up! 🚶🚶🚶🚶🚶🚶🚶🚶🚶🚶🚶

We are looking for young people to link up with students in our partner school in South Africa. The students are all aged between sixteen and eighteen and are studying for their final exams. They want you to email them, so that they can learn more about your lives, families, friends and school. If you are interested, come to the meeting in Room 5 after break on Thursday 16th to hear more about the *Link up* project.

STRATEGY

Checking your writing

When you finish a piece of writing, remember to check your work for mistakes. Always check the following:

a **Punctuation:** commas, full stops, question marks, speech marks, capital letters, exclamation marks, colons, apostrophes.

b **Spelling:** use a dictionary to check the spelling of words.

c **Grammar:** check that you have used the correct tenses.

d **Word order:** check that all the words are in the correct order and that the sentences make sense.

e **Vocabulary:** use a dictionary or a thesaurus to check that you have used the correct word. Watch out for false friends (words that are similar in your own language, but mean something different).

Correction marks

Here are some of the most common correction marks:

p = punctuation   sp = spelling   gr = grammar   wo = word order   ww = wrong word; vocabulary

2 Read the strategy. Then correct the sentences. There is one mistake in each sentence. Match each mistake to a–e in the strategy.

1 I live with my famly in Abingdon, near Oxford.

2 Does your brother like to carry football tops?

3 Im studying for my final exams.

4 I lives with my family in the centre of Bristol.

5 On Saturdays, we go always to the park to play football.

6 What do you like to do in your free time

3 Read Elise's email for the *Link up* project. Then correct the mistakes.

4 Read Bert's first *Link up* email and answer the questions.

1 How does he start the email?

2 What kind of information does he include in each paragraph?

3 How does he sign off?

V **Position**

5 Complete the phrases that Bert uses to identify people in the photo. Then find the phrases in Bert's email and check your answers.

■ ¹.............. the back / front ■ ².............. front of ■ in the middle ³.............. ■ ⁴.............. the left / right of ■ on the right / left ■ ⁵.............. the top / bottom / right-hand / left-hand / corner ■ in the foreground / background ■ behind

6 Look at the photo. Match Bert's friends to descriptions 1–6.

This person is …

1 to the left of Kara. ....

2 in the middle of the top row. ....

3 in front of Ellie. ....

4 in the bottom right-hand corner. ....

5 in the top left-hand corner. ....

6 behind Felix. ....

Hello Adela,

My names Elise and I write to you as part of the Link up project at my school. I'm your new e-pal and I'm very excited about writting to someone in South Africa.

I live in a small flat near the centre of antwerp with my elders, my brother Johan and my dog, Max. I enjoy play hockey and I for a local team play and my school team. We're not very good and we're always losing matches, but we have fun when we play.

I'm ataching a photo of myself and my friends on our last school trip. I'm the dark-haired girl in the middle. My best friend Larissa is the tall one on my right. She wears a white T-shirt and jeans. She's quite shy, but we get on well together and she's got a very good sense of humour.

Please email me back and send me a photo. Tell me about your life and your friends.

Bye for now,

Elise

▶ 🖉 1 photo attached

Hi Peter,

My name's Bert and I'm from Belgium. I'm writing to you as part of the Link up project. I live in Ghent with my parents and brother. There are 900 students in my school, but only eighteen in my class. I usually walk to school with my friends.

I enjoy foreign films and I'm a member of a film club. I'm attaching a photo of me and my friends from one of our film nights. I'm the dark-haired one in the middle of the bottom row. The guy in the top left-hand corner is my friend Yura. The blonde-haired girl to the right of Yura is Marianne. The attractive girl behind me is Ellie. She's very clever, but modest, too. At the back, behind Ellie, is Kara. The guy in the top right-hand corner is Dirk. He's my best mate. We always play football together at the weekend. And my brother Felix is in front of Dirk.

Can you send me a photo of you and your friends when you email me back?

I hope to hear from you soon.

Bye for now,

Bert

WRITING GUIDE

■ **Task** Write an informal email in reply to the online advert below.

Wanted: e-friends

We have a partner school in Rotterdam, Holland. They are looking for e-friends for their sixteen-year-old students. They want to email students in different countries to practise their English and to find out more about life in other places. Tell them about life in your country, school and friends. Please attach photos and describe yourself and your friends.

■ **Ideas** Make notes about:

- yourself and where you live.
- your family.
- where your friends are in the photo.
- what they look like and what they are wearing.
- what they are like: their personalities and what they like doing.

■ **Plan** Follow the plan:

Paragraph 1: Introduction. Write about yourself and your family.
Paragraph 2: Describe a photo of your family or friends.
Paragraph 3: Ask your e-friend to send you a photo.
Paragraph 4: Ask when they will email you and sign off.

■ **Write** Write your email. Use the paragraph plan to help you.

■ **Check** Check the following points:

- Have you used the correct email format and register?
- Have you included all the information asked for in the task?
- Have you followed the paragraph plan?
- Have you checked grammar, vocabulary, spelling, punctuation and word order?

1 Work in pairs. What ways of learning new vocabulary do you know? Rank them from the most useful to the least useful. Give reasons for your ranking.

2 Study vocabulary records A–D and answer the questions.

1 Which method of recording new vocabulary is similar to your own method?

2 Which method do you think is most useful? Which is least useful? Why?

A
stunning = (translation in your own language)

B
S
slender (adj) thin (in an attractive way)
slim (adj) thin (in an attractive way)
status (n) social position
stretch (v) make longer
stunning (adj) very attractive

C
Tue, 10 Oct
Appearance
a handsome man
a pretty woman
overweight / fat
slim / trim

D
stunning (adjective) = (informal) very attractive
/ˈstʌnɪŋ/
Synonym: beautiful
Rosie Huntington-Whiteley is stunning.
(translation in your own language)

STRATEGY

Recording vocabulary: what to record

It is important to keep good records of new vocabulary.

▪ Decide where you will record new words, for example, in a special notebook or in a document on your computer.

▪ Decide what information you need to record about the word. Some things to record are: part of speech, pronunciation, synonyms, antonyms or collocations. You will find all of this information in a good dictionary. Look for other information that tells you about the typical context in which the word is used. For example, the label *informal* tells you that you should only use the word with friends and family.

3 Read the strategy above. Put the information from vocabulary record D in exercise 2 under the correct heading.

1 word .... stunning

2 part of speech ....

3 synonym ....

4 translation ....

5 example ....

6 use (context) ....

4 Study the dictionary entry for *gorgeous* and write your own vocabulary record. Then compare with a partner.

gorgeous /ˈgɔːdʒəs/ *adj* (*informal*) extremely pleasant or attractive: *What gorgeous weather!* ♦ *You look gorgeous in that dress.* ➔ note at **beautiful** ▸ **gorgeously** *adv*

STRATEGY

Recording vocabulary: context

When you make your own vocabulary records, it is important to write when you can use a particular word. Some words have similar meanings, but they are used in different contexts, for example, formal / informal / neutral situations, when referring to men / women / children, or when showing a positive or negative attitude.

A good dictionary will tell you about the situations in which a word is typically used. In the *Oxford Wordpower Dictionary*, notes with the heading 'OTHER WORDS FOR' compare it with words that have a similar meaning. They also tell you the typical context that the word is found in.

5 Read the strategy above. Then study the dictionary entries for *thin* and *fat*. Answer the questions using the words in bold in the entries.

1 Which words would a doctor use?

2 Which word would a friend use to pay you a compliment?

3 Which word would you use to describe a child?

4 Which word is an impolite way of saying that someone is overweight?

5 Which word is an impolite way of saying that someone is too thin?

> **OTHER WORDS FOR**
>
> **thin**
> **Thin** is the most general word for describing people who have very little fat on their bodies. **Slim** is used about people who are thin in an attractive way: *You're so slim! How do you do it?* If you say a person is **skinny**, you mean that he/she is too thin and not attractive. **Underweight** is a formal word, and is often used in a medical context: *The doctor says I'm underweight.*

> **OTHER WORDS FOR**
>
> **fat**
> It is not polite to describe sb as **fat**. **Large** and **overweight** are sometimes used instead: *She's a rather large lady.* ♦ *I'm a bit overweight.* Generally it is not polite to refer to sb's weight when you talk to him/her. **Chubby** is mainly used to describe babies and children who are slightly fat in a pleasant way: *a baby with chubby cheeks.* Doctors use the word **obese** to describe people who are very fat in a way that is not healthy.

6 Choose the correct answers.

1 He's a very cute and **large** / **chubby** baby.

2 The doctor said I was **skinny** / **underweight** and had to put more weight on.

3 'Look at that man. He's so **fat** / **obese**.' 'You can't say that!'

4 Tom's very **skinny** / **slim**. He doesn't look good.

5 Anna is so lovely and **underweight** / **slim**.

7 Find the words below in a dictionary. For each word, write an example sentence that shows it in its typical context.

▪ attractive ▪ beautiful ▪ handsome ▪ pretty

Dictionary entries from *Oxford Wordpower Dictionary*, 4th edition

Vocabulary

1 Complete the sentences with the words below. There is one word that you do not need.

■ elegant ■ handsome ■ overweight ■ plump ■ slender ■ stunning ■ unattractive

1 I think too much make-up is actually ....
2 Stylish and .... clothes don't need to be expensive.
3 Both Robert Pattinson and Taylor Lautner are very ...., but who is more attractive?
4 More than a billion adults globally are unhealthily ...., with many being obese.
5 Most ballerinas are very .... in order to be light.
6 It's official: Ukrainian women are ....! In 2012, they were voted the most beautiful in the world.

Marks .... / 6

2 Complete the sentences with compound adjectives. Use the words in brackets.

1 I'm very .... I never tan. (pale-)
2 Magazines are full of blonde-haired and .... models. (blue-)
3 She had dark hair when she was younger, but now she's .... (blonde-)
4 I'm ...., so I'll need a bigger jacket. (-shouldered)
5 You're .... Have you been on holiday? (-tanned)
6 I'm not .... I'm only 35! (-aged)

Marks .... / 6

3 Complete the sentences using the correct adjective form of six of the nouns below.

■ arrogance ■ assertiveness ■ emotion ■ laziness ■ modesty ■ shyness ■ stubbornness

1 Luke never works hard. He's ....
2 Katie hates meeting new people. She's ....
3 Mark thinks he's better than everyone else. He's ....
4 Jo refuses to change her mind. She's ....
5 Al always says what he wants. He's ....
6 Sofia's very quiet and .... about her success.

Marks .... / 6

4 Replace the words in italics with the words below.

■ chic ■ designer ■ innovative ■ second-hand ■ retro ■ stylish

Trainers are popular because they're both comfortable and [1]........................... (*fashionable*). Converse's early black and white design has become a [2]........................... (*vintage*) classic, and [3]........................... (*owned before*) Converses sell for lots of money. Many top fashion houses now sell [4]........................... (*expensively branded*) ranges. In 2007, American retailers decided to do something [5]........................... (*new and different*) and created some gold Nikes. They cost $50,000 – but they do look [6]........................... (*fashionable and expensive*)!

Marks .... / 6

Grammar

5 Complete the sentences with the present simple or present continuous tense.

1 'Look at that cheetah! How fast .... (it / run)?' 'Over 110 kph!'
2 'How many hours .... (pythons / sleep) every day?' 'Eighteen.'
3 'How long .... (flies / live)?' 'Two to three weeks.'
4 'Which animals eat while .... (they / lie) on their backs?' 'Sea otters.'
5 'Look at that hummingbird!' 'It .... (fly) backwards!'
6 'Male mosquitoes never .... (bite) humans.'
7 'Zebras normally .... (eat) all day.'
8 'That lion .... (not hunt). Why?' 'Male lions .... (not usually / hunt).'

Marks .... / 10

6 Complete the dialogue. Use the present simple or present continuous form of the verbs below and the words in brackets.

■ change (×2) ■ do ■ give ■ leave ■ mean ■ seem ■ think

Jake Do you see that? What [1]........................... (that chameleon)?
Mike It [2]........................... colour. Oh wow. It was green. Now it's purple!
Jake Why [3]........................... (chameleons) colour?
Mike They mainly use colours to communicate.
Jake What message [4]........................... (you) that one [5]........................... us right now?
Mike Darker colours [6]........................... (usually) it's angry.
Jake Well, that chameleon [7]........................... very angry, It's now black!
Mike Oh dear. We [8]........................... now, OK? Sorry for bothering you!

Marks .... / 8

7 Complete sentence b so that it has a similar meaning to sentence a.

1 a Do you want to go to the concert?
  b She suggested ....
2 a I think I might dye my hair red.
  b I'm considering ....
3 a Buying these shoes was a mistake.
  b I regret ....
4 a Packing a swimsuit is essential.
  b Don't forget ....
5 a Buying designer brands isn't compulsory.
  b You don't need ....
6 a Why don't you wear a belt with that?
  b Try ....
7 a It looks like clothes are getting cheaper.
  b Clothes seem ....
8 a I'm getting a piercing when I turn 18.
  b I decided ....

Marks .... / 8

Total .... / 50

Reading and vocabulary The power of tourism

1 SPEAKING Work in small groups. What do most people do on holiday? Agree on the three most typical activities from the list below.

■ find out about local communities ■ learn a new language ■ make new friends ■ eat local food ■ use public transport ■ buy local crafts ■ help with conservation projects ■ relax by the pool ■ try to save water ■ get a good suntan ■ read a good book

2 Read the definition of responsible tourism. What things in exercise 1 would a responsible tourist do? Then read the text. Why is Guludo Lodge a good example of 'responsible tourism'?

> **Responsible tourism (n)** Travel that does not harm the cultural or natural environment. It can improve the life of local people and help protect the environment.

3 Read the text again and put the events in the correct order.

1 Education and health projects changed people's lives.
2 A charity was set up to help local people.
3 Amy completed her studies at college.
4 She worked in a school for free.
5 Amy and Neal decided to use tourism to help people.
6 Their work was recognized by the tourist industry.
7 They found a place for their lodge.
8 Jobs were created for people in the village.

4 Answer the questions.

1 What gave Amy the idea to help people through tourism?
2 Why did Amy and Neal decide to go to Mozambique?
3 What helped Amy and Neal to achieve their dream?
4 In what ways did the new beach lodge help local people?
5 How can you get to Guludo Lodge?
6 What can you see and do there?
7 What does the word 'nema' mean?

5 SPEAKING Discuss the questions.

1 What do you think about Amy and Neal's achievements?
2 In what other ways can we be responsible tourists? Think about:
 ■ how you get to a holiday destination.
 ■ what you use when you are there.
 ■ what you do when you are there.
 ■ what you leave behind.
 ■ what you bring back.

A ROAD LESS TRAVELLED

Amy Carter-James is small, blue-eyed and blonde, with a friendly smile. She doesn't look like she could change the lives of thousands of people but, remarkably, she has.

It all started when Amy took a gap year in Africa
5 after she finished university. 'I spent eight months volunteering in a very poor rural school in Kenya,' she says. 'That was the first time I saw poverty, I was so young and so easily inspired and I thought, "Why can't tourism do the same thing for community
10 development?" '

On her return to England, twenty-two-year-old Amy and her boyfriend Neal decided to take 'the road less travelled'. They drove across Mozambique, one of the poorest countries in Africa, but it wasn't exactly a
15 holiday. Mozambique had two qualities which appealed to them: great potential as a travel destination and local people who desperately needed help. Once there, the couple got off the beaten track and headed for Quirimbas National Park, where they found a tiny
20 stretch of white sand close to a village called Guludo. Life in Guludo was hard: there was little clean water and not enough food. Healthcare was poor and people in the village had a life expectancy of thirty-eight years. Amy and Neal had no qualifications in tourism or
25 healthcare but they had common sense, enthusiasm and determination. They talked to the villagers about their plan to create a small beach resort which would provide employment for people and lift families out of poverty. 'We took a translator with us,' says Amy. 'Their only
30 question was: 'When can you start?'

Vocabulary: compound nouns: travel; travel; types of journey; verbs+prepositions: trave
Grammar: narrative tenses; *used to* and *would*

Speaking: discussing ideal holidays, memorable journeys; persuading and negotiating
Writing: a story

2A

The couple set to work on a beach lodge, building beach huts from local materials and employing people from the surrounding area. Once the lodge was complete, they set up a charitable foundation called NEMA, which received 5% of its revenue. This money was used to create clean water points, fund healthcare projects, build two primary schools and support conservation projects – it helped to improve the lives of thousands of people. 'We wanted to show the world the power of tourism, that it could be a vehicle for change,' says Amy.

It isn't easy to get to Guludo. It's not a typical package holiday with airport pick-ups and drop-offs. There's no public transport, either. The nearest city is Pemba and once there, you have to take a helicopter, a boat or go on a three-hour car journey along bumpy roads. But Guludo Lodge is worth the effort. Today the lodge has nine 'bandas', or beach huts, with beautiful sea views. There are no overpriced souvenir shops and other tourist traps. It's the perfect place to take time out, escape the crowds and soak up the sun. Visitors can see the sights – explore Ibo island with a tour guide, go scuba diving or observe African wildlife at the Mogandula Bush Lookout. But the highlight for many is getting to know people in the village, taking part in festivals and learning about NEMA's work. 'People who stay with us often come for the diving or the beach,' says Amy, 'but it's the communities that really blow them away.'

People like Amy and Neal believe that the tourist industry can do much good in the world and Guludo Lodge is leading the way, winning many awards for its responsible tourism. Back in the village, people are talking about NEMA. In the local dialect, it's a word with a special meaning. 'It's difficult to explain,' says Amy, 'but it means that kind of hope that accompanies the end of suffering.'

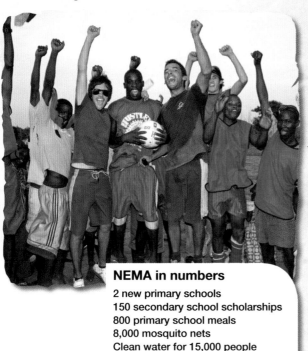

NEMA in numbers

2 new primary schools
150 secondary school scholarships
800 primary school meals
8,000 mosquito nets
Clean water for 15,000 people

V insight **Compound nouns: travel**

6 Match the words in A to the words in B to make compound nouns. Then check your answers in the text.

A ■ beach ■ national ■ package ■ public ■ tourist
■ tour ■ travel

B ■ destination ■ guide ■ holiday ■ park ■ resort
■ trap ■ transport

7 Read the text. Then replace the phrases in italics with compound nouns in exercise 6.

The world's highest rubbish dump

It's one of the most famous places in the world and thousands of people have been there. But it isn't a [1]*place for a holiday by the sea* and you can't use [2]*a regular bus or train service* to get there. It isn't [3]*an organized holiday from a travel agent*, with the usual [4]*shops that sell overpriced souvenirs* and the [5]*person who shows tourists around* will probably be a sherpa! As a [6]*place for holiday makers*, it's pretty unusual – it's Mount Everest.

Everest is part of a [7]*protected area of land* in Nepal. Many endangered species live there, such as snow leopards and black bears, but the park and these animals are suffering. The problem is rubbish.

Every year, hundreds of climbers leave rubbish on the mountain, everything from food cans to oxygen cylinders and even fridges! A group of climbers do regular clean ups, but there is still more than a hundred tonnes of waste to collect. Even the world's highest mountain can't escape the negative impact of tourism!

V Travel

8 Complete the descriptions with the correct form of the verbs below. Then check your answers in the text.

■ escape ■ get off ■ get to know ■ see ■ soak up ■ take
■ take part in

When we go away, we like to [1]................ the beaten track, away from the usual tourist destinations. That's the point of a holiday – to [2]................ from the crowds and have an adventure!

I like to [3]................ time out, lie on the beach, read a good book and [4]................ the sun. The weather isn't great at home, so I never usually sunbathe.

My family like to [5]................ guided tours and activities – we always [6]................ the sights. Last year, I tried snowboarding with my brother. It was fun because we [7]................ some local people and made new friends.

9 SPEAKING Work in pairs. Which description in exercise 8 is your idea of a good holiday? Give reasons for your answer.

Vocabulary bank Types of holiday page 135

ATLANTIC CHALLENGE
... the world's toughest
rowing race

From Tenerife to Barbados:
3,000 km, two rowers, one boat.

Are you tough enough to compete?
Apply online at www.row...

1 SPEAKING **Read the advert for the Atlantic challenge and discuss the questions.**

   1 What type of event is it?
   2 What might the challenges be?
   3 If you took part in the event, who would you choose as your rowing partner?
     ■ your best friend ■ your mum / dad ■ your teacher ■ someone famous

2 **Read part 1 of the story. Who was supposed to be Daniel's rowing partner? What happened? What do you think happened next?**

Part 1
[1]Jan Meek usually **got** home from work at 6 o'clock and today was no different. [2]She **made** herself a cup of tea and **looked** out of the kitchen window. [3]It **was raining** and cold outside – not good weather for building a boat. Jan had an uneasy feeling and decided to check her answering machine. There was a message from her son, Daniel, and it wasn't good news. [4]At the time, 21-year-old Daniel **was preparing** to compete in the Atlantic challenge with a friend. Unfortunately, his friend had just called him with some bad news. He didn't have the time to prepare for the race, so Daniel had to find another partner, someone with enough free time to raise money, build a boat and to train! [5]The boat **was** very small and the race was long, so it also had to be someone he could get on with. [6]Jan phoned her son and asked him what **had happened**. Then [7]while Jan **was suggesting** solutions, Daniel **interrupted** her …

Narrative tenses

3 **Read part 1 of the story again. Then match sentences 1–7 to rules a–g.**

We use the past simple for:
a a past state.
b a past habit.
c a sequence of actions in the past.
We use the past continuous for:
d background descriptions.
e an action or actions in progress at a specific time in the past.
We use the past simple and the past continuous for:
f a longer action interrupted by a shorter action.
We use the past perfect for:
g an action or event that happened before another action in the past.

Reference and practice 2.1   Workbook page 106

4 **Complete part 2 of the story with the correct form of the verbs in brackets. Then answer the questions.**

   1 Who did Daniel ask and why?
   2 Why did they agree?
   3 What was good / bad about the journey?

Part 2

Surprisingly, Daniel ¹................................ (ask) his fifty-year-old mum to be his rowing partner. His mum ²................................ (never / row) in her life, but she was very adventurous. The previous year she ³................................ (study) Chinese in Taiwan, then she had gone backpacking round the world on her own. Jan said 'yes' because she ⁴................................ (know) that the race was a 'once-in-a-lifetime' opportunity.

Two years and many hours of training later, Jan and Daniel ⁵................................ (arrive) in Tenerife. At last they were ready to take part in the race – they ⁶................................ (raise) enough money and they ⁷................................ (build) a good boat. On the boat, there was enough food for 100 days, as well as books and music for entertainment. They ⁸................................ (also / ask) friends to write them letters and poems, so they had something to open during the difficult days ahead.

Once the race ⁹................................ (start), Jan and Daniel realized just how hard it was going to be. The rowing was tiring, they couldn't wash and they were constantly soaked with salt water. There were terrible days when they wanted to give up, but there were also good days. While they ¹⁰................................ (row), they saw dolphins, whales, and flying fish. They also ¹¹................................ (get) to know each other extremely well.

In the end, the journey ¹²................................ (take) 101 days – two months longer than the winners of the race. Jan and Daniel thought that everyone ¹³................................ (forget) about them. But when they arrived in Barbados, people ¹⁴................................ (wait) on boats to greet them. Everyone ¹⁵................................ (cheer) and waving, and there was music and fireworks. People wanted to congratulate them on their amazing achievement!

5 🔊 **1.06** **Listen to a radio show about Jan and Daniel. What did they do next?**

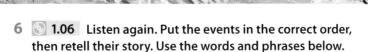

6 🔊 **1.06** **Listen again. Put the events in the correct order, then retell their story. Use the words and phrases below.**

■ before (the expedition) ■ by the time (they arrived) ■ first ■ next
■ then ■ after ■ while ■ when ■ in the end

Jan and Daniel thought about giving up.
They went on a course to learn survival skills.
They had a bad accident.
Jan suffered from frozen hands.

They learned how to use a gun.
Friends followed their blog posts.
They were ready to start the expedition.
They broke another world record.

7 **Choose the correct answers.**

1 Jan and Daniel **had been** / **were** on an adventure together before the polar challenge.
2 Before they left, they **were starting** / **started** a blog about their expedition.
3 They were well-prepared because they **had trained** / **trained** for over a year.
4 They took a gun because a polar bear **had attacked** / **attacked** another team.
5 One of the tents that they **brought** / **had brought** burnt down.
6 They packed up their remaining tent, then **carried on** / **were carrying on** with their journey.
7 Halfway through their journey, they realized that they **hadn't packed** / **didn't pack** enough food.
8 By the time they reached the pole, they **had raised** / **raised** a lot of money for charity.

8 **SPEAKING** **Work in pairs. Ask and answer questions about a memorable journey you have had. Use the ideas below.**

Think about:

■ where you went.
■ what you had packed / read / done before your journey.
■ who you travelled with.

■ what you did / saw on the journey.
■ how you were feeling before, during and after.
■ what you thought about the journey.

1 SPEAKING Work in pairs. What are the differences between these travellers? Where do they normally spend their holidays? What are the pros and cons of each type of travel?

■ armchair traveller ■ staycationer ■ adventure tourist ■ globetrotting backpacker ■ holidaymaker

STRATEGY

Identifying purpose

When you listen to people talking, try and identify the purpose of the conversation. Listen for:

■ the context. How many people are speaking? Who are they? Where are they?

■ how the speakers feel. Are they angry, happy, bored, interested, worried?

■ why they are speaking: to make an arrangement / give an opinion / give instructions / make suggestions, etc.

2 ◎ 1.07 Read the strategy. Listen to the radio show. Which of the travellers in exercise 1 are speaking? Why are they calling in?

3 ◎ 1.07 Listen again and match each speaker 1–4 with two sentences a–h.

1 Luca   2 Noah   3 Katrina   4 Jed

a likes to visit places that aren't popular.
b says travelling is hard work.
c thinks typical tourist holidays are boring.
d finds out about places on a computer.
e likes to tell stories about his / her travels.

f disapproves of people on package tours.
g is aware of the environmental impact of travel.
h doesn't like to go away for a long time.

V Types of journey

4 Study the highlighted words in sentences 1–7. Then match them to definitions a–g.

1 Last summer, I went on a trek through the Alps.
2 I also went on a ten-day voyage around Antarctica, whale watching.
3 I'm not an explorer. I've never been on a polar expedition.
4 I also prefer short trips or weekends away to local places.
5 A flight to Thailand would produce a lot of CO_2.
6 They go on coach tours which stop off at popular tourist attractions.
7 They go on planned excursions to crowded museums.

a A journey by air.
b A long journey which is often scientific.
c A journey in a ship or a spacecraft.
d A difficult walk, lasting several days or weeks.
e Travelling from place to place with an organized group.
f A short outing to one place for pleasure.
g A short or long journey for business or pleasure.

5 SPEAKING Work in pairs A and B. Choose a role card and prepare a dialogue between a travel agent and a tourist.

Student A
You are a travel agent. Think about what visitors can see and do in your town. Decide which activities and places would appeal to different types of tourist. Listen to Student B, then give advice about what they can see and do.

Student B
You are a tourist. Tell student A what you want from your holiday and what type of activities you enjoy. Ask them for advice about what you can see and do.

Persuading and negotiating

6 **SPEAKING** Work in pairs. Read the adverts. Which tour of London would you like to try? Give reasons for your answer.

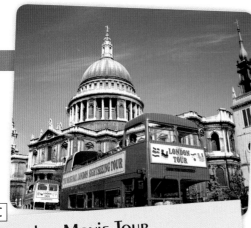

A

City Jogging Tours

Join us as we guide you through 2,000 years of history on London's most exciting sightseeing tour. Our 6 km running tour stops off at many of London's most famous sights, such as Trafalgar Square, the London Eye, Big Ben and the Houses of Parliament. Experience London in a memorable and healthy way – book a City Jogging Tour now!

2 hour tour £8

B

EAST END EXPLORER

An insider tour of East London. Discover:
* colourful street art down tiny side streets
* fascinating shops, including London's best record store
* the story behind Brick Lane, Spitalfields Market and more

We guarantee you'll see loads of places you'll want to visit again … and again!

2 HOUR TOUR £12

C

LONDON MOVIE TOUR

Visit different film locations in and around London. See locations for *The Dark Knight*, *The Bourne Ultimatum*, *Pirates of the Caribbean 4* and many more. Our guides are all local actors and actresses and great storytellers!

3 HOUR TOUR £25

7 🔊 **1.08** Listen to a dialogue between a tour guide and two tourists. Which tour in exercise 6 are they talking about? How does the tour guide persuade them to join the tour?

8 🔊 **1.08** Complete the phrases from the dialogue. Then listen again and check.

Persuading and negotiating	Reaching agreement
If you …, I'll give you … . You've got [1]................................. to lose. That sounds [2].................................., but … . I'm not so [3]................................. . I still think … . You won't be [4].................................. .	Well, you've [5]................................. me. OK, let's [6]................................. for it.

9 🔊 **1.09** Put the dialogue in the correct order. Then listen and check.

.... **Nick** OK, but I still think we should go on a tour. Look, here's another one. It's called East End Explorer and there's a local person as the tour guide.

.... **Fran** Hmm, I prefer to explore things on my own. It's more fun and you get to meet local people.

.... **Nick** Why don't we go on a tour?

.... **Fran** We've got a free morning tomorrow. What shall we do?

.... **Nick** Yes, and you can go shopping, too!

.... **Fran** That sounds interesting, but the weather forecast isn't great and I don't fancy running in the rain.

.... **Nick** Maybe, but we haven't got much time and a tour is a good way to see the sights quickly, don't you agree? Look, here's a leaflet for a city jogging tour.

.... **Fran** OK, you've persuaded me! Let's book it.

.... **Nick** Great! You won't regret it!

.... **Fran** So we would get to know local people.

10 Read the dialogue again. Underline more ways of persuading and negotiating, and reaching agreement.

11 **SPEAKING** Work in pairs A and B. Choose one of the tours in exercise 6 and persuade your partner to go with you.

Student A
You are very sporty and like to be active. You also like visiting famous places and ticking them off your '100-things-to-see-before-you-die' list. You think the idea of a jogging tour is great. It's also cheap and you don't want to spend loads of money. Persuade your friend.

Student B
You are really interested in film and think the film tour sounds amazing. It's expensive, but you're willing to pay because it's a 'once-in-a-lifetime' experience. Your friend is not that interested in film, they'd rather go jogging. But they do want to see the sights. Persuade them.

1 SPEAKING Look at the photos and discuss the questions. Then read the text and check your ideas.

1 What type of places do the photos show?
2 What other things might you see along the road? Think about natural and man-made attractions.

2 Read the text again. Are the sentences true (T) or false (F)? Correct the false ones.

1 Route 66 connects the East coast of America with the West coast.
2 The road made life easier for people in big cities.
3 Unusual weather conditions caused the great migration.
4 In the 1930s, it was easy for farmers to find work in California.
5 In the 1940s, the road was given a new name.
6 The road became popular because of its tourist attractions.

3 SPEAKING Are there any famous routes in your country? What are the most popular tourist attractions? Are they connected to any historical events?

V insight Verbs + prepositions: travel

4 Choose the correct prepositions. Then check your answers in the text.

1 It was getting dark so we headed **with** / **for** the nearest motel and booked a room for the night.
2 We followed the path and it led us **to** / **for** a small river, deep in the forest.
3 The interstate highway connects **to** / **along** Route 66 at Williams, Arizona.
4 When we came to the crossroads, we decided to travel **around** / **down** the road to California.
5 To get to the service station, you have to drive **along** / **with** the main road and turn left.
6 The road winds **around** / **for** mountains and lakes. The views are spectacular.
7 We were late, so we cut **down** / **through** the park.

DVD extra | Chicago to LA

used to and would

5 Study sentences 1–5 in *The Mother Road*. Then complete the rules with *used to*, *would* or the past simple.

a We use .... or .... for repeated past actions or habits that do not happen now.
b We can also use .... or the past simple tense for states (= state verbs) in the past, that have changed or are different now.
c We can't use .... or .... when something only happened once.
We use ....

Reference and practice 2.2 | Workbook page 107

The Mother Road

It's over 4,000 km long and crosses two-thirds of the USA. It's been called 'The Mother Road' and 'The Main Street of America'. It's been in films, books and songs and there's even a piece on display at the Smithsonian Museum in Washington. Welcome to Route 66.

Route 66 starts in the hustle and bustle of Chicago. Outside the city, it cuts through cornfields and the open plains of the West, into gold mining towns and ghost towns, over deserts and through valleys, winding around lakes and mountains, until it arrives in Los Angeles on the Pacific Ocean. Midwest America is connected with the West coast, and the past is connected with the present. Let's go back to the 1920s to see how it all began.

1920s

In the early 1920s, life in Midwest America was very different. ¹People didn't use to travel much because there were no highways* near the small towns – ²a trip to LA would usually take weeks. But in 1926, things started to change thanks to a new road called Route 66. This new road opened up the American West to hundreds of thousands of people. ³Agricultural communities that used to be isolated started to grow and develop into towns. Farmers were also able to sell their produce to big cities.

1930s

In the mid-1930s, hard times returned. America was suffering from the Great Depression and across the country, millions of people were out of work. In the Midwest, severe drought conditions and dust storms destroyed farmland and thousands of families were forced to leave their homes. They headed for California, along Route 66, where they had heard there were agricultural jobs. Unfortunately, the mother road led them to shanty towns* outside towns and cities, where they lived in terrible poverty. Route 66 became associated with the pain and misery of this great migration.

1940s–1950s

[4]When the Great Depression came to an end after World War II, there was a new age of optimism and thousands moved from East to West, looking for a better life. People had more free time and many owned cars. [5]Families wouldn't stay at home during hoildays. Instead, they would drive along Route 66 to the beaches of California, visiting the Grand Canyon and other attractions along the way. It was boom time for the road and hundreds of diners, motels and service stations lined the route. Billboards and huge statues tempted tourists to stop at man-made and natural attractions, such as the giant Blue Whale in Oklahoma or the Meramec Caverns in Missouri. Then jazz musician Bobby Troupe wrote the hit song Route 66. The mother road had a brand new image – one of freedom and fun.

1956–present day

As more people travelled from East to West, a newer, bigger road was needed and work began on a national interstate highway. Sadly, the towns and attractions along Route 66 began to die out. Then in the 1990s, people started campaigns to preserve the old road, new signs were put up and tourists began to travel down it once again.

Today, the mother road still offers an amazing journey through the American West. Whether you want the freedom of the open road, a trip into the past, or simply a greasy burger from an all-American diner, you can still 'get your kicks* on Route 66'.

* highways = main roads in America, usually 8 lanes wide

* shanty towns = areas outside a town where poor people live in homes made out of cardboard and wood

* get your kicks = have a good time

---

6 Complete the text with the correct form of the verbs in brackets and *used to* or *would*. Sometimes both may be possible.

WILLIAMS, ARIZONA

Williams, Arizona, on Route 66, is a small town 50 miles from the Grand Canyon National Park. Today, the town is a popular tourist attraction, with steam train rides and Route 66 memorabilia. But in the past, life [1] .... (be) very different in Williams, Arizona.

In 1882, 250 people [2] .... (live) in Williams. The town had a few dirt streets with log cabins and tents and everyday life [3] .... (be) very dangerous. Cowboys [4] .... (often / have) 'gunfights' in the streets and outside the town outlaws [5] .... (often / rob) stagecoach passengers or travellers on horseback.

Day-to-day life was hard, too. Back then, there [6] .... (not be) a school, so children [7] .... (stay) at home. They [8] .... (help) their parents to milk cows, collect wood and grow vegetables. They [9] .... (not play) much because there were so many chores to do. When they did have free time, families [10] .... (entertain) themselves with picnics in the forest, violin music, or simply reading aloud from a book.

7 SPEAKING Write sentences using *used to* or *would* about life in your town in the past.

Think about:
- houses and homes.
- transport: how people got around.
- free time and entertainment.
- everyday life.

Vocabulary bank Travel and transport page 135

1 SPEAKING Work in pairs. Look at the photos and answer the questions.

1 Where are these places?

2 What type of traveller would go there?

3 What adjectives would you use to describe these places?

2 Read about a competition from a travel magazine. Then read extracts A–D from four competition entries. Match them to photos 1–4.

Travellers' Tales Writing Competition

This month is all about Travellers' Tales. Send in tales of your weird or wonderful journeys and you might appear in next month's magazine. One lucky winner will go on the trip of a lifetime – a Greyhound Bus Tour round the USA!

A

The Australian Outback is a very big place. It went on as far as the eye could see. I tried to start the car again, but the engine died. 'That's it,' said Jez. 'What do we do now?' He was starting to panic. 'Just wait,' I replied calmly. 'And if nobody comes? It's hot out here and we only have one bottle of water.' 'Look,' I replied angrily, 'I don't know, OK? Let's just hope someone comes along.' That's when we noticed the small sign a few hundred metres down the road. We ran over to it and read: 'William's Creek 20 km'. 'We could walk there …,' I thought.

B

'How much?' I asked, pointing to the bottle of water. '10 rupees' replied the street vendor, smiling. I gave him a couple of coins, then walked back towards the platform, just in time to see my train leave the station. 'Hey!' I yelled as I ran after it, pushing through the crowds of people. But it was too late. By the time I got to the platform, the train had gone, along with my backpack. I had to think fast – the next stop was Delhi, at least an hour away. But how could I get there in time?

C

It was raining hard as we drove along Route 66. It was late and we were tired and looking for a place to stop. After a while we saw some neon lights ahead. They belonged to a motel, so we decided to take a break. The motel café was deserted. The waitress behind the counter looked up, but she didn't smile. 'We're out of pancakes and fries,' she said as she handed us the menu 'but I can do y'all a hamburger.' We were eating our hamburgers, when a motorcycle gang stopped outside. 'Time to move on,' I thought, but the rain was getting worse. Suddenly, the lights went out.

D

Some time ago, we went to Guatemala on holiday. While we were there we took a trip to the rainforest, to take photos of monkeys and exotic birds. Sounds like a typical traveller's tale, doesn't it? But it isn't. At first, everything went smoothly. Backpacks were packed, cameras were ready and the guide arrived on time. We jumped into his jeep and eventually we were driving along a narrow track deep into the forest … that's when we saw it.

STRATEGY

Starting a story

When you write a story, your opening sentence should grab the reader's attention and get them interested.

Start with:

1 a quote from a character in the story, that introduces a main event.
2 a description of the weather, the time of day and how you were feeling. It establishes the atmosphere.
3 a description of the location, especially if it's unusual.

Try not to start with:

4 when the event happened, like *Last summer, A few weeks ago, The year before last* … etc. But if you do, make it interesting by adding something surprising.

3 Read the strategy. Then read extracts A–D again and match them to 1–4 in the strategy. Which story do you think will be the most interesting? Why?

Ordering events in a story

4 Complete 1–4 with the highlighted words and phrases in extracts A–D.

   1 Start of a sequence of events: In the beginning, To start with, … .
   2 Show how a story moves on: A few minutes later, Just then, … .
   3 Show that two events happen at the same time: As, … .
   4 End of a sequence of events: In the end, Finally, …

5 Work in pairs. Discuss what happens next in each story A–D.

6 Read the rest of story A. Were your ideas similar or different?

---

¹ .... we were still walking. ² ...., we'd felt confident, but ³ .... we'd run out of water. Our road trip round Australia was turning into the holiday from hell. The sun was hot and ⁴ .... we stopped talking and just walked. Then ⁵ .... something hopped onto the road ahead. It was a red kangaroo, about two meters tall. ⁶ .... we got closer it didn't move, it just sat there looking at us. 'Don't show that you're afraid,' I said, as we carefully took a detour around it. There was something strange about it.

We carried on walking, but a few kilometres later Jez had had enough. 'We're never going to get out of here,' he complained. ⁷ .... we heard a distant buzzing noise. 'Look!' I cried excitedly. There in the distance was an old red truck, speeding down the road. ⁸ .... it reached us and stopped, and a farmer jumped out. 'What are you boys doing here?' he asked. 'Is that your car back there?' 'Yes, it is …' 'Well, you're lucky,' he interrupted. 'Don't use this road much, but we're looking for a kangaroo, a sick one and nasty – it attacked the dogs on the farm this morning.' I looked at Jez and he looked at me. 'Get in,' the farmer added. We did, of course. It was a long time before we visited the Outback again.

---

7 Complete the story in exercise 6 with the words and phrases below. There might be more than one possible answer.

   ▪ eventually ▪ two hours later ▪ finally ▪ at first ▪ after a while ▪ suddenly ▪ as ▪ just then

---

WRITING GUIDE

▪ **Task** Write your own entry for the travel competition.

▪ **Ideas** Brainstorm ideas for your story. Think of questions beginning with *Who / Why / What / Where / When*. Then answer them.
   Decide how you are going to start your story. Use the strategy to help you.

▪ **Plan** Decide which ideas you are going to use and match them to these paragraphs.
   Paragraph 1: Begin your story in an interesting way. Introduce the main character(s), the place and the type of journey.
   Paragraph 2: Develop the story, describing the events in the order that they happened. Use the words and phrases in exercise 7 to help you.
   Paragraph 3: Bring your story to an end. Did anything happen to end your journey? Did someone help you continue it? Did anything funny, strange, scary happen?

▪ **Write** Write your story. Use the paragraph plan to help you.

▪ **Check** Check the following points:
   ▪ Does the story start in an interesting way? Is there a variety of adjectives and adverbs?
   ▪ Is the story divided into logical paragraphs? Does the sequence of events make sense?
   ▪ Have you checked grammar, vocabulary, spelling and punctuation?

1 Work in pairs. Study the highlighted words in the extract from the text on page 17. What part of speech are all the words?

It isn't easy to get to Guludo. It's not a typical package holiday with airport pick-ups and drop-offs. There's no public transport, either. The nearest city is Pemba and once there, you have to take a helicopter, a boat or go on a three-hour car journey along bumpy roads. But Guludo Lodge is worth the effort. Today the lodge has nine 'bandas' or beach huts, with beautiful sea views.

STRATEGY

Using a dictionary to find compound words

A compound is a word made up of two or more words. The meaning of the compound word is different from the meaning of its individual parts. Compounds can be written as one word or as separate words (sometimes hyphenated). A good dictionary will tell you how to write them.

The most common compounds in the English language are compound nouns. Typical compound noun combinations are:

1 noun + noun
2 adjective + noun
3 noun + verb
4 verb + preposition

2 Read the strategy above. Then match the highlighted compound nouns in exercise 1 to types 1–4 in the strategy.

3 Study the dictionary entry for *tour*. How many compound nouns does it list? What types of compound nouns are they?

tour /tʊə(r); tɔː(r)/ *noun* **1** [C] a tour (of/round/ around sth) a journey that you make for pleasure during which you visit many places: *to go on a ten-day coach* **tour** *of/around Scotland* ✦ *a sightsee-ing tour* ✦ *a* **tour** *operator* (= a person or company that organizes tours) ➲ note at **travel 2** [C] a short visit around a city, famous building, etc: *a* **guided tour** *round St Paul's Cathedral*

4 Complete the sentences with compound nouns from the dictionary entry in exercise 3.

1 We were taken on a .... around the museum and learned a lot about the various pieces of art.
2 We didn't enjoy the .... because we sat in one place for too long and there was no space to stretch our legs.
3 During the .... we saw the most important monuments in the city.
4 We normally book our holiday with a .... because they arrange everything for us.

STRATEGY

Word order in compound nouns

The first word in a compound noun is like an object, and it is usually in the singular, even if it has a plural meaning. For example:

holidays that schools have = school holidays (not schools holidays)

5 Read the strategy above. Study the dictionary entries for *resort* and *holiday*. Then complete the sentences with the correct singular or plural form of the compound nouns.

resort[1] /rɪˈzɔːt/ *noun* [C] a place where a lot of people go to on holiday: *a seaside/ski resort* ➲ note at **holiday**

holiday /ˈhɒlədeɪ/ *noun* **1** (*AmE* vacation) [C,U] a period of rest from work or school (often when you go and stay away from home): *We're going to Italy for our summer* **holidays** *this year.* ✦ *How much holi-day do you get a year in your new job?* ✦ *Mr Phillips isn't here this week. He's away* **on holiday**. ✦ *I'm going to* **take a** *week's* **holiday** *in May and spend it at home.* ✦ *the school/Christmas/Easter/summer holi-days* **2** [C] a day of rest when many people do not go to work, school, etc. often for religious or nation-al celebrations: *Next Monday is a holiday.* ✦ *New Year's Day is a* **bank/public holiday** *in Britain.*

1 resorts on the beach ....
2 holidays in the summer months ....
3 a resort where skiers go ....
4 a holiday during Christmas ....
5 a resort by the seaside ....

6 Match the words in A to the words in B to make compound nouns. Check your answers and the spelling in a dictionary.

A ▪ holiday ▪ school ▪ travel ▪ theme ▪ guide
B ▪ park ▪ resort ▪ book ▪ holiday ▪ agency

7 Complete the sentences with the compound nouns in exercise 5.

1 We always buy a .... to read about the places we're travelling to.
2 My class went to a .... last week. Everyone had a great time and we tried all the rides.
3 The .... we booked our holiday with specializes in coach tours abroad.
4 I can't wait for the .... to start. No homework for six weeks!
5 The .... we stayed in last time didn't have any sports facilities, so we decided to go somewhere else this year.

Dictionary entries from *Oxford Wordpower Dictionary*, 4th edition

Vocabulary

1 Match the words in A to the words in B to make compound nouns. Then use the compound nouns to complete the sentences.

A ▪ national ▪ package ▪ public ▪ tour ▪ travel ▪ tourist

B ▪ destination ▪ guide ▪ holiday ▪ trap ▪ park ▪ transport

1 Thomas Cook invented the first .... with travel and accommodation in 1841.
2 Disneyland, Paris, is Europe's most popular ....
3 The first kind of .... was the ferry boat.
4 Polar bears live in the world's biggest .... in Greenland.
5 Before becoming an author, John Steinbeck worked as a ....
6 The souvenir shop in the museum was a real .... – everything was overpriced.

Marks .... / 6

2 Complete the collocations with verbs.

1 We prefer to .... off the beaten track.
2 We .... time out from school.
3 I love to .... up the sun on the beach.
4 I try to .... to know the local people.
5 We explore the area and .... the sights.
6 I like to .... the crowds and go somewhere peaceful.

Marks .... / 6

3 Complete the sentences with the words below. Use each word only once.

▪ expedition ▪ flight ▪ tour ▪ trek ▪ trip ▪ voyage

1519–1522	Magellan led the first sea ¹.................. round the world.
the 1700s	Art and history ².................. s of Europe became fashionable for rich young people.
1903	The Wright brothers made the first ³.................. in an aeroplane.
1911	Machu Picchu was rediscovered. Now thousands of walkers go on ⁴.................. s there every year.
1911	Roald Amundsen's ⁵.................. reached the South Pole, using boats, dogs and horses.
today	A short day ⁶.................. from London to Edinburgh and back takes less than a day.

Marks .... / 6

4 Complete the text with the correct prepositions.

'Turn left here and head ¹.................. Ballyrigg. Drive ².................. this road for 10 km. It winds ³.................. fields and plains and cuts ⁴.................. a valley. Keep going until the road connects ⁵.................. the B105. Go east here, and the road will eventually lead you ⁶.................. the castle.'

Marks .... / 6

Grammar

5 Complete the text with the past simple, past continuous, or past perfect form of the verbs in brackets. Include a time word where given.

In April 2012, Laura Dekker ¹.................. (become) the youngest person to sail around the world. Journalists ².................. (hurry) to interview her as soon as she ³.................. (complete) her voyage. The sixteen year old ⁴.................. (just / spend) 518 days at sea, so at the time of the interviews she ⁵.................. (feel) quite tired! But she ⁶.................. (say) she was very happy. Just before Laura finished her journey, she ⁷.................. (celebrate) her sixteenth birthday – by eating doughnuts for breakfast! While she ⁸.................. (travel), she also ⁹.................. (spend) time surfing, diving, and playing the flute. She explained that the flute was easier to play than a guitar while strong winds ¹⁰.................. (blow)!

Marks .... / 10

6 Complete the sentences. Use the past simple, past continuous or past perfect form of the verbs below.

▪ already leave ▪ climb ▪ download ▪ lie ▪ listen ▪ lose ▪ not go ▪ take

1 They .... maps from the internet yesterday.
2 This time yesterday I .... on the beach.
3 It was a place that I .... to before.
4 The coach .... when I arrived.
5 We .... part in a tour. Then we went shopping.
6 When the plane landed they .... to music.
7 I broke my leg while I .... the mountain.
8 She was upset because she .... her passport.

Marks .... / 8

7 Complete sentence b so that it has a similar meaning to sentence a. Use between two and five words, including *one* of the words in brackets.

1 a We had a daily swim in the sea. (would / use)
  b We .... in the sea every day.
2 a My first meeting with Alice happened last summer. (met / meet)
  b I first .... last summer.
3 a We went to the beach resort every summer. (use / would)
  b We .... every summer.
4 a The idea of 'responsible tourism' is new. (use / wouldn't)
  b The idea of 'responsible tourism' .... exist.
5 a 2012 was the year of my holiday to Peru. (used / went)
  b In 2012 .... Peru on holiday.
6 a Travelling by coach was a regular habit of ours. (would / didn't)
  b .... by coach.
7 a I've only just started to enjoy family holidays. (would / to)
  b I .... family holidays.
8 a Were you keen on camping when you were young? (use / used)
  b .... like camping when you were young?

Marks .... / 8

Total .... / 50

Listening

1 🔊 **1.10** Listen and match speakers 1–4 to options A–E. There is one option that you do not need.

Which speaker's holiday:

A did not have good facilities? ....

B was quite expensive? ....

C did the speaker not book ahead? ....

D was very relaxing? ....

E does the speaker regret taking? ....

Speaking

2 Work in pairs. Look at the photos of different holiday accommodation. Speculate about where these places might be, why people might choose to stay in them and what a stay might be like.

3 Work in pairs and follow the instructions.

1 Each choose a different photo from exercise 2. Imagine you are planning a holiday with your partner. Try to persuade him / her to choose your accommodation.

2 Negotiate a compromise with your partner. Agree a place to stay, but make sure both of you feel happy!

Reading

4 Complete the text *House swapping* with sentences A–H.

A Firstly, there are the profiles.

B They cost a fortune!

C Luckily, she seemed to like what we'd written, too.

D By the time my boyfriend came home from his Saturday job, it was spotless.

E Well, yes and no. It isn't for everyone.

F A flat above an all-night bar didn't make the list, either.

G What if they make a mess?

H Thanks to them, we discovered a wonderful jazz café – and a roller disco!

House swapping

by Annie Toase

It was the night before my holiday and I was already exhausted. I'd just spent the whole day frantically cleaning the flat. [1]............... I'd even dusted the lights! My easier-going other half found my efforts very amusing. 'Aren't holidays meant to be relaxing?' he asked.

We'd joined *HouseExchange.com* a few weeks ago, when we'd been searching for cheap holidays online. Package holidays were out of the question. [2]............... I'm a student nurse and Max is a musician, so money is tight. But *HouseExchange.com* allows you to stay in someone's home in a beautiful tourist destination – for free!

So what's the catch? Well, while you're away, strangers will be staying in your home. [3]............... Or laugh at your bad taste in furniture? The worries don't end there. What if *you* don't like *their* home? It's important to choose your house swap with care!

HouseExchange.com is a bit like a dating service in two respects. [4]............... Everyone has to write one of these in order to 'sell' their home and neighbourhood. Secondly, site users are often quite fussy! After all, few of us want to swap with just 'anyone'.

5 Read the text. Choose the correct answers.

Paris

Paris is a 'dream' destination for many foreign tourists. Some love shopping in the boutiques and admiring the fashions. Parisians are famous for their **1**................, modern style and effortless elegance. Other tourists immediately **2**................ for the museums and art galleries, especially the astonishing *Louvre*. Other people simply enjoy spending their time relaxing and soaking **3**................ the atmosphere. But, like all big cities, Paris can **4**................ a lonely place at times! If you'd like to meet other travellers during your stay, why not attend our 'Polyglot Picnic'? We **5**................ this free event every Sunday at 3 p.m., for visitors who **6**................ for language exchange, food and fun. You can **7**................ the noise and crowds in a beautiful city park near the university. It's a great way to **8**................ to know people in the area and to make friends from around the world. Everyone is very welcome, so there's no need to be **9**................. No one is a stranger here and you'll quickly feel welcome. We **10**................ a small group in the past, but now hundreds of people join us every summer. We hope you'll join us, too. Please bring a frisbee, badminton racket, game or music to share. And of course, a smile!

	a		b		c	
1	a	chic	b	vintage	c	trim
2	a	head	b	journey	c	travel
3	a	with	b	on	c	up
4	a	to be	b	be	c	being
5	a	are holding	b	held	c	hold
6	a	like to look	b	look	c	are looking
7	a	listen	b	escape	c	join in
8	a	take	b	get	c	become
9	a	shy	b	modest	c	sensitive
10	a	were being	b	would be	c	used to be

For this reason, I'm afraid I rejected the home of a charming middle-aged couple, who had a rules list that was thirty pages long! **5**................ I even dismissed an exquisite house in the heart of Paris 'which you can share with my pet snakes' – for obvious reasons.

However, Rika's Berlin flat looked stylish and clean in the photos – and Rika herself sounded refreshingly 'normal'! **6**................ At least, she sounded very positive! I think the house-swap worked out well for all of us. We admired Rika's amazing collection of art and she said she loved our stylish 'retro' furniture (I think she was being kind – we bought it second-hand because it was cheap!).

As well as all the benefits of staying in a home-from-home, house swapping is a great way to feel like a local on holiday. Many of Rika's neighbours said 'hello', and recommended places to visit. **7**................ Neither were mentioned in the guidebook, so we felt like real 'explorers'.

Would I recommend it? **8**................ Being open-minded is a must and yes, you do have to be prepared to do quite a bit of housework before you travel! But as a way to travel for virtually nothing, you can't beat it.

6 Imagine you are joining *HouseExchange.com*. Write a profile for the website. Include information about:

* you (your name, where you live, your personality and interests).
* your home (this can be your real home or an imaginary one).
* your neighbourhood or town and what visitors can see and do there.
* your ideal holiday with HouseExchange (where you would like to go and why).

1 SPEAKING Look at the photos. Which of the things make you happy? What other things make you happy?

STRATEGY

Identifying main ideas of paragraphs

A paragraph usually has two types of sentences: a topic sentence which summarizes what the paragraph is about and detail sentences which provide more information, explanations or examples. Identifying the main ideas of paragraphs will help you to understand the key points in a text and this will help you to understand the overall message of the text.

- The topic sentence is usually the first, second or last sentence of the paragraph.
- It is usually more general than the other sentences in the paragraph.
- Identify it, by comparing it to the other sentences.
- When you find the topic sentence, turn it into a question and check if the other sentences in the paragraph answer this question.

2 Read the strategy. Then read the text and find the topic sentence in each paragraph. Match headings 1–6 with paragraphs A–D. There are two headings that you do not need.

1 Recharge your body and mood
2 Short-lived happiness
3 A natural remedy
4 Can having more and more make you happy?
5 Help and be helped
6 Do well at school and be happy

3 Read the topic sentences again and choose the best summary of the text.

a An opinion about what society should do to make people happy.
b An article about what makes people happy.
c A study showing why people find it impossible to be happy.

4 Answer the questions.

1 According to the text, what are the three basic needs which are essential for happiness?
2 What kind of happiness do material objects provide?
3 What does the sentence 'Happiness means you have to give and take' refer to? Give some examples.
4 What effect does exercise have on a person's mood?
5 According to the text, what happens if you do not get enough sleep? Is this true in your experience?
6 What do you agree with in the text? Is there anything you don't agree with?

Is chocolate the answer?

Have you ever wondered what makes people happy? Why are some people on cloud nine while others are always down in the dumps? What's the secret?
5 Is it pots of money, good health, loving relationships, owning the latest gadget or simply chocolate?

A
The latest World Happiness Report says that
10 prosperity is not the main reason for happiness. If you suffer real hardship, you are unlikely to be happy, but once your basic needs are met, money and material things become less of a necessity. Happiness depends more on recognizing the things you have and
15 appreciating them, rather than getting more things. Yes, money can buy you the latest smartphone, tablet or fashion item, and you might get a kick out of the ownership of these material objects, but this enjoyment is usually short-lived. Remember all those
20 presents you got for Christmas when you were little? You were over the moon when you opened them, but not for long. A month later, they were lying abandoned at the bottom of a drawer. And have you forgotten those delicious chocolates that made
25 you feel really happy when you were eating them, but ill after you'd finished them all?

B
It seems that deep, long-lasting happiness comes from intangible things rather than things like
30 chocolates and smartphones. One essential factor is human relationships. People who have the support

Vocabulary: idioms; suffixes: *-ness, -ity*; values; adverbs
Grammar: past simple and present perfect; present perfect continuous

Speaking: discussing tips for a happy life; giving and reacting to news
Writing: a personal letter

3A

of family members and also have strong friendships are more likely to be happy. Feeling protected and respected and knowing you can trust in the people around you is vital. But happiness means you have to give and take. Performing acts of kindness and generosity on a regular basis, for example, listening to a friend in need or carrying a neighbour's shopping, will make you <u>feel on top of</u> the world. Even a simple smile can work wonders. In fact, they say that one smile makes a person feel as good as eating 2,000 bars of chocolate (not all at once, of course!). 35

40

C

It's not surprising that health is another key contributor to happiness. Poor health will certainly make you <u>feel down in the mouth</u>. But being healthy and staying healthy requires some effort. A healthy diet is crucial and so is regular exercise. Laziness will not make you happy. Exercising for twenty to thirty minutes a day helps to reduce stress and anxiety and makes you feel more positive and optimistic because it releases endorphins (feel-good chemicals). So, if you've been <u>feeling blue</u> and worrying too much about your exams, get exercising. You'll also find that you sleep better. 45

50

55

D

Talking of sleep, do you often wake up feeling miserable? If so, it's probably because you haven't had enough of it. Teenagers tend to go to bed too late and have to get up early, so many suffer from a lack of sleep. Tiredness will certainly affect your happiness levels and put you in a bad mood. It also affects your ability to concentrate and may slow your growth. So if you want to be happy and do well at school, try to get at least eight hours a night. 60

65

Now you know the theory, it's time to put it all into practice. Smile, everyone!

50

55

V insight Idioms: happiness and sadness

5 An idiom is a group of words which form an expression. The meaning is different from the literal meanings of the individual words. Study the underlined idioms in the text. Which ones are about happiness and which about sadness?

V insight Noun suffixes: *-ness, -ity*

6 Put the noun forms of the words below in the correct part of the table. Then check your answers in the text.

- lazy ■ kind ■ necessary ■ prosperous ■ tired
- generous ■ happy ■ able

-ness	*-ity*

7 Read the tips and choose the correct answers.

Tips for a happy life

Be ¹kind / kindness to others. The ²able / ability to help someone will make both you and them feel good.

Offer your time to people in need – ³generous / generosity will make you feel good about yourself!

Try to get up early – ⁴lazy / laziness will make you feel ⁵tired / tiredness – you will feel more positive after an early start.

It's not ⁶necessary / necessity to have more and more things. ⁷Prosperous / Prosperity isn't the key to happiness. Be ⁸happy / happiness with what you have and who you are.

8 SPEAKING Work in groups of three. Prepare a list of three more tips for a happy life. Then work with another group and select the top three tips. Present them to the rest of the class.

Vocabulary bank Feelings: intensity page 136

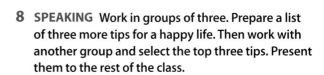

1 SPEAKING Work in pairs. Which of these things can help you to study better?

■ singing ■ listening to music ■ chatting to friends ■ doing sport ■ eating chocolate ■ sleeping longer ■ exercising before class

2 🔘 **1.11** Listen to a radio programme about how fitness helps us to perform better and answer the questions.

1 What two experiments are mentioned in the programme?
2 What do some students in the USA do before they start their lessons?
3 What do some students have to do during their lessons?
4 What are some of the results of introducing physical exercise in school?
5 Did you find any of the information surprising?

Past simple and present perfect

3 Read the comments about exercise programmes at school. Which comments are by teachers and which by students? Match the highlighted verbs in comments 1–7 to rules a–g.

1 I've completed a forty-minute workout this morning and I'm about to go and do a test. I feel full of energy!

2 We've just heard that we'll be sitting on exercise balls during some of our lessons.

3 I'm exhausted. I've just done 'Wake up and shake up'.

4 We did the programme for one term, but our students didn't like it.

5 I've done the programme for a year and I'm still attending all the classes.

6 We began the programme a week ago and we've already seen the benefits among the students.

7 I've never done this sort of thing before, but I'm really enjoying it.

We use the past simple:
a to talk about actions that happened at a known time in the past.
b to talk about completed past actions and states.

We use the present perfect:
c to talk about experiences in the past, usually with *ever* or *never*.
d for recent events or states that have a connection with the present, usually with *already*, *just* or *yet*.
e to talk about actions and states that started in the past and have not changed, usually with *for* or *since*.
f to talk about actions that happened during a time which still continues; usually with *this morning*, *this week*, *this year*.
g to give news.

4 Compare the two sentences. In which sentence is it still morning? Which tense is used?

1 I've completed a forty-minute workout this morning and I'm about to go and do a test.

2 I completed a forty-minute workout this morning. It was tiring, but I worked better in my classes after it.

Reference and practice 3.1 Workbook page 108

5 Work in pairs. Study the pairs of sentences. Why are different tenses used in sentences a and b?

1 a I was a teacher for three years.
   b I've been a teacher for three years.
2 a Have you ever used an exercise ball in class?
   b Did you use an exercise ball in class yesterday?
3 a I finished my workout before school.
   b I haven't finished my daily workout yet.
4 a I've never played tennis.
   b I didn't play tennis last night.
5 a I didn't speak to Julia at the party last Saturday.
   b I haven't spoken to Julia for ages.
6 a Have you seen Dan this morning?
   b Did you see Dan this morning?

6 SPEAKING Complete the sentences with the past simple or the present perfect form of the verbs in brackets. Then work in pairs and answer the questions.

1 .... you .... all your homework yet? (finish)
2 .... you .... your friends after school yesterday? (see)
3 I .... any exercise before class. What about you? (never do)
4 .... you .... your arm? (ever break)
5 .... you .... any sport last weekend? (play)
6 .... you .... raw fish? (ever eat)
7 .... you .... a comment on any blogs this week? (post)
8 What .... you .... in geography last year? (learn)

7 Complete the interview with the present perfect or past simple form of the verbs below.

■ be ■ cycle ■ do ■ go ■ have ■ help
■ join ■ not learn■ not get ■ sign up
■ spend ■ start ■ work

Millie The *Healthy Schools* project is part of a government plan to get Britain active. It **1**................... in schools a few years ago. Last term, I **2**................... hard on the 'healthy eating' part, but this term I **3**................... a lot of time on the 'physical activity' part.

Journalist So, what **4**................... you .... last term for 'healthy eating'?

Millie Well, I **5**................... in early each morning for 'Wake and shake' classes, then I **6**................... a healthy breakfast with a group of friends. Both those things **7**................... my concentration in class and I **8**................... tired towards lunchtime.

Journalist And what classes **9**................... you .... this term?

Millie I **10**................... never .... a big fan of exercise, but I **11**................... for street dance at lunchtimes. It is a good opportunity to learn something new, get fit and be with friends. It's difficult! I **12**................... all the moves yet!

Journalist And what about getting to school?

Millie Well, I usually get the bus, but this week, I **13**....................

8 SPEAKING Work in pairs. Interview each other about how healthy you are at school. What can you do to have a healthy body and a healthy mind?

Feeling good 33

1 SPEAKING Work in pairs. Do you agree with the statements?

In team sports, like football:
1 apart from the sport, you also learn life skills.
2 the individual team members are more important than the team.
3 you can make a lot of friends.

In individual sports, like tennis:
4 you have to rely on your own skills.
5 players are more likely to behave badly.
6 your rivals often become your friends.

2 🔊 **1.12** Listen to two young sportspeople talking about their sport. Which opinions in exercise 1 do they agree with?

3 🔊 **1.12** Listen again and answer the questions.
1 When did Georgina start playing football?
2 What is she aware of when she scores a goal?
3 What does she like most about being in a team?
4 What is the only disadvantage she mentions?
5 What is Carl's ambition?
6 How does Carl feel when he wins?
7 What kind of stamina do tennis players need?
8 Why do some tennis players throw their rackets and shout?

V Values

4 Study the words below. Which ones do you think refer to team sports, which to individual sports and which to both? Match the words to sentences 1–9.

> ■ commitment ■ discipline ■ self-esteem ■ self-reliance ■ self-sacrifice ■ single-mindedness ■ sportsmanship ■ stamina ■ team spirit

1 I respect myself and am confident about my abilities.
2 We all work together and share the same aims.
3 I have one aim and I'm determined to achieve it.
4 I can keep exercising even if I'm tired.
5 I give all my time and hard work to the team.
6 I always put the needs of the group before my own.
7 I have a very strict lifestyle. I always eat healthy food and train regulary.
8 I don't depend on others, only on myself.
9 I respect my opponents. I don't behave badly if I lose.

5 SPEAKING Work in pairs. Your school has received money to start one of the sports in the photos and it has asked you to choose the sport. Discuss the advantages and disadvantages of your chosen sport. Then work with two other pairs and decide on one sport that the school should choose.

Giving and reacting to news

6 SPEAKING Work in pairs. Discuss the questions.

1 How often do you tell someone good or bad news?
2 How do you react when someone tells you good or bad news?

7 🔊 **1.13** Listen to the dialogue. What good news does Evie have? What values does she demonstrate? Listen again and complete phrases 1–5 in the table.

Giving news	Reacting to bad news
You'll never ¹..................!	I'm sorry to hear that.
I've got bad news.	You must be feeling upset.
I've got some good news.	
	Exclamations
Reacting to good news	Oh no! How awful! How terrible! How exciting! What rubbish!
You're ²..................!	
That's ³..................! / fantastic news!	
You ⁴.................. it.	
I'm really ⁵.................. for you.	
Congratulations! Well done!	

8 🔊 **1.14** Put the dialogue in the correct order. Then listen and check.

.... **Olly** What rubbish! You love playing rugby.

.... **Sean** Nothing really serious, but he says that I'm not disciplined and committed enough.

.... **Olly** You look upset. What's wrong?

.... **Sean** Yes, I am. I'm going to miss being part of the team.

.... **Olly** Come on, cheer up. It's not the end of the world. Let's go and play football. It will take your mind off it.

.... **Sean** Well, yes, but in a way, he's right. I haven't been to all the training sessions recently. I missed one last week when I went into town with Haley, and the week before I was too tired, and the week before that, I had a toothache … .

.... **Olly** But, still, I don't think it's fair just to throw you out like that. You must be feeling upset.

.... **Sean** I've got bad news. The coach has thrown me out of the rugby team.

.... **Olly** Well, try to look on the bright side. At least you'll have more time for your friends!

.... **Olly** Oh no! I'm sorry to hear that. What did you do?

.... **Sean** Yes, I suppose so.

9 Read the dialogue in exercise 8 again and underline three more phrases that Olly uses to make Sean feel better. Which of the exclamations does Olly use?

10 SPEAKING Work in pairs. Give and react to news. Use the ideas below or your own ideas.

- You and your family are moving to another country.
- You have just won a sports competition.
- You have been chosen to appear on a television programme.
- Your youth club has decided to stop the afternoon sport activities.

1 SPEAKING Complete the factfile with the numbers below. Then read the text and check your answers. Did any of the facts surprise you?

▪ 2,700 ▪ 12.2 ▪ 22 ▪ 2 ▪ 50 ▪ 25

In numbers ...

How much do you know about an American teenager's lifestyle?
1 Number of overweight teenagers (millions) ....
2 Percentage of teens living in the suburbs ....
3 Number of hours spent in cars per day ....
4 Number of hours watching TV per week ....
5 Percentage of teens who exercise each week ....
6 Daily calories consumed by an American teen* ....

* recommended daily calories for a teenager = 2,000

2 Read the text again and answer the questions.

1 Why did Americans start living in the suburbs?
2 Why do you need a car in the suburbs?
3 Why don't American teens exercise much?
4 Why does food from fast food restaurants taste good?
5 Why was supersizing introduced?
6 What do you think will happen to overweight teens in the future?

3 SPEAKING Think about your lifestyle. How does it compare to an American teen's lifestyle? Who has the healthiest lifestyle and why?

V insight Adverbs

4 Study the highlighted adverbs in the text and answer the questions.

Which adverbs are:
1 sentence adverbs (adverbs that introduce a whole sentence)?
2 adverbs of manner (adverbs that describe the way we do something)?
3 adverbs of degree (adverbs that make an adjective or verb stronger or weaker)?

5 Choose one word that you <u>cannot</u> use to complete each sentence.

1 ...., in America, children as young as two suffer from obesity.
   a Really   b Worryingly   c Surprisingly
2 You can make pizzas at home easily and ....
   a cheaply   b quickly   c comfortably
3 The new burger restaurant .... became a big success.
   a incredibly   b rapidly   c quickly
4 Healthy food is .... expensive compared to fast food.
   a really   b extremely   c similarly
5 Jordan sat down .... on the sofa and turned on the TV.
   a comfortably   b incredibly   c quickly
6 More than 30% of teens in the USA are overweight. ...., 30% of teens in the UK are overweight, too.
   a Similarly   b Extremely   c Worryingly

FAT AMERICA

America is getting fatter. Back in the 1970s only 10% of teens were overweight, but today, one in three teenagers (or more than 25 million) are overweight or obese. Let's take a look at the reasons why.

5 ## Car culture

In the 1940s, the population inside cities grew rapidly and American families started to move into the suburbs. Today, more than 50% of American teenagers
10 live there. In the suburbs, houses are bigger, gardens are bigger, and teenagers are bigger, too. It's easy to see why – they go everywhere in cars. Suburbs are a long way from shopping centres, schools and friends' houses. They often have no pavements, making it
   23 times more dangerous to walk or cycle than to
15 drive. As a result, families spend an average of two hours a day in their cars. And, when they reach their destination, drive-through supermarkets, restaurants and banks keep them comfortably in their seats.

'Screenagers'

20 A typical American family has three TVs and the average teenager, or 'screenager', watches 22 hours of television every week. By the time they leave High School, most teenagers will have spent more time in front of a TV than in the classroom. But it's not just
25 TV that makes kids extremely inactive. The average US home has 24 electronic gadgets, including smartphones, computers and games consoles. It's not surprising that only 12.2% of American teenagers actually exercise each week.

30 ## Fast food

Fast food is one of America's great success stories and [1]Americans <u>have been eating</u> hamburgers for decades. The first burger bar opened in 1921, but it wasn't until the 1950s that fast food became incredibly successful.
35 Women started to work, people had less time and restaurants like McDonald's fed families quickly and cheaply. Today, 50% of meals are eaten outside the home and more than three quarters of American teenagers eat a fast food meal at least once a week.
40 [2]People <u>have known</u> about the problems of fast food for years, but they still eat it. Why? Probably because the salt, fat and sugar makes it taste really good.

DVD extra Live well, play well

Supersizing

In the 1960s jumbo-sized popcorn went on sale in a movie theatre in Chicago. The manager wanted people to spend more, but he noticed that customers only bought one bag of popcorn because they didn't want to look greedy. However, they didn't mind buying a bigger-sized bag. The idea of supersize portions was born. In the 1970s, fast food restaurants adopted the same approach and introduced larger fries and sodas. Surprisingly, today's 'small' fries are the same size as large fries in 1970. Similarly, the largest soda in 1955 was much smaller than today's child-size soda. Over the last three decades the average teenager's calorie consumption has risen by 25% to 2,700 a day. Worryingly, that's 700 calories more a day than they need.

So what does the future hold for America? Doctors fear an epidemic of illnesses like diabetes, heart disease and cancer. Many think this could be the first generation that doesn't outlive its parents. But health centres for obese children are starting to make a difference. At the centres are children like 12-year-old Conchita. [3]Conchita's tired today because she's been exercising. 'It's hard work, but I'm feeling good,' she says. [4]How many times has she exercised this week? 'Three,' she replies, 'and [5]I've given up fast food, too.' 'These kids want long lives and they want to do a lot of things,' explains a doctor at the centre. 'Clearly, that's not going to happen unless they change their lifestyle.'

Present perfect simple and present perfect continuous

6 Study the rules. Then match sentences 1–5 in the text to rules a–e.

We form the present perfect continuous with *have / has* + *been* + *-ing* form of the verb.

We use the present perfect continuous:

a to talk about a situation or action that began in the past and is still in progress. The emphasis is on the duration of the activity. We can use *for* and *since* to show how long.

b to talk about a recent activity that explains a present situation.

We use the present perfect simple (not the continuous):

c when we focus on the **result** of an action or **how often** it has happened.

d when an action is **finished** and **complete**.

e with **state verbs**, for example: *be, like, believe, have*.

Reference and practice 3.2 Workbook page 109

7 Complete the text with the present perfect simple or present perfect continuous form of the verbs in brackets.

Touchdown!

17-year-old Austin Walker looks happy. He [1] .... (play) American football all morning and he [2] .... (score) two touchdowns. It's pretty good and I tell him so during the break. 'How long [3] .... (you / be) a member of the Johnson Eagles football team?' 'Six months,' says Austin, 'and I'm getting good.' When Austin Walker joined the school football team he weighed over 120 kilos. Today, he's a lot slimmer – he [4] .... (lose) weight bit by bit and he's almost reached his goal. He [5] .... (stop) eating fast food, too. 'It's something I [6] .... (want) to do for a long time,' he says. 'I just didn't have the discipline before.' So what changed his mind? 'Six months ago my mum was diagnosed with diabetes,' explains Austin. 'It was a shock, so my family decided to make some lifestyle changes – we [7] .... (eat) less food and exercising more.'

'It [8] .... (not be) easy,' he adds, 'but I want to be with my family for as long as I can and that means living a healthy life.'

8 SPEAKING Make questions. Use the present perfect and the present perfect continuous tense. Then work in pairs and answer the questions.

1. you / ever / be / to America
2. how long / study / English
3. how many times / exercise / this week
4. how long / know / your best friend
5. you / ever / eat / a supersize meal
6. how often / walk / to school / this week

Vocabulary bank Health problems page 136

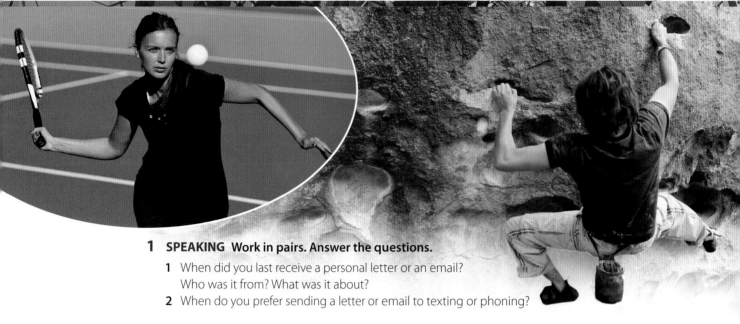

1 SPEAKING Work in pairs. Answer the questions.

   1 When did you last receive a personal letter or an email?
      Who was it from? What was it about?

   2 When do you prefer sending a letter or email to texting or phoning?

2 Read Simon's letter to his friend Abby and her reply. Answer the questions.

Who:

   1 has tried something new recently?

   2 has made an important decision?

   3 has had a frightening experience?

   4 has been worried about other people's feelings?

   5 is worried about their future?

   6 feels optimistic about the future?

STRATEGY

Showing your attitude

You can show your attitude or opinion on something using adverbs and prepositional phrases. With these words and phrases you can, for example, show that:

a you did not expect something to happen.

b it is not good that something happened.

c something is clear.

d you are saying what you really think.

e it is good that something happened.

3 Read the strategy. Study the highlighted words and phrases in Simon's letter. Match them to categories a–e.

4 Replace the highlighted words and phrases in Simon's letter with the words and phrases below.

   ■ frankly ■ clearly ■ unfortunately ■ to my surprise ■ fortunately

5 Read Abby's letter again and choose the correct answers.

Expressing reason and purpose

6 Study the four sentences from the letters. Which two sentences express a reason and which two express a purpose?

   1 Felix suggested that I needed to do something different **so that** I can relax.

   2 **Since** everyone's got exam fever, I haven't got much else to write about.

   3 I've got to go now **because** I've got a revision class in ten minutes, but write soon!

   4 My dad is relieved that he no longer has to wake up at 5 a.m. **in order to** drive me to tennis practice.

7 Complete the sentences with an appropriate reason or purpose.

   1 Simon has taken up rock climbing, because …

   2 Abby decided to give up competitive tennis so that …

   3 Simon and his friends are studying hard at the moment in order to …

   4 Since Abby's dad is happy, …

   5 You have to concentrate very hard when you're climbing so that you don't …

   6 Abby is looking forward to the summer, because …

Hi Abby,

How are you? I'm sorry I haven't been in touch for a while. I can't believe summer is nearly here! How's the tennis going? I remember you had a big tournament in April. How did it go?

I've been studying hard for my exams and, to be honest, I'm getting pretty stressed out about the results. Felix suggested that I needed to do something different so that I can relax and forget about everything, so I've taken up rock climbing! I'm not very sporty, so obviously, the thought of hanging off a rock face on the end of a rope was quite scary. But, surprisingly, I've been enjoying it and it's helped me take my mind off things. It was also an exciting experience, the scenery was beautiful and, luckily, I haven't hurt myself. I actually really like it!

Since everyone's got exam fever and all we do is study, I haven't got much else to write about. By the way, Felix says 'hello'. Sadly, he can't go to the lakes with us this summer. You are coming back to the lakes again with your parents, aren't you? I've got to go now because I've got a revision class in ten minutes, but write soon!

Take care,

Simon

Hi Simon,

Thanks for your letter. I'm really sorry that you're so worried about your results, but the rock climbing sounds great. I'd love to try it myself one day.

Guess what, I've decided to give up competitive tennis! I realized that I didn't want to make it my whole life; there are too many other things I want to do. ¹**Surprisingly / Obviously**, I was terrified of telling my parents, because I thought they'd be disappointed in me. But, ²**to be honest / luckily**, I knew I wasn't committed enough. ³**Fortunately / Unfortunately**, they took the news very well. ⁴**Sadly / Frankly**, I think my dad is relieved that he no longer has to wake up at 5 a.m. in order to drive me to tennis practice or to tournaments around the country!

Anyway, I'd better go now – I've got to get ready for a party! For years, I haven't had time to do anything except play tennis, so I'm enjoying my new social life! ⁵**To be honest / Luckily**, I still have some friends left.

In answer to your question, of course we're coming to the lakes this year, but it's a shame I won't see Felix.

Write soon!

Love, Abby

WRITING GUIDE

■ **Task** Write a letter to a friend or relative telling them your news.

■ **Ideas** Decide who you are going to write to and make notes about:
- questions you could ask the person.
- past experiences you could describe.
- recent events you have taken part in.
- information you could request from the person.

■ **Plan** Decide which ideas you are going to use and match them to these paragraphs.

Paragraph 1: Start the letter and ask some questions about how the person has been.

Paragraph 2: Describe a recent past experience and say how you felt about it.

Paragraph 3: Describe a recent event you have been to and its consequences.

Paragraph 4: Ask the person you are writing to for some information.

■ **Write** Write your letter. Use the paragraph plan to help you.

■ **Check** Check the following points:
- Is the tone of your letter friendly and informal?
- Have you used the appropriate beginnings and endings?
- Have you expressed the reason and purpose of the actions you describe?
- Have you checked grammar, vocabulary, spelling and punctuation?

1 Work in pairs. Study the dictionary entries below. How many different forms of the word *sad* are there? What part of speech are they?

> **sad** /sæd/ *adj* (sadder; saddest) **1** sad (to do sth); sad (that ...) unhappy or causing sb to feel unhappy: *We are very sad that you are leaving.* • *I'm very sad that you don't trust me.* • *That's one of the saddest stories I've ever heard!* • *a sad poem/song/film* **2** bad or unacceptable: *It's a sad state of affairs when your best friend doesn't trust you.* ▶ **sadden** /'sædn/ *verb* [T] (*formal*): *The news of your father's death saddened me greatly.* ▶ **sadness** *noun* [C,U]

> **sadly** /'sædli/ *adv* **1** unfortunately: *Sadly, after eight years of marriage they had grown apart.* **2** in a way that shows unhappiness: *She shook her head sadly.* **3** in a way that is wrong: *If you think that I've forgotten what you did, you're sadly mistaken.*

STRATEGY

Word-building: suffixes

Words that have similar forms can be grouped into a 'family', for example, *happy*, *happily*, *happiness*, *unhappy*. Every family is built around a 'root' word. In this case, it is *happy*.

You can form new words by adding **prefixes** (to the beginning of the root word) or **suffixes** (to the end of the root word). When you come across a new word, it is good to record other forms of that word as this will help you to develop your vocabulary.

2 Read the strategy above. Then use a dictionary to complete the table.

noun	adjective	adverb
happiness		
	sad	
beauty		
		generously
	necessary	
		memorably

3 Study the suffixes in the table in exercise 2. Then complete the rules.

1 Typical noun suffixes are: ...., ...,
....

2 Typical adjective suffixes are: ...., ...,
..................., ..., ...

3 Typical adverb suffixes are: ...., ...

4 Choose the correct answers.

1 Does great wealth always bring **happiness / happy / happily**?

2 My little sister often plays **happiness / happy / happily** for hours with her toys.

3 We were amazed by the **beauty / beautiful / beautifully** of the countryside.

4 The musician played the piano **beauty / beautiful / beautifully**.

5 She's very **generosity / generous / generously** and spends a lot of time helping the elderly.

6 Living **generosity / generous / generously** makes people feel happier.

7 If **necessity / necessary / necessarily**, I can help you with the shopping on Saturday.

8 There's no **necessity / necessary / necessarily** to give lots and lots of money to charity. Even a small amount will help.

5 Complete the table with the correct verb forms. Use a dictionary to help you. What are the typical verb suffixes?

adjective	verb
sad	
beautiful	
memorable	
different	

6 Complete the sentences with the correct forms of the words in brackets. Use the suffixes on this page.

1 We were all .... (sad) to hear that our teacher left the school.

2 It was a very .... (memory) experience – I'll never forget it.

3 My brother can't .... (different) between red and orange. He always gets them mixed up.

4 She .... (kind) offered to carry my bags.

5 The class was very .... (friend) and kind to the new students.

6 The school is really old, so the classrooms will be .... (modern) next year.

7 Use the suffixes on this page to make word families built around the words below. Use a dictionary to help you. Then write your own example sentences with each word.

■ prosper ■ respect ■ kind

Dictionary entries from *Oxford Wordpower Dictionary*, 4th edition

Vocabulary

1 Complete the idioms in the text with one word in each gap.

Are you feeling [1]................ in the mouth? Clothes you wear can stop you feeling down in the [2]................ . Studies suggest that if you wear colourful clothes, you'll soon feel on [3]................ of the world again. Blue is effective for many, and yellow helps others to feel [4]................ the moon. You can be on cloud [5]................ when you wear red, though some people find it stressful! Green is a good choice if you're feeling [6]................ .

Marks .... / 6

2 Complete the sentences with the correct form of the words in brackets.

1 The best gift you can give is .... (kind)
2 Love is a .... for small children. (necessary)
3 .... today means hard work tomorrow. (lazy)
4 Don't wait for .... – go and find it. (happy)
5 We should measure .... in friendships, not in money. (prosper)
6 Success is the .... to learn from failure. (able)

Marks .... / 6

3 Complete the text with the words.

▪ commitment ▪ self-esteem ▪ discipline ▪ self-reliance
▪ stamina ▪ team spirit

Gym trainer Mart Hardy says, 'If you *really* want to get fit, you need [1]................ – a determination to succeed. That means [2]................ , for example, waking up early in the morning, so you can exercise. You'll soon build up [3]................ , so you can exercise for a long time without getting tired. Exercising alone demands [4]................ – you've only got yourself to depend on. If the gym isn't for you, take up a sport, like basketball. It's fun and you'll enjoy the [5]................ of playing with others. Being part of a winning team boosts your [6]................ , so you feel great about yourself!'

Marks .... / 6

4 Choose the correct answers.

Surfing is an [1]**extremely** / **rapidly** popular sport, enjoyed by millions of people. It started in ancient Hawaii, and [2]**quickly** / **worryingly** spread worldwide. For ancient Hawaiians it had religious significance, so [3]**rapidly** / **clearly**, it wasn't just a sport. Surfing was [4]**incredibly** / **worryingly** important, too, as the chief ruler was usually a [5]**comfortably** / **really** good surfer. [6]**Clearly** / **Surprisingly**, Hawaiians who surfed badly were not as well-respected as good surfers!

Marks .... / 6

Grammar

5 Complete the sentences with the past simple or present perfect simple form of the verbs in brackets.

1 I .... (try) two new sports so far this year.
2 I tried badminton first, and last week I .... (wear) skates for the first time.
3 I .... (want) to try skating since February.
4 I .... (watch) a really cool skating video on YouTube back then.
5 I .... (find) a skating class last month.
6 The teacher .... (win) lots of awards for skating since she began.
7 However, my first lesson .... (be) a disaster!
8 In my first lesson, I .... (fall) over a lot.
9 I .... (not become) an expert yet.
10 But I .... (get) better since my first try!

Marks .... / 10

6 Write sentences and questions. Use the past simple or present perfect simple.

1 I / never / swim / in the sea
....
2 you / drive / or / walk / to school / today ?
....
3 she / not win / any games / yet
....
4 they / beat / our team / in the last match
....
5 I / not do / any sport / last year
....
6 you / ever / ride / a mountain bike ?
....

Marks .... / 6

7 Complete the text with the present perfect simple or continuous form of the verbs below.

▪ be ▪ believe ▪ dream ▪ encourage ▪ forget ▪ join
▪ play ▪ practise ▪ run ▪ watch

I [1]................ football all day, and I've got another hour to go. I'm exhausted! The whole team [2]................ around the pitch for hours. I [3]................ (just) the Manchester United Youth team – that's why I [4]................ so intensively. I [5]................ (always) of being a famous footballer one day.
Dad [6]................ my biggest fan ever since I first kicked a ball. He [7]................ me to train for the last 15 years, and he doesn't show any signs of stopping! He [8]................ me train all day today – he's still looking at me right now. He [9]................ (always) in me, even when I doubted myself. He remembers all my best goals – even the ones I [10]................ (already)!

Marks .... / 10

Total .... / 50

1 SPEAKING Look at the photos and discuss the questions. Then read the text and compare your ideas.

1 Have you ever visited an island? Can you name some islands?

2 What do you think life is like on the island in the photos? Think about the climate, food, work and free time.

2 Read the text again and choose the correct answers.

1 Why is John Sailike sad?
   a He regrets his childhood.
   b He misses friends from his community.
   c He doesn't want to leave the island.
   d He can't hear the sea at night.

2 What do people do on the island?
   a Men and women do similar work.
   b They have frequent contact with the outside world.
   c They use a lot of electricity.
   d They try to provide their own food.

3 What first impressions of the island does the writer give?
   a Life on the island is very simple.
   b People on the island are unhappy.
   c Islanders need more help from the outside world.
   d It's difficult for islanders to live there.

4 Which of these things is <u>not</u> a problem for the islands?
   a Fresh water shortages.
   b More risk of illnesses.
   c A poor food supply.
   d Too many people.

5 What might happen when the islanders relocate?
   a There won't be enough food and shelter.
   b People will forget Carteret traditions.
   c They won't be able to communicate.
   d They won't be able to find work.

6 How have people helped the islanders?
   a They have built them new homes.
   b They have supported the younger generation.
   c They have tried to protect their traditions.
   d They have researched climate change.

3 SPEAKING Work in pairs. Discuss the questions.

1 What did you learn about Carteret culture?
2 Did any of the challenges the islanders face surprise you?

V The environment

4 Study the highlighted words in the text and match them to definitions 1–9.

1 to stay alive, despite difficult conditions
2 when water destroys something
3 to move to another place
4 to disappear forever
5 to leave a place because of danger
6 destroying something
7 to protect something for the future
8 poisoning and making something bad
9 to affect a larger area or a bigger group of people

Island story

'When I was a little boy, I loved to go fishing in the sea with my spear,' says John Sailike, sadly. 'When I leave the island, I'll lose the sea and the happiness of this place. I'll miss the sound of the
5 waves at night … I won't hear it any more.'

[1]John is a fisherman from the Carteret islands in the South Pacific, an idyllic <u>semi</u>-circle of white sand, palm trees and crystal clear waters. Each day, he goes out in a canoe to catch fish for
10 his family, while his wife looks after the children and grows vegetables in their garden. The family lives in a wood hut with sand floors and they don't use much electricity, so when the sun goes down, it is usually time for bed. [2]This peaceful,
15 <u>under</u>developed place has a tiny population and only one contact with the outside world – a ship which brings supplies from Bougainville, a large island 86 km away. But all this is about to change, because John, along with 3,000 other people, is
20 leaving his island home. The question is, why?

Take a closer look at the islands and the reason becomes clear. The Carterets are the victim of global warming. High tides often flood across the villages and wash away people's homes.
25 [3]Salt water from the sea is <u>over</u>flowing into vegetable gardens and devastating fruit trees. It's contaminating the fresh water supply, too. Islanders are struggling to survive on coconut milk and fish, and children are suffering from

Vocabulary: the environment; prefixes: *semi-, under-, over-, re-, co-, inter-*; verbs + prepositions; collocations: charities
Grammar: expressing the future; future perfect and future continuous

Speaking: discussing cultural identity; comparing types of protest; asking for and expressing opinions
Writing: an opinion essay

4A

malnutrition. The dying trees are home to mosquitoes that spread diseases, like malaria. People know that life on the island is coming to an end. [30]

Experts predict that the Carterets will be under water by 2015. Before then, [4]the islanders will relocate to places like Bougainville and rebuild their lives. This move will provide people with food and shelter, but what will happen to their culture? The islanders have songs for different everyday activities, and traditions and celebrations linked to the sea. They also have their own language, called 'Halia'. [5]If they co-exist with other cultures, this may die out. [35] [40]

'We're losing our home, our identity, our whole life,' says islander Ursula Rakova. 'We hope the world is listening.' It is. [6]Over the last few years, articles in international newspapers, YouTube videos and an Oscar-nominated documentary film called *Sun is Up* have talked about the Carteret islands. People have supported the islanders and as a result, they have turned their anger and frustration into action. 'Tulele Peisa' is a project which is helping to evacuate people like Ursula. It's also looking for ways to preserve their way of life and record their language and traditions for future generations. [45] [50]

Back on the island, John Sailike is getting into his boat for the last time. He's saying goodbye to his home and to his ancestors. He does not know what the future will bring; he does not know if his culture will survive. He is the human face of climate change. [55]

Factfile: Carteret Islands

Location: South Pacific, off the north-east coast of Papua New Guinea
Population: 3,300
Total area: 0.6 square km (83 football fields)
Highest point: 1.2 metres above sea level
History: Discovered by Philip Carteret in 1767

5 Complete the article about blue gold with the correct form of the highlighted verbs in *Island story*.

Blue gold

Did you know that 97% of all the world's water is salt water? 3% is drinkable, but we can only use 1% of this because the rest is trapped in glaciers or deep underground. The bad news is this percentage is getting smaller because of overpopulation, pollution and climate change. It's a scary situation: rising sea levels [1]............... homes and sometimes whole islands on one side of the world. Floods and high tides [2]............... fresh water and [3]............... disease. Governments are forced to [4]............... communities from danger zones and [5]............... them to higher ground. But, in other parts of the world, droughts [6]............... crops and kill farm animals. And as people move to other areas in search of food, traditions and cultures [7].............. . It's a man-made problem, so what's the solution? We have to learn to [8]............... this valuable resource. In 2030, almost 50% of the world's population will probably experience water shortages, and experts predict the first water wars. Who will be the winners and losers? Will we [9]............... the battle for blue gold?

V insight Prefixes: *semi-, under-, over-, re-, co-, inter-*

6 Study sentences 1–6 in *Island story*. Then match the underlined prefixes to definitions a–f.

a again or back
b together
c between
d not enough, below
e half, partly
f too much

7 Complete the sentences with the words in brackets and a prefix in exercise 6.

1 The island was .... Too many people were living there. (crowded)
2 Once the Carterets are under the sea, they will never .... (appear)
3 If the islanders ...., there might be enough food for everyone. (-operate)
4 It's difficult to .... with people who speak a different language. (act)
5 The fish smelt bad and it was .... It wasn't safe to eat. (cooked)
6 Their new homes on Bougainville were .... They could only live there for a few months. (-permanent)

8 SPEAKING Work in pairs. Think about the place where you live. Choose the things that make up your cultural identity, then put them in order of importance. Give reasons for your order.

■ language ■ music (songs and dance) ■ festivals
■ beliefs ■ land / geographical features ■ houses ■ food

Vocabulary bank Global issues page 137

1 SPEAKING Work in pairs. Discuss the questions.

1 How often do you:
- ▣ send instant messages or chat with a friend on a social networking site?
- ▣ post comments on other people's pages?
- ▣ post a status update on a social networking site?
- ▣ upload photos or videos?

2 Do you ever use social media for other reasons, for example, to organize something?

2 Read the text and answer the questions.

1 What are flashmobs?
2 Why do people organize them?
3 Why is Joel organizing his flashmob?
4 How will people find out about it?

Expressing the future

3 Read the text again. Then match sentences 1–7 in the text to uses a–g.

Ways of expressing the future:
- **a** present simple for scheduled events, timetables
- **b** present continuous for arrangements
- **c** *will* for promises and hopes for the future (often with *hope, promise*)
- **d** *will* for predictions about the future (often with *think, probably*)
- **e** *going to* for intentions
- **f** *going to* for predictions based on evidence
- **g** *may / might* for uncertain predictions about the future.

| Reference and practice 4.1 | Workbook page 110 |

4 Read the sentences and choose the correct answers.

1 I might go to the eco festival in the park this weekend.
- **a** I have a definite plan to go to the festival.
- **b** I haven't decided on my plans yet.
- **c** I probably won't go.

2 What are you doing tonight?
- **a** I want to know about your arrangements for tonight.
- **b** I want to know about your activities now.
- **c** I'm asking you to make a prediction about the future.

3 The protest starts at 7.30 a.m.
- **a** The protest has just started.
- **b** The protest might start at that time.
- **c** The protest will definitely start at that time.

4 I'm meeting Anna at the café to talk about the protest.
- **a** I might meet Anna in the café.
- **b** Anna and I have decided the time and place to meet already.
- **c** I hope I'll see Anna in the café.

5 I think that flashmobs will become more popular in the future.
- **a** I predict that this will happen.
- **b** This will definitely happen.
- **c** I want this to happen.

Crowd power – the flashmob phenomenon

Flashmobs are public performances given by groups of strangers who find out about events through social media, networking sites and text messages. Flashmobbers meet at a precise time and perform a short action together when a signal is given. The performance finishes suddenly, at an arranged time and the people then move away immediately. For some people, flashmobs are about having fun. But for others, they're a way of getting together a group of people to make a political point. We asked Joel to tell us about his next flashmob event.

Joel is a 19-year-old Canadian and he's a strong advocate of recycling. 'On Saturday, **[1]I'm organizing** a flashmob event to promote recycling. **[2]It starts** at ten in the morning. **[3]How will we organize** the event? Probably through Twitter, Facebook and other websites. According to the weather forecast, **[4]it's going to be** really hot on Saturday, so **[5]I hope that lots of people will be there**. **[6]We're going to leave** some rubbish near a recycling bin and then wait in the park. I hope we'll look

like ordinary people, enjoying a day out. But everyone's going to start clapping and cheering as soon as someone picks up the rubbish and puts it in the recycling bin. Some people **⁷may not understand** what we're doing, but I think that it will be fun. Flashmobbing is possible because of the way that people continually share information around the world now. It's the future of political protest.'

5 Complete the text with *will, going to* or *might* and the correct form of the verbs in brackets.

Jason, 21, lives in San Francisco. Tomorrow afternoon, he's **¹**.................................. (take part) in a 'carrotmob' event. In carrotmob events, a group of people spend their money to support a business and in return the business agrees to do something good for the environment. For tomorrow's event, lots of people **²**.................................. (buy) food at the MiniMart store in Pine Street between 2 and 3 p.m. In return, the store promises it **³**.................................. (spend) 50% of the hour's revenue on new energy-efficient lighting. 'Four hundred people have promised to visit the store tomorrow,' says Jason, 'so it **⁴**.................................. (be) very busy! I really hope that my sister, Sadie, **⁵**.................................. (join) me. She **⁶**.................................. (come), but it depends on whether her teacher lets her leave early, says Jason. 'But, even if she's not there, I think that we **⁷**.................................. (have) a lot of fun tomorrow!' Next month Jason **⁸**.................................. (organize) another carrotmob event at a local sports centre. **⁹**.................................. lots of people .... (support) the next event? 'I don't know yet,' says Jason. 'But it's a great idea.'

6 🔘 **1.15** **Listen to Melanie talking about a Critical Mass bike ride and answer the questions.**

1 What is a Critical Mass bike ride?
2 What is the aim of the ride?

7 🔘 **1.15** **Make sentences about the event. Then listen and check.**

1 Melanie / join / a Critical Mass bike ride
2 The ride / start / eight in the morning
3 It / be / very busy
4 They / cycle / through the streets
5 People in cars and buses / get / annoyed
6 They / not be able to move fast
7 Hopefully more people / decide / to hop on a bike

8 SPEAKING **Work in pairs. Discuss the questions.**

1 Which of the three types of protest (flashmobbing, carrotmobs, Critical Mass bike rides) will become more / less popular in the future?
2 What other ways of protesting might become popular?
   ▪ using Twitter, Facebook ▪ organizing marches
   ▪ signing petitions ▪ writing letters to the government

1 SPEAKING Work in pairs. Look at the photos and discuss the questions.

1 Where do you think this school is?
2 Why are the students protesting?
3 What problems do you think students might experience at this school?

2 🔊 **1.16** Listen to the radio programme about Attawapiskat Elementary School and check your ideas. Then answer the questions.

1 Who was Shannen Koostachin?
2 Why is she inspirational?

3 🔊 **1.16** Listen to the radio programme again. Are the sentences true (T) or false (F)? Correct the false ones.

1 Kate thinks that Shannen is very famous around the world.
2 Shannen believed that children needed education as preparation for life.
3 Shannen wrote to children all over Canada and asked them to support her campaign.
4 The announcement from the Minister for Aboriginal Affairs in 2008 was probably very disappointing for Shannen.
5 The Attawapiskat community cancelled the school trip in order to pay for their representatives to travel to Ottawa.
6 Shannen thought that the First Nation children had special rights to education.
7 Shannen moved to New Liskeard because the school there had better facilities.
8 The new school in Attawapiskat will probably not have a gym or a music studio.

STRATEGY

Identifying facts, opinions and speculation

When you listen to people discussing a subject, it is important to identify:

■ facts: *The government spent $5 million on the environment last year.*
■ opinions: *I think / I believe / In my opinion / It's my view that the government didn't spend enough money on the environment last year.*
■ speculation: *The government will probably / might / may focus on the environment in the next year. Perhaps / Maybe the government will spend more money on the environment next year.*

4 Read the strategy. Then study the statements in exercise 3 again. Are they facts (F), opinions (O) or speculation (S)?

V insight Verbs + prepositions

5 Choose the correct prepositions.

1 to believe **in / at / for** global warming
2 to protest **after / over / against** climate change
3 to belong **about / to / for** a community
4 to insist **on / at / for** freedom of speech
5 to rely **in / on / at** the government for help
6 to set **in / on / up** a campaign
7 to care **about / with / after** a situation

6 SPEAKING Discuss the questions.

1 What do you think about Shannen's campaign? Would you insist on the same facilities for your school?
2 What school facilities do you rely on?
3 Why might you set up a campaign in your school? Is there anything you might protest against?

DVD extra Protest

A
BASKETBALL COURTS CANCELLED!
Plans for a new basketball court in North Park have been cancelled.

B

PROTEST IN THE PARK
200 people protest against plans to build a waste recycling facility in the skatepark.

C
SCHOOLS SHORTEN SUMMER HOLIDAYS
Students and teachers at Park School are horrified at the decision to shorten summer holidays to three weeks.

Asking for and expressing opinions

7 **SPEAKING** Read the newspaper headlines. What do you think about these issues? Which is the most important? Which is the least important?

8 🔊 **1.17** Listen and match the dialogue to one of the three headlines in exercise 7.

9 🔊 **1.17** Complete the phrases from the dialogue. Then listen again and check.

Asking for opinions	Reacting to opinions and suggestions
What do you ^{1}.................?	I'm not so ^{6}................. (it is a bad idea).
What do you ^{2}.................?	That's just what ^{7}................. .
	That's a ^{8}................. .
Expressing opinions	
^{3}................., I think … .	
As far as I'm ^{4}................., … .	
It ^{5}................. a good idea to … .	

10 Add the phrases below to the table in exercise 9.

■ I agree with you about that. ■ I take your point, but … . ■ In my opinion … . ■ What's your view on this? ■ To tell you the truth, … . ■ I see what you're saying, but … . ■ If you want my opinion, … .

11 🔊 **1.18** Choose the correct answers. Then listen and check.

Leo I don't believe this – the council decided not to build the basketball courts in the park.

Ella ^{1}................., it's probably a good idea. We already have a football pitch and tennis courts, so we don't need another outdoor facility. ^{2}................. they should build a youth club.

Leo ^{3}................., but a basketball court is much cheaper than a youth club.

Ella You're probably right. ^{4}.................

Leo How about we organize a protest?

Ella ^{5}................. . That sounds very serious. How about we just write a letter to the council?

Leo OK, that's a great idea.

1 a I'm not so sure   b To tell you the truth   c I take your point
2 a That's just what I was thinking   b That's a great idea   c In my opinion
3 a What do you reckon?   b As far as I'm concerned   c I see what you're saying
4 a I'm not so sure   b What do you think?   c If you ask me
5 a I'm not so sure   b I agree with you about that   c That's a great idea

12 **SPEAKING** Work in groups of four. Choose an issue that you all feel strongly about. Discuss how you are going to organize a campaign to support your cause. You have a campaign budget of €150. Use the ideas below or your own ideas.

■ more cycle paths ■ recycling
■ more youth facilities ■ helping the elderly

1 Look at the price list and decide how to spend your budget.
2 Discuss how you will use social media.
3 Discuss other ways of protesting (for example, writing letters to the government, organizing a march, a sit-in, a flashmob).

Campaign price list
Leaflets: €10 for 100 black and white leaflets or 50 colour leaflets
Posters: €15 for 50 posters
T-shirts: €8 per T-shirt
Advertisement on bus: €250
Using a local celebrity: €100
YouTube video: €120

1 SPEAKING Work in pairs. Discuss the questions.

1 How do you find out about global and local issues – from the internet, a newspaper or TV?

2 How can charities make a difference?

2 Read the text and compare your ideas.

3 Complete the text with sentences A–G. There is one sentence that you do not need.

A Other people buy products from their online shops.

B She can hear her schoolmates cheering and she knows she has to finish.

C They don't make donations because they haven't got much money.

D It's cool and clear and Mohammed has not been ill for weeks.

E By the end of this year, people will have completed more than 350 events.

F They give up their free time and volunteer.

G Over the next few years, this money will be helping people like Mohammed.

4 SPEAKING Discuss the questions.

1 Which charities are popular in your country?

2 Have you ever been to an event that supports a good cause? What was it? What did the event achieve?

V │ insight Collocations: charities

5 Find the verbs in the text and write the nouns that go with them.

1 take part in .... / a marathon

2 raise .... / awareness

3 transform .... / a situation

4 donate .... / clothes

5 volunteer .... / help

6 aid .... / developing countries

7 address .... / a problem

8 support .... / a campaign

6 Complete the text with verbs in exercise 5.

Be humankind

Since the 1960s, charities have put slogans on T-shirts to ¹ .... awareness of social problems and encourage people to take action. In the past, these slogans were often about world peace, but today slogans ² .... many different issues, such as environmental problems, poverty and social injustice.

T-shirts with slogans show that we ³ .... a charity or a campaign. Sport Relief slogans like 'Rise to the Challenge' and 'Go the Extra Mile' encourage people to ⁴ .... events. Other slogans such as Oxfam's 'Change, not Charity' encourage us to ⁵ .... our time and not just ⁶ .... money. And although slogans don't ⁷ .... people's lives on their own, they are an important part of the process. In the words of another Oxfam slogan, they persuade us to 'Be humankind'.

Go the Extra Mile

London, UK: It's two o'clock in the afternoon and Sophie Hanson is running a marathon. She's wearing a T-shirt that says 'Go the Extra Mile', but she's feeling tired. ¹...............
She grabs a bottle of water, takes a long drink and carries
5 on. By the time she finishes, she will have raised £200.

Halfway around the world, in Sierra Leone, Africa, Mohammed Koroma is thirsty. It's 30 degrees outside, so he picks up a cup of water and takes a long drink. The water is from a new well in his village, so it isn't
10 contaminated. ²............... He will be going to school again at 8 a.m. tomorrow.

Sophie and Mohammed are two teenagers with very different lives, but their lives are connected through charity. Sophie is taking part in a huge national event
15 that raises money for people in the UK and abroad – a sponsored run for Sport Relief. Mohammed's village has a new well that was paid for with money from the same event. Every year, Sport Relief and its sister charity, Comic Relief, raise money for good causes. ³............... These events
20 include marathons and football matches, talent shows and baking competitions, and when they are all completed, they will have raised over £50 million. That's enough money to transform the lives of thousands of people.
⁴...............

25 According to recent research, the UK is the fifth most generous nation in the world. Charities are an important part of British society, and some of the world's biggest and most famous organizations, such as Oxfam and Save the Children, started in the UK. Today, there are over
30 160,000 charities, and more than three quarters (79%) of people donate money or volunteer time every month.

Many people make regular donations to big charities that aid poor people in different countries. **5**............ Smaller charities, such as sports projects or hospices, address more local issues and rely on smaller events, like car boot 35 sales and fun runs. They also rely on volunteers for the day-to-day running of these projects.

Teenagers play a big role in this culture of giving. A recent World Vision study showed that 69% of teens are aware of the needs of others thanks to the internet and globalization. 40 And although teens may not have much money to give, they often help in other ways. **6**............ In the UK, more than a third of teenagers have given time to charities in the last year. In fact, supporting a charity is part of everyday life, and young people are the new champions of this culture. 'I feel 45 good when I do something,' explains Sophie after the race. 'I read about so many problems in the news – at home and abroad. Often, I feel helpless. I don't have a lot of money, but then I can volunteer, I can get sponsors and I can make a difference.' Back in Sierra Leone, Mohammed is smiling. 50

Charity in numbers

160,000 charities in the UK raise £37 billion every year.

13.2 million people volunteer for charities.

Charity shops raise £200 million every year.

The biggest charities like Oxfam, Cancer Research and the RSPCA raise more than £10 million a year.

Future perfect and future continuous

7 Study sentences 1–3 from the text and match them to rules a–c. Then complete the rules.

1 By the time she finishes (the marathon), she **will have raised** £200.
2 Over the next few years, this money **will be helping** people like Mohammed.
3 He **will be going** to school again at 8 a.m. tomorrow.

We use the future continuous:
a to talk about an action in progress at a definite time in the future.
b to talk about an action in progress over an extended period of time in the future.
Form: *will / won't + be +* ....
We use the future perfect:
c to talk about an action that will be finished before a definite time in the future.
Form: *will / won't + have +* ....

Reference and practice 4.2 | Workbook page 111

8 A school magazine interviewed Sophie before the race. Complete the interview. Use the future continuous or the future perfect.

Interviewer What **1**............ (you do) at 1 p.m. on Saturday?
Sophie I **2**............ (run) in the marathon and hopefully by 6 p.m. I **3**............ (finish).
Interviewer How far **4**............ (you run) by the end of the race?
Sophie About 42 km.
Interviewer That's impressive. **5**............ lots of people .... (take part) in the event on Saturday?
Sophie Yes, I **6**............ (not do) it alone. Hundreds of people will be there.
Interviewer **7**............ (you celebrate) with your friends after the event?
Sophie Yes, I will. I **8**............ (collect) their money, too!
Interviewer How much money **9**............ (you raise)?
Sophie About £200, I hope!

9 SPEAKING Work in pairs. Discuss the questions.

What will you be doing:
1 after school today?
2 at 2 p.m. on Saturday?
3 this time next week?
4 during the summer holidays?

What will you have done:
5 in two hours' time?
6 by this time tomorrow?
7 by the end of this year?
8 in five years' time?

Vocabulary bank | Charities page 137

Support our charity!

This year, Hepworth school will be organizing fundraising events throughout the school year.

We want YOU to help us decide which of these two charities we will support with our funds this year:

WaterAid
WaterAid works in 26 of the world's poorest countries. It aims to improve access to safe, clean drinking water for hundreds of thousands of people.

World Wide Fund for Nature (WWF)
The World Wide Fund for Nature aims to protect endangered animals and plants by conserving their habitats and fighting against climate change and pollution.

Write an essay to tell us which charity you want to support and why.

1 SPEAKING Read the poster and answer the questions.

1 Why does Hepworth school want students to choose one of the charities?
2 Have you heard of these charities?
3 Which charity would you choose to support? Why?

2 Read Nick's essay and answer the questions.

1 According to Nick, what is a basic human right?
2 How many people around the world cannot get safe, clean water?
3 How does WaterAid help communities to be more independent?
4 Which charity is bigger, WaterAid or WWF?

STRATEGY

Organizing an opinion paragraph

When you write an opinion essay, the main part of it will be paragraphs expressing your opinion. Each opinion paragraph should include:

1 **The main point:** *My first reason for choosing WaterAid is that in many parts of the world the poorest people don't have taps or even wells.*
2 **Support:** *Often their only source of water is dirty and dangerous and very far from their homes.*
3 **Specific example:** *In fact, 884 million people do not have access to safe, clean water.*

3 Read the strategy. Then study paragraphs C and D in Nick's essay and find examples for each point 1–3 in the strategy.

4 Study Nick's essay again. In which paragraph(s) A–E does he do 1–4?

1 Presents an opposing viewpoint.
2 Introduces the topic and states his opinion.
3 Summarizes and restates his opinion.
4 Supports his opinion by presenting arguments and examples.

A   Hepworth school has asked the students to choose its main charity for the year. In my opinion, we should choose WaterAid, because access to safe, clean water is a basic human right.

B   My first reason for choosing WaterAid is that in many parts of the world the poorest people don't have taps or even wells. Often their only source of water is dangerous because it's dirty and it's very far from their homes. In fact, 884 million people do not have access to safe, clean water and 5,000 children die each day from water-related diseases. I am convinced that by supporting WaterAid, we can help to reduce these numbers.

C   Another argument for donating our money to WaterAid, is that it helps communities to set up and maintain their own water and hygiene projects. By doing this it educates people and encourages communities to look after their own needs. Better hygiene can reduce childhood deaths by 35%.

D   My final point is that many people might say that WaterAid is a much smaller charity than the World Wide Fund for Nature, so it can't make as much of a difference as WWF can. In fact, annual total donations to WWF are nearly ten times the donations to WaterAid. However, this is why I feel that WaterAid needs our money more.

E   To conclude, I believe that Hepworth should choose WaterAid as its charity, because it helps the poorest people around the world and it will really benefit from our donations.

Nick Jones

Introducing arguments and giving opinions

5 Study the phrases in the table. Then put the highlighted phrases in Nick's letter under the correct heading in the table.

Introducing arguments	Giving opinions
The main argument for / against is … .	My point of view is that … .
First of all, … .	To my mind, … .
It is also important to note that … .	

6 Complete Monica's essay with phrases in exercise 5. Sometimes more than one answer is possible.

Our school wants to choose one charity to support this year. ¹_____ we should choose the World Wide Fund for Nature (WWF), because it helps to conserve the environment and protects animals and plants, and there is nothing more important than the future of our planet.

²_____ supporting the WWF is that climate change is a major issue for our planet. The WWF works in many ways to fight against climate change. It supports energy efficiency and is promoting a new international climate agreement.

³_____ donating money to this charity is that the WWF does a lot of important work to preserve huge areas, for example, the Amazon rainforest and the Arctic.

These areas are under threat because of global warming, deforestation, or overfishing. If we don't protect these places now, it will be too late! That's why ⁴_____ the WWF's work is so necessary.

⁵_____ the WWF protects a large number of endangered species, including tigers, rhinos and polar bears. These beautiful animals share our planet and ⁶_____, it's our duty to look after them and to prevent their extinction.

In conclusion, ⁷_____ our charity for this year should be the WWF because it is doing the most important work – protecting life on our planet and protecting the planet itself.

Monica Du Pont

WRITING GUIDE

■ **Task** Your school wants to give €500 to one of the two charities below. Find out more about both charities and decide which one you want to support. Write an opinion essay to explain why your school should choose this charity.

UNICEF (The United Nations Children's Fund)
UNICEF is an international charity which defends children's rights. It works with families, communities and governments in more than 190 countries and aims to protect children from exploitation, violence and poverty.

Friends of the Earth
Friends of the Earth is one of the largest environmental charities in the world. It fights for solutions to environmental problems, supports fair trade and campaigns against climate change, pollution and genetically modified crops.

■ **Ideas** Make notes about:

■ what the charity does.
■ why it is an important issue.
■ why this charity deserves your school's money more than any other charity.

■ **Plan** Follow the plan:

Paragraph 1: Write an introduction and give a clear statement of your opinion.

Paragraphs 2–4: Give at least three reasons for your opinion. Write each reason in a separate paragraph. Add support and specific examples.

Paragraph 5: Write a conclusion to the essay. Restate your opinion and summarize the reasons for it.

■ **Write** Write an opinion essay. Use the paragraph plan to help you.

■ **Check** Check the following points:

■ Have you used a clear paragraph structure?
■ Have you included all arguments supporting your opinion?
■ Have you used language for introducing arguments and giving opinions?
■ Have you checked grammar, vocabulary, spelling and punctuation?

1 Work in pairs. Study the dictionary entry for *over-*. Then match the words in bold in sentences a–d to meanings 1–4 in the dictionary entry.

> **over-** /ˈəʊvə(r)/ [in compounds] **1** more than usual; too much: *to oversleep* ◆ *over-optimistic* ◆ *overactive* **2** completely: *overjoyed* **3** upper; outer; extra: *overcoat* ◆ *overtime* **4** over; above: *overcast* ◆ *to overhang*

a A balloon flew **overhead**.

b When he heard the good news, he got **overexcited**.

c The train was **overcrowded**, so I couldn't get a seat.

d I left my **overcoat** on the bus.

STRATEGY

Word-building: the meaning of prefixes

Many words in English are made up of a prefix (e.g. *over-*) and a root word (e.g. *flow*). The prefix + the root word produce a new word (e.g. *overflow*).

A lot of prefixes carry meaning. If you understand the meaning of prefixes, it will help you to understand new words. A good dictionary will have entries for prefixes. Prefixes can be grouped into the following categories:

a numbers
b time
c size
d position

---

2 Read the strategy above. Then match the prefixes in bold to a–d in the strategy.

1 The **trans**atlantic flight from London to New York takes six hours. ....

2 There are many **pre**-war buildings in my street. ....

3 The **mini**bus picks us up at 7 a.m. every morning. ....

4 A **tri**cycle has three wheels. ....

5 In the **fore**ground of the picture, you can see the idyllic beach. ....

6 We usually do our shopping at the **super**store on the outskirts of town. ....

7 He's **bi**lingual – he speaks two languages fluently. ....

8 The **ex**-footballer is giving a talk at our school today. ....

3 Match the prefixes in exercise 2 to meanings 1–8.

1 three ....
2 two ....
3 before ....
4 small ....
5 former ....
6 front ....
7 extreme; large ....
8 across; through ....

4 Add the prefixes below to categories a–d in the strategy.

■ post- ■ maxi- ■ mono-■ sub-

5 Answer the questions.

1 If a word is a monosyllable, how many syllables has it got?
2 What's bigger – a market, a minimarket or a supermarket?
3 Is an ex-friend still your friend?
4 What's longer – a maxi-dress or a mini-dress?
5 Where is a subway?
6 How many languages does a trilingual person speak?

6 Complete sentence b so that it has a similar meaning to sentence a. Use one of the prefixes from exercises 2 and 4 and the correct form of the words below.

■ president ■ weekly ■ eaten ■ atlantic ■ lingual ■ mature

1 **a** The first flight across the Atlantic was from Canada to Ireland in 1919.
  b The first .... flight was from Canada to Ireland in 1919.
2 **a** Although her baby was born before its expected time, he is doing well.
  b Although her baby was ...., he is doing well.
3 **a** I'm so full – I've had too much food.
  b I'm so full – I've ....
4 **a** When learning vocabulary, it's good to use a dictionary which is only in English.
  b When learning vocabulary, it's good to use a .... dictionary.
5 **a** We went to a talk given by our former president.
  b We went to a talk given by our ....
6 **a** We have meetings twice a week.
  b We have .... meetings.

7 Use a dictionary to find three words with each of the prefixes *mono-*, *multi-* and *sub-*. Write your own example sentence with each new word.

1 ....
....
....

2 ....
....
....

3 ....
....
....

Dictionary entries from *Oxford Wordpower Dictionary*, 4th edition

Vocabulary

1 Complete the sentences with the correct form of the verbs below.

▨ contaminate ▨ devastate ▨ die out ▨ evacuate ▨ spread
▨ relocate

1 The bird called the dodo .... in the 17th century.
2 Infected insects can .... dangerous diseases.
3 Oil .... water, making it dangerous for animals.
4 In 1956, the US government paid Native Americans to .... from the country to the city.
5 Hurricane Katrina .... New Orleans in 2005.
6 After the 2011 tsunami, Japanese authorities .... local people to places of safety.

Marks .... / 6

2 Complete the text with the correct form of the words in brackets. Add the correct prefixes (co-, inter-, over-, under-, re-, semi-).

Brazilian *favelas*, which are poor, [1] ....
(developed) places, are often also [2] ....
(crowded). *Favela Painting* is a charity with [3] ....
(national) support from many countries. It helps
favelas to [4] .... (build) lost hope and pride by
painting their houses. Artists and local people
[5] .... (operate) to create unique designs. In just
one street you can see a fish, a kite, and a half
moon in a perfect [6] .... (circle)!

Marks .... / 6

3 Complete the text with the correct prepositions.

I care [1] .... animals. I believe [2] ....
treating them with respect. That's why I
belong [3] .... an animal rights charity, the
League Against Cruel Sports. We protest
[4] .... hunting animals for sport. We've
set [5] .... an anti-hunting campaign and
now we're relying [6] .... your donations for
success. Please help!

Marks .... / 6

4 Complete the sentences with the verbs below. There is one verb that you do not need.

▨ address ▨ aid ▨ donate ▨ raise ▨ take part ▨ transform
▨ volunteer

1 Over 30,000 people .... in the Tokyo marathon every year.
2 Please .... for just an hour a week to help elderly people.
3 Live Aid tried to .... awareness of Africa's problems.
4 I know I should .... more money to charities.
5 We need to .... the problem of global warming.
6 Education can .... people's lives for the better.

Marks .... / 6

Grammar

5 Complete the sentences with the verbs below.

▨ 's going to be ▨ will be ▨ may be ▨ starts ▨ might start
▨ will come ▨ 'm speaking ▨ 'll speak ▨ may join

1 I hope the rain .... soon. My garden is very dry.
2 You .... right about climate change – I'm not sure.
3 Look at that rain! The river is already full. There .... a big risk of floods tonight.
4 I .... the campaign. I haven't decided yet.
5 I promise I .... to her about it soon, OK?
6 I think life in the future .... better than now.
7 I .... to the Environment Minister at 3.00 p.m. tomorrow.
8 The lecture on environmentalism .... at 11.00.
9 It's possible that countries .... a war over water.

Marks .... / 9

6 Choose the correct answers.

Today, I [1] .... try doing an RAK ('random act of
kindness') with a friend. We made plans last night. We
[2] .... at my house this morning. We [3] .... discuss
what to do then. We have a few ideas already. We
[4] .... to the bus stop and pay for a stranger's ticket.
According to my timetable, the next bus [5] .... in an
hour. Alternatively, we [6] .... up litter in the park.
The sky is blue – it [7] .... be a lovely day. You know
what? Let's do that. I think it [8] .... more fun!

1 a might   b will   c 'm going to   d may
2 a 'll meet   b meet   c 're meeting   d might meet
3 a won't   b may   c will   d 're going to
4 a might go   b go   c 're going   d will go
5 a is leaving b won't leave c may leave   d leaves
6 a will pick b might pick c 're picking   d pick
7 a 's going to b may   c might   d will
8 a is being   b will be   c is   d may not be

Marks .... / 8

7 Complete the sentences. Use the future perfect or future continuous form of the verbs in brackets.

1 'What .... you .... at this time tomorrow?' 'I .... at the charity shop.' (do / volunteer)
2 The anti-war march .... by 11.00. After that, we .... outside the town hall. (finish / protest)
3 At 6.00 tonight, I .... the documentary on global warming. .... you .... home by then? (watch / get)
4 In a year's time, the city .... by 50%. 10,000 more people .... here then. But by the end of this year, the authorities .... just 1,000 more homes. (grow / live / build)

Marks .... / 9

Total .... / 50

Listening

1 Read the sentences. Are they facts (F), opinions (O) or speculations (S)?

1 Volunteering was Alice's own idea.
2 Alice thought it would help her to get into university.
3 Her work might help Tanzanian teachers to feel more enthusiastic about sport.
4 In Alice's opinion, the main benefit of sport is learning key life skills.
5 The charity may teach martial arts for the first time next year.
6 Not everyone will be a good volunteer for the charity.

2 🔊 **1.19** Listen to a radio programme. Are the sentences in exercise 1 true (T) or false (F)? Correct the false ones.

Speaking

3 Work in pairs. Take it in turns to give and react to news. Use the ideas below or your own ideas.

1 You raised lots of money in a charity marathon, but you didn't finish it.
2 Your parents won't let you volunteer at a sports camp in Tanzania this summer.
3 Your local youth centre has offered you a part-time job teaching sport this summer.

4 Work in pairs. Imagine that your class is going to spend a weekend volunteering. Discuss each volunteering option below, giving your opinions. Then decide together what you think the class should do and why.

1 helping disabled children to take part in activities on a sports camp
2 going on a two-day sponsored walk to raise money for better school facilities
3 cleaning up your local park

Reading

5 Read the text. Then choose the best description of the text type a–d.

a a report making recommendations
b an article promoting a particular service
c a factual description for an encyclopedia
d a review of a service the writer has tried

6 Match headings 1–8 to paragraphs A–F. There are two headings that you do not need.

1 Introducing a new alternative
2 Maximizing your workout
3 An easier, gentler kind of exercise
4 Skills and personal development
5 An unpleasant chore
6 A job well done
7 Studying nature
8 Harming the planet

Go green and get fit!

A ....

Going to the gym or the sports centre often feels like a joyless necessity. The sweaty rooms and irritating music seem to be the part of the price you pay for getting fit. You won't have much fun in the process, perhaps, but at least you'll be doing something worthwhile. Or so you *think*.

B ....

In actual fact, your exercise routine will have some devastating side-effects and we don't just mean aching muscles! Gyms and sports centres need huge amounts of energy for lights, air conditioning, heating – and of course, pools and machines. While you've been running, your treadmill has been burning as much electricity as fifteen 75-Watt light bulbs.

C ....

Luckily, there's now another way for people who care about more than calorie-counting. *Green Fitness* allows you to exercise in the open air, surrounded by birdsong, for the fraction of the price of a leisure club membership. What's more, rather than devastating the planet, you'll be helping to preserve it. How? By doing conservation work in some of the most beautiful parts of the country.
Click here for locations.

D ....

If you've never done any gardening before, don't worry. We'll give you all the training you need. Volunteers cooperate to achieve tasks together, so you won't be on your own. The team spirit is amazing – something which you're never going to find at the gym! What's more, many volunteers have reported that taking part in sessions has boosted their self-esteem and happiness. Click here for reviews.

E ....

However, be warned: this is not a 'soft' alternative and laziness is not an option! An hour's moderate gardening is at least as demanding as a six-kilometre jog and builds strength and stamina in *all* parts of your body. The only thing you might miss is fast, aerobic exercise. That's why *Green Fitness* also leads optional 'military fitness' style runs at the end of each session for weekend volunteers – for no extra cost. Click here for prices.

F ....

Still not sure? Then think about this. At the end of every session you'll have achieved something truly special. No, not just a trim waist or more muscular arms! You'll be able to see the flowers you've planted, or the walls that you've repaired and think: 'I did that.' You might leave covered in mud (sorry!), but you'll also leave feeling on top of the world. How many gym users can say the same? Click here to join!

7 **Read the text. Choose the correct answers.**

People volunteer for different reasons, but probably most of us volunteer ¹.......... try to improve life for others. However, generosity brings a reward. It seems that volunteers can expect ².......... themselves as well!

In the past few years, studies ³.......... that people who volunteer typically experience greater levels of self-esteem than those who don't. ⁴.........., their overall health and well-being also improves. People who volunteer regularly today ⁵.......... longer in the future, and they tend to suffer from fewer diseases – although of course there are no guarantees!

Partly, these health benefits are ⁶.......... to the extra exercise, as volunteers are usually fairly active people. Helping others burns calories! What's more, it seems that we generally enjoy ⁷.......... others happy, which in turn boosts our energy and fitness levels. It is now generally agreed that being ⁸.......... in the dumps for extended periods of time is bad for our health, as depression weakens us physically as well as mentally.

So how much time should we volunteer for? Some studies suggest that we ⁹.......... volunteer for at least 100 hours a year to enjoy the full advantages. At the end of our first year of volunteering, we ¹⁰.......... our own lives for the better, too.

1	a in order to	b because of	c so that
2	a benefit	b to benefit	
	c benefitting		
3	a have been showing	b had shown	
	c have shown		
4	a Similarly	b Really	c Extremely
5	a are living	b will live	c may live
6	a because	b due	c so as
7	a making	b to make	c make
8	a under	b below	c down
9	a can	b need to	c may
10	a will be transforming	b are transforming	
	c will have transformed		

8 **Read the statement below. Then write an opinion essay. Use the plan to help you.**

'Not all students enjoy school sports lessons. Should older teenagers have the option of doing volunteer work in their local communities instead?'

Paragraph 1: Introduce the topic and briefly state your own opinion.

Paragraph 2: Give arguments to support your opinion. Use a different paragraph for each main idea.

Paragraph 3: Present an opposing viewpoint and comment on it.

Paragraph 4: Summarize your opinion, giving reasons.

5 Rights and wrongs

Reading and vocabulary Teenage gangs

1 **SPEAKING** **Why do teenagers join gangs? Discuss the reasons below and add your own ideas. Then read the text and compare your ideas.**

- to make money - because of peer pressure
- for the excitement - to have somewhere to hang out
- to belong to a group - to feel safe

STRATEGY

Using referencing to understand a text

Reference words link different parts of a text together. They can refer back to a word, a phrase or a whole sentence or idea.

- pronouns, for example: *he, him, it, they, them, that, this, these, those*
- possessive adjectives, for example: *his, its, their, her*
- relative pronouns, for example: *who, whose, which*

2 **Read the strategy. Study the underlined words in the text. Who or what do they refer to?**

1	That (line 3)	**5**	him (line 31)
2	She (line 10)	**6**	whose (line 35)
3	its (line 17)	**7**	his (line 59)
4	who (line 26)	**8**	them (line 61)

3 **Study the underlined reference words in A–F. Who or what do you think they refer to? Complete the article with sentences A–F. There is one sentence that you do not need.**

A <u>He</u> was shot in the arm, but luckily he survived.

B There are 169 gangs <u>there</u>, with more than 5,000 members.

C <u>They</u> were easy to get and easy to use.

D <u>His</u> father left home when he was a baby, and Joshua and his sisters were brought up by their mother.

E <u>Its</u> members had code names like P-Man or Stepz, and they looked after each other.

F <u>That</u>'s when he met Ben.

4 **Read the article again and answer the questions.**

1 What problems did Joshua's family have when he was young?
2 What didn't he like about the gang?
3 How did Joshua's gang send warnings to other gangs?
4 Why was Joshua attacked?
5 How did his mum feel when she saw him? Why?
6 In what ways was Ben similar to Joshua?
7 How did the Youth Inclusion Project help Joshua?

V Crime

5 **Study the people below. What are the crimes that they commit?**

- mugger - shoplifter - armed robber - vandal - thief
- offender

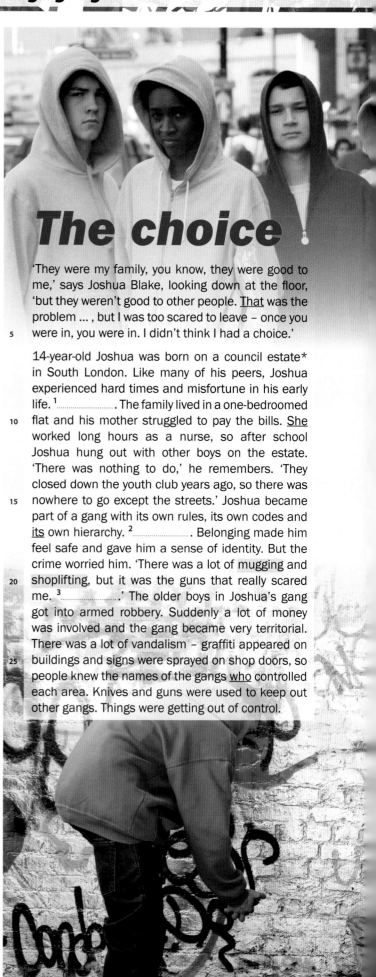

The choice

'They were my family, you know, they were good to me,' says Joshua Blake, looking down at the floor, 'but they weren't good to other people. <u>That</u> was the problem ... , but I was too scared to leave – once you
5 were in, you were in. I didn't think I had a choice.'

14-year-old Joshua was born on a council estate* in South London. Like many of his peers, Joshua experienced hard times and misfortune in his early life. ¹......................... . The family lived in a one-bedroomed
10 flat and his mother struggled to pay the bills. <u>She</u> worked long hours as a nurse, so after school Joshua hung out with other boys on the estate. 'There was nothing to do,' he remembers. 'They closed down the youth club years ago, so there was
15 nowhere to go except the streets.' Joshua became part of a gang with its own rules, its own codes and <u>its</u> own hierarchy. ²......................... . Belonging made him feel safe and gave him a sense of identity. But the crime worried him. 'There was a lot of mugging and
20 shoplifting, but it was the guns that really scared me. ³..........................' The older boys in Joshua's gang got into armed robbery. Suddenly a lot of money was involved and the gang became very territorial. There was a lot of vandalism – graffiti appeared on
25 buildings and signs were sprayed on shop doors, so people knew the names of the gangs <u>who</u> controlled each area. Knives and guns were used to keep out other gangs. Things were getting out of control.

Vocabulary: crime; noun prefixes: *mis-*, *dis-*; phrasal verbs with *to* and *with*; synonyms: the law
Grammar: first and second conditionals; modals of obligation, prohibition and permission; *should* and *ought to*

Speaking: discussing teenage crime; solving moral dilemmas; apologizing and accepting apologies
Writing: a letter to a newspaper

5A

Then, one day, something changed. 'I was walking home from school when a boy rode past on a bike,' says Josh. 'I didn't recognize <u>him</u>, but he called out my name and when I looked round, he pulled out a gun.' Joshua was the victim of a revenge shooting. ⁴............................. . The boy on the bike was from a rival gang, <u>whose</u> leader had been attacked the day before. 'My mum was devastated when she found out,' says Joshua. 'She knew about my misbehaviour at school, but she had no idea about the gang. She just looked at me in disbelief, she couldn't stop crying.'

Three weeks in hospital gave Joshua time to reflect on the choices he had made. He decided he wanted a different life, he wanted to change. ⁵............................. .

Ben Magoro is a mentor* at a Youth Inclusion Project, a programme which helps kids escape from gang culture and get back into education. Ben, like many mentors, was a gang member himself. He was involved in car theft and he'd been sent to prison for the offence. Ben understood 'gang mentality'. 'It is like a family,' says Ben, 'it's a family where the mistreatment of "outsiders" is OK, but show a gang member disrespect and you'll be seriously hurt. It's a family where crime and dishonesty are OK and any disagreement is solved with a gun. It's a family that thinks committing crime is an acceptable way to make a living, but belonging to that family is a big mistake – all it does is destroy your life.'

The Youth Inclusion Project offered Joshua a way out and gave him the courage to turn <u>his</u> life around. Projects focus on teenagers' interests, such as music, sport or fashion. Mentors help <u>them</u> to express themselves, reflect upon their past and make better life choices. 'In the gang my choice was either die young or go to jail,' says Joshua, 'But now I can choose to get an education, I can choose a future … I can choose life.'

* council estate = an area of houses built and rented out to people by the local government
* mentor = an experienced person in an educational institution who trains and advises new students

6 Choose the correct answers.

1 The **mugger** / **shoplifter** looked around the store, then quickly put the watch into her pocket.
2 A person who is charged with a crime is called **an offender** / **a thief**.
3 The play area in the park has been destroyed by **vandals** / **muggers**.
4 Last night a **shoplifter** / **thief** broke into our house and stole the TV.
5 The news headlines were all about the **theft** / **mugging** of a famous painting from an art gallery.
6 There was **an armed robbery** / **vandalism** at our local supermarket last night. £10,000 was taken.

V insight Noun prefixes: *mis-* and *dis-*

7 Read the sentences, then match the prefixes *mis-* and *dis-* to definitions a and b.

1 Joshua experienced hard times and misfortune in his early life.
2 It's a family where crime and dishonesty are OK.

a the opposite of something, not **b** wrong or bad

8 Complete the text with the words in brackets and *mis-* or *dis-*. Then check your answers in *The choice*.

The campaigner

19-year-old Alexander Rose had the ¹............................. (fortune) to grow up on a bad council estate. Whenever there was ²............................. (agreement) between people, someone got hurt. School was impossible – there was constant ³............................. (behaviour) in the classroom and ⁴............................. (respect) for teachers. Kids that turned up didn't want to learn. Their lessons were on the street, and they were lessons in ⁵............................. (honesty) and crime.

'A lot of these kids suffered from ⁶............................. (treatment) at home, so they didn't care about other people,' says Alex. Alex tried to ignore the violence until he lost a 16-year-old friend. His first reaction was ⁷............................. (belief) – how could this happen to someone he knew? Then he decided to do something about it. Alex designed the STOP logo, which stands for Stop This Ongoing Problem. He printed the logo on some T-shirts, then sold them to friends to get his message onto the streets. 'I'm just one person putting in ten per cent,' says Alex. 'If everyone put in ten per cent, that really would bring about change.'

9 SPEAKING Discuss the newspaper headlines. What do you think are the causes and solutions?

'A third of children believe that gangs and knives are a threat to their safety'
'Youngsters turning to gangs instead of parents'
'Make school day longer to stop pupils joining gangs'

Vocabulary bank Crime and punishment page 138

Rights and wrongs 57

Lie, lie, lie!

- 98% of teens say they lie to their parents.
- 96% of teens say that lying is wrong.
- Younger teens are better at lying than older ones.
- 40% of parents believe it is normal to sometimes lie to their children.
- 65% of people think it's OK to lie in order not to hurt someone's feelings.
- Most people lie three times in ten minutes of conversation.
- Men and women lie the same amount, but about different things.
- We lie most frequently to the people we love.

1 SPEAKING Work in pairs. Read the facts about lying. Which facts surprise you and why? Which one is not true?

2 ⊚ 1.20 Listen to three teenagers talking about lies. Match statements 1–6 to Charlie (C), Sean (S) and Elly (E).

1 If my best friend asks me if I like her new haircut tomorrow, I'll say yes.
2 If they didn't ask so many questions, I wouldn't tell so many lies.
3 If he ever found out, he'd be really furious.
4 If I said what I really thought, they might get upset.
5 If you tell the truth all the time, you'll offend people.
6 Unless she learns that lying is wrong, she might become a compulsive liar.

3 ⊚ 1.20 Listen again. What are Charlie's, Sean's and Elly's opinions on telling lies?

First and second conditionals

4 Study sentences 1–6 in exercise 2 and decide which ones talk about situations likely to happen and which ones talk about situations unlikely to happen. Then answer the questions.

1 Which conditional talks about a real or very likely situation in the present or the future?
2 Which conditional talks about an imaginary or unlikely situation in the present or the future?
3 What tenses do we use to form each conditional?
4 What does *unless* mean in sentence 6? How can you rephrase this sentence using *if*?

Reference and practice 5.1 Workbook page 112

5 Complete the questions with the correct form of the verbs in brackets. Then work in pairs and answer the questions.

1 If you .... (realize) your friend was shoplifting, would you tell anyone?
2 What would you do if you .... (see) some people vandalizing your local park?
3 If you .... (go out) this evening, what time will you come home?
4 What .... (your parents / do) if you come home later than you should?
5 If someone .... (ask) your friends if you were an honest person, what might they say?
6 What .... (you / do) if it rains a lot this weekend?

6 Read the text *How to spot a liar* about lie detection and complete the conditional sentences.

How to spot a liar

If we ¹........................ (not lie), we ²........................ (not be) human. But how can you tell if a person is lying? Only about one in a thousand people can spot a really good liar and many of these so-called 'deception wizards' work for the police. So, what signs ³........................ (you / look for), if you ⁴........................ (be) a deception wizard?

Firstly, there are many common beliefs about liars that aren't true. For example, 'liars never look you in the eye'. When you're talking to someone, if they ⁵........................ (not look) you in the eye, it just ⁶........................ (mean) that they're shy, not that they're lying. Liars are clever and they know that if they ⁷........................ (not make) eye contact, people ⁸........................ (suspect) them, so they make sure they do.

The way we tell stories can also give a lot of clues. If you ⁹........................ (invent) a story about why you haven't done your homework today, it ¹⁰........................ (be) short, in the right order and without much detail. Surprisingly, a true story won't be in the correct order and will have lots of corrections and contradictions. A liar ¹¹........................ (need to) learn these things if they ¹²........................ (want) to convince a deception wizard.

If you ¹³........................ (train) to be a deception wizard, you ¹⁴........................ (learn) to watch for other important clues, too: the number of times a person blinks, touches their face, scratches their head or moves their hands. The tone of voice can also be a sign. Speaking in a higher voice than usual can indicate a lie. Imagine your mother asked, 'Did you break this cup?' If you ¹⁵........................ (be) guilty, you ¹⁶........................ (shout), 'No, I didn't break it!' in a very high tone. If you ¹⁷........................ (be) innocent, you ¹⁸........................ (answer) just, 'No', in your natural voice.

7 🌐 **1.21** Listen to two stories. What lies did Jody and Simon tell?

8 Complete the questions with the correct second conditional form of the verbs in brackets. Then work in pairs and answer the questions. Give reasons for your answers.

1 If you .... (be) Jody, how .... (you / feel) about your mother changing her mind?
2 If you .... (be) Louise, ... (you / tell) your mother about Jody?
3 If Jody's mother .... (find out) about the lie, how .... (she / react)?
4 If Simon .... (offer) you a memory stick, ... (you / take) it?
5 If Simon .... (find out) that Jack knows the truth, what .... (he / do)?
6 If Jack .... (tell) his classmates about Simon, what .... (happen)?

9 **SPEAKING** Work in pairs. Read situations 1–4 and discuss what you would do. Think of at least three possible options for each situation. Then compare your ideas with another pair.

1 You see your older brother or sister stealing some money from your mother's purse.
2 You are at a friend's house. By accident, you break a very expensive porcelain vase, but nobody sees you do it.
3 You are taking an exam. Your friend is having problems and asks you to tell him / her the answers to some of the questions.
4 Your friend has given you a birthday present. You open it in front of him / her and you see a horrible jumper.

1 ◉ **1.22** **SPEAKING** Work in pairs. Do you agree with the statements about apologizing? Listen to the introduction to a radio show and choose the things that they mention.

1 It's a sign of weakness to apologize to people.
2 Saying sorry can be difficult for some people.
3 Men apologize more than women.
4 Some people are worried about apologizing in case the apology is not accepted.
5 Accepting an apology is difficult for some people.

2 ◉ **1.23** Listen to the whole radio show and choose the correct answers.

1 The presenter says that
  a some people never make mistakes.
  b he never makes mistakes.
  c everybody makes mistakes and no one is perfect.
2 People often don't like apologizing because
  a they don't like dealing with other people's problems.
  b they don't like saying they are wrong.
  c they don't like rejecting other people.
3 For some people, not apologizing is a sign of
  a weakness.
  b strength.
  c power.

4 Avoiding situations where you have to apologize
  a is not realistic at all.
  b is easy to achieve.
  c is possible in childhood.
5 If people decided not to apologize,
  a nothing would happen.
  b they wouldn't trust each other.
  c they would still have lots of friends.
6 According to the psychologist, it's more important to
  a make things right than to be right.
  b be right than to lose friends.
  c have lots of friends than to keep apologizing.

V insight Three-part phrasal verbs with *to* and *with*

3 **SPEAKING** Study the highlighted phrasal verbs in questions 1–8. Match them to meanings a–h. Then work in pairs and answer the questions.

1 If you make a mistake, do you always own up to it immediately?
2 Have you fallen out with anyone recently? Who was it and why?
3 Have you ever had to come up with an excuse for not doing something?
4 Do you think you live up to your parents' expectations?
5 Are you good at putting up with situations that you don't like?
6 If you have a lot of homework, do you get round to doing it straight away or do you leave it until the night before it's due?
7 Can some people get away with telling lies more than others?
8 If you don't do well at something, do you put it down to lack of experience?

a tolerate someone or something that is unpleasant without complaining
b admit you are responsible for something bad or wrong
c to understand that something is caused by something else
d do as well or be as good as other people expect
e do something wrong and not be punished for it
f find the time to do something
g have an argument with someone, so you are not friendly with them any more
h to think of an idea, suggestion

4 **SPEAKING** Work in pairs. Discuss the questions below.

1 Is it easy or difficult for you to apologize to people?
2 Who do you apologize to most often? What for?

Apologizing and accepting apologies

5 SPEAKING When might you make a formal apology and when might you make an informal one? When might you hear a formal apology?

6 🔊 **1.24** Listen to dialogues 1–6 and match them to speakers a–f:

a a teacher and a parent
b a parent and a child
c a shop assistant and a customer
d a teacher and a student
e two friends
f train station announcer

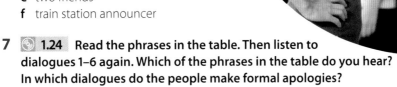

7 🔊 **1.24** Read the phrases in the table. Then listen to dialogues 1–6 again. Which of the phrases in the table do you hear? In which dialogues do the people make formal apologies?

Apologizing	Accepting apologies
Informal apologies	**Accepting informal apologies**
I'm very / so / really sorry.	That's OK.
I'm sorry. I didn't mean to.	It (really) doesn't matter.
	Don't worry about it.
Formal apologies	Never mind.
I (do) apologize for … .	
I'd like to apologize for … .	**Accepting formal apologies**
Please accept our apologies.	That's quite all right.
We regret to inform you that … .	Let's say no more about it.
It was very inconsiderate of me.	
	Showing the speaker you are not happy
	Don't let it happen again.
	You've really let me down.

8 🔊 **1.25** Complete the dialogue with phrases a–f. There is one phrase that you do not need. How does Ben feel? Then listen to a different version of the dialogue. How does Ben feel now?

a I regret to inform you
b I didn't expect that from you.
c I'm really sorry,

d Please forgive me.
e you've really let me down.
f I feel really bad about it.

Ben Hi, Kate. I'm really looking forward to Saturday. What time did we say we'd meet?
Kate Saturday? We didn't arrange to meet on Saturday, did we?
Ben Don't you remember? You said you'd help me choose a suit for my brother's wedding.
Kate Oh, no! I'd completely forgotten, Ben. ¹……………………………… but I've made other plans. I'm going to visit my cousins in Oxford. Perhaps we could go the following Saturday?
Ben No, that will be too late. The wedding's next weekend. I can't believe you forgot.
Kate ²………………………… .
Ben Well, you should because ³………………………… .
Kate ⁴………………………… . You know I've got an awful memory.
Ben Yes, I know, but ⁵………………………… .

9 SPEAKING Work in pairs, A and B. Choose a situation and prepare a dialogue. Student A explains the situation and apologizes, student B listens and accepts or does not accept the apology. Then swap roles and choose a new situation.

1 You borrowed your friend's jacket for a party. You ripped it.
2 You were using your dad's laptop to do some homework when you spilt some tea on it.
3 You work in a shop. A customer brings back some new jeans he / she bought at the weekend. There is a problem with them.
4 You broke one of the pictures in the school corridor while you were playing with a ball during the break.

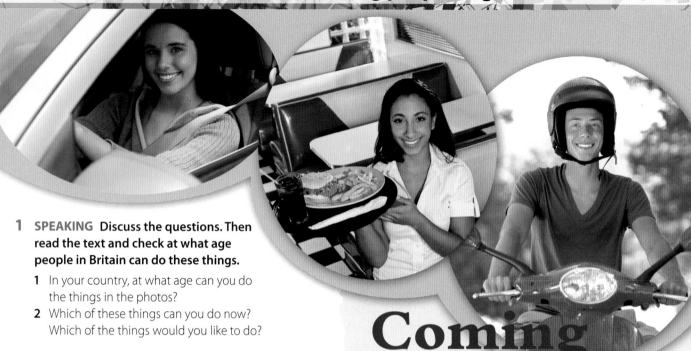

1 SPEAKING Discuss the questions. Then read the text and check at what age people in Britain can do these things.

1 In your country, at what age can you do the things in the photos?
2 Which of these things can you do now? Which of the things would you like to do?

2 Read the text again. Which paragraph A–F mentions the things in 1–7? There is one thing that you do not need.

1 The age of criminal responsibility.
2 The kind of part-time jobs young teenagers often do in the UK.
3 The age British teenagers have to be to drive a car.
4 The rights of a child if they break the law.
5 The impact of adults' decisions on children.
6 The move from being a child to an adult.
7 Voting rights.

V insight Synonyms: the law

3 Study the highlighted adjectives in the text. Then replace the adjectives in italics in sentences 1–6 with the correct words.

1 Many laws are *limiting* for teenagers and don't give them enough freedom.
2 School uniforms are *compulsory* in a lot of schools in the UK, but many students would prefer to choose what they wear.
3 According to law, every person has the right to a *just* trial, no matter what they've done.
4 Some people in England say that it should be *illegal* for teenagers to use tanning beds.
5 Wearing seat belts in the back seat of a car is *voluntary* in many countries, so people can decide if they want to do it or not.
6 In USA, teenagers under 16 can't live on their own. Is this *allowed (by law)* in your country?

4 SPEAKING Work in pairs. Discuss the questions.

1 What similarities and differences are there in the laws for the things mentioned in the text in your country?
2 What do you think an appropriate age for criminal responsibility should be? Why?
3 Why do you think age limits are necessary?

DVD extra UK Youth Parliament

Coming of age

A Some laws make sense. Others don't. In Britain, for example, the law states that you <u>can</u> get married at the age of sixteen (with your parents' approval), but you <u>may not</u> have a tattoo. You can choose
5 your life partner, but not a piece of body art. Age limits vary hugely around the world due to different historical, political, social and cultural factors. Here, we examine some rules, regulations and prohibited activities in the UK and explore
10 where childhood ends and adulthood begins in different areas of life.

The law

B The United Nations Convention on the Rights of the Child says that children have the right to help
15 from a lawyer and a fair trial that takes account of their age or situation.

C The age of criminal responsibility is ten years old in England, Wales and Northern Ireland and in Scotland it is twelve. Some people believe that a
20 low age of responsibility acts as a deterrent and stops young people from committing crimes. However, there is concern about how children between the ages of eight and twelve can fully understand the consequences of their actions.
25 Recent research has shown that the age of ten is probably too low because the part of the brain that has to make decisions and judgements is still developing.

D However, there is one area where teenagers' decisions
30 and opinions are taken into account and that is voting. In the UK, voting is optional and it is not a legal duty. Teenagers do not have the right to vote until the age of eighteen, but even then they <u>don't have to</u> vote in any election if they don't want to.

Modals of obligation, prohibition and permission

5 Study the underlined modal verbs in the text and answer the questions.

Which modal verbs mean:

1 it is necessary to do this? .... , ...
2 you are allowed to do this? .... , ...
3 it is not necessary to do this, but you can if you want to? ....
4 you are not allowed to do this? .... , ... , ...

> We usually use *must* when the speaker has decided that something is important and *have to* when someone else has decided this. However, in many situations, we can use *must* and *have to* in the same way.

Reference and practice 5.2 | Workbook page 113

6 Study the sentences. What is the difference in meaning between sentences a and b?

1 a I have to wear a school uniform.
 b I must buy a new school uniform because this one is too small.
2 a You don't have to tell anyone about this.
 b You mustn't tell anyone about this.
3 a You can't walk on the grass.
 b You must not walk on the grass.
4 a You can leave your bike here.
 b You may leave your bike here.

7 Rewrite the sentences using the words in brackets so that they have a similar meaning. Do not change the given words.

1 It is compulsory at my school to stand up when a teacher walks into the classroom. (have to)
2 You are allowed to fly a plane with a pilot's licence. (can)
3 During a trial, witnesses are not allowed to tell lies. (mustn't)
4 You do not have permission to leave the exam room before you finish. (may not)
5 The bus leaves at 6.30 a.m. It is essential that you arrive by 6.25 a.m. or the bus will leave without you. (must)
6 It is not necessary to wear a helmet when you ride a bike in England. (don't have to)

8 SPEAKING Which of these things is it necessary / not necessary for you to do? Which of them are you allowed / not allowed to do?

- have a credit card ▪ open a bank account ▪ fly a plane
- buy a pet ▪ give blood ▪ choose your own doctor
- leave home ▪ buy a lottery ticket ▪ go to school

Vocabulary bank | Law and order page 138

For many, this is a waste of a vote and a lot of UK teenagers feel voting should become obligatory so that it has more value. They feel they <u>must</u> take more responsibility if they want things to change and voting is an effective way to do this. ⁳⁵

Transport ⁴⁰

E British law authorizes sixteen-year-old Britons to ride mopeds with a small engine and quad bikes off road, but they can't drive a car or a quad bike on the road until the age of seventeen. Although Britain has some of the safest roads in the world, ⁴⁵ car accidents are the biggest cause of death of young people between the ages of seventeen and twenty-one. For this reason many people feel that twenty-one is a more appropriate age to hold a driving licence. ⁵⁰

Education and work

F Compulsory education in Britain continues until a child is sixteen and all students <u>have to</u> stay in full or part-time education until then, but this will probably soon increase to eighteen. Some school- ⁵⁵ leavers continue to work in jobs that they were doing part-time while they were at school. Young workers <u>may</u> start a part-time job at the age of thirteen in Britain and the most common jobs are babysitting and doing paper rounds. Young people ⁶⁰ <u>mustn't</u> work for more than two hours on a school day or a Sunday and they <u>can't</u> work for more than twelve hours during a school week. There is a view that such laws are restrictive and that younger children need to be encouraged to work more, ⁶⁵ especially if they are willing and able.

CURFEW FOR TEENAGERS

Local police announced yesterday that they are planning to introduce a curfew scheme during the school summer holiday period. Under this scheme, anyone under the age of sixteen will have to be home by 9 p.m. According to the police, the aim of the scheme is to cut the risk of teens becoming victims of crime or becoming offenders themselves. 'If we see teenagers on the streets after this time, we'll take them home,' said PC Davis. 'Most teenage crime takes place early in the evening and this scheme will certainly help to stop it. If it's successful, we'll introduce it into other parts of the country.'

1 SPEAKING **Work in pairs. Answer the questions.**

   1 Why do people write to newspapers?

   2 If you wrote a letter to your local newspaper, what would you write about?

2 **Read the newspaper article and answer the questions.**

   1 What is the main aim of the curfew scheme?

   2 What do you think about the scheme?

   3 Do you think it will be effective? Why / why not?

STRATEGY

Making suggestions and expressing results

When you write a letter to a newspaper, you might have to make suggestions and express results. In order to do this, you need to:

■ understand the problem and its cause.

■ prepare suggestions on how to solve the problem.

■ support the suggestions with possible results.

■ use specific phrases to introduce the suggestions and results.

3 **Read the strategy. Then read the letter that Jon wrote in response to the article and answer the questions.**

   1 What problem is he writing about?

   2 What does he think about the scheme?

   3 What suggestions does he make?

   4 What possible results does he mention?

4 **Study sentences 1–8 in the letter. Which ones make suggestions and which express results?**

Dear Sir / Madam,

I am writing to express my views on the proposed curfew scheme reported in your newspaper last week. I am strongly against this scheme and I believe it will cause more harm than good.

Police say that the scheme will help to protect teenagers and also reduce crime. But what about those teenagers who never get into trouble? A curfew would punish us and some could react in a negative way, which would make the problem worse.

[1]I recommend that they focus on the people that commit crime, rather than all teenagers. [2]This would mean that a lot of innocent teenagers would not feel like they are being punished for things they have not done.

[3]Another good idea would be to talk with us and our families. Many young offenders have difficult home lives or parents who do not look after them properly. Social services should give these families more support. [4]In this way, they would be able to identify the reasons some teenagers break the law and deal with the root of the problem. [5]If they did this, it would help to solve the problem in the long term.

[6]Another suggestion would be to organize activities for us, rather than lock us up at home. [7]If we had more worthwhile things to do, we would not be causing problems. Nobody can deny that there is nothing for us to do in our town, except hang out on the streets. The local council ought to provide some places for us to meet. [8]Perhaps they could offer free activities for us to do in the afternoons and at weekends.

I look forward to hearing the opinions of your other readers.

Yours faithfully,

Jon Rogers

should and ought to

We use *should* and *ought to* when we want to say that something is right or the best thing to do. They express a mild obligation. *Ought to* is more formal than *should*.

Reference and practice 5.3   Workbook page 113

5 **SPEAKING** Work in pairs. Discuss the possible results of the alternatives to the curfew scheme below. Use the expressions for making suggestions and expressing results.

- have regular discussions between young people, the council and the police
- set up sports activities and arts programmes
- install more security cameras and employ people to watch them
- have more police officers on the streets

WRITING GUIDE

- **Task** Write a letter to the newspaper expressing your views on the proposed scheme below.

> The local council is planning to create 'dispersal zones' in certain areas of the city to try to reduce street fighting. Under this scheme, if the police see a group of more than two young people in the street, they can ask them to separate and move. They can also remove people who do not live in the area and arrest them if they return within 24 hours.

- **Ideas** Make notes about:

1 How you feel about the proposed scheme. Do you agree or disagree with it?
2 Things you want to include. Think about:
   - the causes of street violence.
   - alternatives to the dispersal zones.
   - possible results.
   - what should happen to people that do not live in the area.

- **Plan** Decide which ideas you are going to use and match them to these paragraphs:

   Paragraph 1: Say why you are writing and express your opinion on dispersal zones.
   Paragraph 2: Explain the reason for your opinion and show you understand the problem and its cause.
   Paragraph 3: Present the first suggestion and result.
   Paragraph 4: Make another suggestion and a possible result.
   Paragraph 5: Add a final point.

- **Write** Write your letter. Use the paragraph plan to help you.

- **Check** Check the following points:

   - Have you included all the information from your notes?
   - Have you used a variety of phrases for making suggestions and expressing results?
   - Have you checked grammar, vocabulary, spelling and punctuation?

Rights and wrongs 65

1 Read part of the listening extract from unit 3C and find six phrasal verbs. What do they mean?

For some people it's all about power and being in control. They think that if they apologize they will lose that. Sometimes issues with apologizing can be put down to experiences in a person's childhood: perhaps a child was criticized a lot by their parents while they were growing up and felt they never lived up to their parents' expectations. As they get older they can take two approaches to this to avoid all the negative associations from childhood. One is to try and avoid situations where they may end up having to apologize at all. This is a very difficult strategy to get away with because it is completely unrealistic. The other, simpler approach, is to avoid admitting they have made mistakes or come up with excuses time after time not to apologize.

STRATEGY

The grammar of phrasal verbs

A phrasal verb is a combination of two or three words: a verb and at least one particle (a preposition or an adverb). The particle changes the meaning of the verb. There are three main types of phrasal verbs:

1 Intransitive – these verbs do not need an object.

2 Transitive, separable – these phrasal verbs can be separated by an object (in a dictionary, there is usually *sb / sth* <u>between</u> the two parts of the phrasal verb).

3 Transitive, inseparable – these phrasal verbs cannot be separated by an object (in a dictionary, there is usually *sb / sth* <u>after</u> the phrasal verb). Three-part phrasal verbs cannot be separated.

2 Read the strategy above. Study the dictionary entries for phrasal verbs with *fall*. Match them to categories 1–3 in the strategy.

> **PHR V** **fall apart** to break (into pieces): *My car is falling apart.*
> **fall back on sb/sth** to use sb/sth when you are in difficulty: *When the electricity was cut off we fell back on candles.*
> **fall for sb** (*informal*) to be strongly attracted to sb; to fall in love with sb
> **fall for sth** (*informal*) to be tricked into believing sth that is not true: *He makes excuses and she falls for them every time.*
> **fall out (with sb)** (*BrE*) to argue and stop being friendly (with sb)
> **fall through** to fail or not happen: *Our trip to Japan has fallen through.*

1 fall apart ....
2 fall back on sb / sth ....
3 fall for sb ....
4 fall for sth ....
5 fall out ....
6 fall out with sb ....
7 fall through ....

3 Choose the two sentences that are incorrect. Why are they incorrect?

1 They have fallen out.
2 They fell out with each other.
3 Luke fell out with.
4 She fell out with her best friend.
5 He has fallen his mother out.
6 Why have they fallen out?

4 Study the dictionary entries for phrasal verbs with *put*. Which ones are separable and which inseparable? Match sentences 1–4 to a–d to make mini dialogues.

> **put sb up** to give sb food and a place to stay: *She had missed the last train home, so I offered to put her up for the night.*
> **put sth up 1** to lift or hold sth up: *Put your hand up if you know the answer.* **2** to build sth: *to put up a fence/tent* **3** to fix sth to a wall, etc. so that everyone can see it: *to put up a notice* **4** to increase sth: *Some shops put up their prices just before Christmas.*
> **put up sth** to try to stop sb attacking you: *The old lady put up a struggle against her attacker.*
> **put up with sb/sth** to suffer sb/sth unpleasant and not complain about it: *I don't know how they put up with this noise.*

1 Can you put us up for a night when we're in New York?
2 The school is putting up the price of school lunches.
3 I'm going to put up that painting.
4 I can't put up with his behaviour.

a But they're already so expensive!
b I know. He's very unpleasant.
c Let me help you with that – I'll make sure it's straight.
d Sure. You can stay for as long as you need.

5 Put the words in the correct order to make sentences. Write two sentences if more than one order is possible. Add a particle to every sentence.

1 have / fall / I / a problem / Whenever / can / back / always / I / my mum

2 a fight / She / the attacker / put / against

3 bus tickets / They've / the price / of / put

4 fell / Maggie / with / her sister

5 can't / I / put / that noise / with

6 holiday / fallen / Our / have / plans

6 Use a dictionary to find the phrasal verbs below. Check if they are transitive or intransitive, and separable or inseparable. Then write your own example sentence with each phrasal verb.

■ get away ■ get away with sth ■ get sb down
■ get down to sth ■ get round sb ■ get round to sth

Dictionary entries from *Oxford Wordpower Dictionary*, 4th edition

Vocabulary

1 Complete the sentences with the correct form of the words in brackets.

1 .... is a big problem in many cities. (thief)
2 Graffiti isn't art, it's .... (vandal)
3 The .... stole a T-shirt. (shoplift)
4 They sent the .... to prison. (offend)
5 They used guns during the .... (rob)
6 The ....took her mobile phone and watch. (mug)

Marks .... / 6

2 Use a word with a negative prefix for each definition.

■ behaviour ■ belief ■ agreement ■ respect ■ fortune ■ honesty

1 the feeling of not believing in something: ....
2 the act of showing that you don't think someone is important: ....
3 bad luck: ....
4 the act of not telling the truth: ....
5 the act of behaving badly: ....
6 a refusal to agree: ....

Marks .... / 6

3 Complete the phrasal verbs in the text with one word in each gap.

Dear Agony Anne,

Help! I've fallen ¹............... with my mum after an argument. She's always criticizing me and I never live up ²............... her expectations. She says I never get ³............... to tidying my room, but I do it every year! She says I'm always coming up ⁴............... excuses for avoiding housework, but I'm allergic to cleaning products! Of course, I know I'm not perfect, but I always own ⁵............... to my mistakes. Well, eventually, anyway.

I can't put ⁶............... with the situation any more. What should I do?

Marks .... / 6

4 Replace the words in italics with the words below.

■ fair ■ obligatory ■ legal ■ optional ■ prohibited ■ restrictive

There are lots of rules about driving in the UK, saying what is ¹............... (*lawful*) and what isn't. It is ²............... (*illegal*) to hold a mobile phone while driving. Wearing a seat belt is also ³............... (*compulsory*). Drivers also need to obey strict speed limits. Some people complain that speed cameras are not ⁴............... (*just*), and that the maximum speed limits in the UK are too ⁵............... (*limiting*). However, the police argue that staying safe should not be ⁶............... (*voluntary*)!

Marks .... / 6

Grammar

5 Complete the first and second conditional sentences with the correct form of the verbs below.

■ ask ■ feel ■ get ■ introduce ■ not laugh ■ not send ■ not tell ■ see

1 If you .... a friend stealing, would you tell anyone?
2 If you do some volunteering, you .... good.
3 My parents will help me if I .... into trouble.
4 If I ruled the country, I .... some new laws!
5 Life would be easier if we .... any lies.
6 If Jo .... for help today, what will you say?
7 I .... any shoplifters to prison if I were a judge.
8 If you tell me your secret, I .... at you, I promise.

Marks .... / 8

6 Complete the sentences with the first or second conditional form of the verbs in brackets.

1 Girl: I .... on holiday if I .... the lottery. (go / win)
2 Shoplifter: If I .... something I like, I .... it. (see / take)
3 Shop owner: If we .... anyone shoplifting, we .... the police. (see / call)
4 Teacher: I .... cheating in exams illegal if I .... the world. (make / rule)
5 Politician: The streets .... safe if we .... crime. (not be / not reduce)
6 Good liar: My mum .... me if I .... the dog broke it. (believe / say)
7 Elderly man: If I .... a policeman, I .... to be an athlete. (not be / like)
8 Friend: I .... for your coffee if you .... me. (pay / forgive)
9 Stupid thief: I .... a palace if I .... the Mona Lisa. (buy / steal)
10 Judge: If people .... any crime, I .... an easy life. (not do / have)

Marks .... / 10

7 Complete sentence b so that it has a similar meaning to sentence a. Use the words in brackets.

1 a It's compulsory for students to wear a tie.
  b Students .... (must)
2 a Joining after-school clubs is optional.
  b Students .... (don't have to)
3 a We insist that students arrive on time.
  b Students .... (have to)
4 a We allow students to bring in mobile phones.
  b Students .... (can)
5 a Making calls in lessons is prohibited.
  b Students .... (mustn't)
6 a Having school lunches isn't compulsory.
  b Students .... (don't have to)
7 a Students aren't permitted to eat in class.
  b Students .... (may not)
8 a Students have permission to wear rings.
  b Students .... (can)

Marks .... / 8

Total .... / 50

1 SPEAKING Which of these things might influence you to buy a product? Put them in order from 1–5.

■ a TV advertisement ■ a celebrity ■ a special offer
■ a friend's recommendation ■ a review on a blog

2 Read the text and choose the correct answers.

1 The girl in the café
   a is being sold something.
   b has the same conversation with a different boy.
   c is working with the boy.
   d will probably buy the computer game.

2 The tourist in the street wants
   a someone to help them.
   b to help someone.
   c to advertise something.
   d to give something away.

3 Stealth marketing is
   a marketing through personal recommendation.
   b advertising in magazines.
   c marketing by teenagers.
   d expensive and difficult to do.

4 When companies use stealth marketing, they
   a sell their product in an illegal way.
   b give away their product for customers to try.
   c use people that customers 'trust' to sell something.
   d only use people on the streets to sell their products.

5 What does Tanya say about stealth marketing?
   a It makes her feel uncomfortable.
   b She often has to pay for products.
   c She enjoys making videos of shopping trips.
   d It makes her feel better than her friends.

3 SPEAKING Work in pairs. Answer the questions.

1 What examples of stealth marketing are there in the text?

2 What do you think about stealth marketing? Is it dishonest? What if the product is genuinely good?

3 Would you like to be a stealth marketer? Why / why not?

V Advertising

4 Study the underlined words in the text. Then match them to definitions 1–8.

1 to talk someone into doing something
2 to study something in more detail
3 to lie to someone
4 to have an effect on someone's ideas and choices
5 to advertise something for the first time
6 to show something, so people can look at it
7 to advertise a product and encourage people to buy it
8 to aim something at someone

The influencers

Imagine this: you are in a café when you hear a teenage boy talking about a new computer game. He's explaining its amazing features to a girl and the girl wants to know where she can buy it. Nothing unusual, you might say, until after fifteen minutes, the boy and girl move to another café and have an identical conversation. On your way home, a 'tourist' in the street asks you to take a photo with their camera. You do and, afterwards, they tell you how they bought the camera recently and how it's on special offer. New friend or fraud? Welcome to the world of stealth marketing. You may say you haven't met a stealth marketer yet, but that's the point. The chances are that you have.

Stealth* or 'word of mouth' marketing isn't like normal advertising. We can recognize adverts on billboards or in glossy magazines, but it's difficult to spot stealth marketing – it just tricks us. Studies have shown that people are more likely to trust a person on the street, who they think is giving free advice, rather than an advert. In fact, in a recent poll of teenagers, only 5% believed adverts, compared with 52% who trusted their peers.

More than $500 billion a year is spent on advertising worldwide, but compared with conventional advertising campaigns, stealth marketing is cheap and effective. So how does it work? Well, let's look at company X. Company X wants to launch a new product for teens. They need their product to look 'cool' and interesting, so they decide to pay young people to talk about it.

Vocabulary: advertising; describing amounts; trade; addition and contrast
Grammar: the passive; *have / get something done*

Speaking: discussing stealth marketing; discussing fair trade; talking about photos
Writing: a formal letter of complaint

6A

These young marketers are carefully selected – company X <u>researches</u> teen websites and <u>targets</u> the most popular people or 'trendsetters'. These teens then <u>persuade</u> their peers to buy the cool new product. Seventeen-year-old Tanya Fulham is one of them. 35
Tanya Fulham is beautiful, sporty and clever. She's interested in fashion, loves shopping, and listens to the latest pop music. She has more than 150 friends on her social media page and she often <u>influences</u> their choices and opinions. She's the latest recruit 40 of an undercover marketing agency. People like Tanya <u>promote</u> brands in blogs and on social media websites. 'Products which are fashionable or have a strong brand image are easy to sell,' explains Tanya. 'I can usually get people to buy everything 45 from make-up to luxury goods, like designer jeans.' Other teen marketers upload videos of themselves, which describe recent shopping trips and <u>display</u> their 'hauls'*. They show people how a product works or what it looks like up close. 50
'It's great getting free samples of cool, new products that my friends haven't heard about,' adds Tanya. 'It makes me feel important because I have insider knowledge.' But do her friends know that she is paid to promote them? 'No, they don't,' she admits. 'But 55 I don't think it's dishonest. If I find something I like, I talk about it. It doesn't make any difference whether I'm paid or not.'
Perhaps Tanya is right. Lots of people tell others about the new book they're reading, a new place they've 60 discovered or a cool gadget they've just bought. We're also a 24/7 generation and see more than 3,000 ads a day, so what difference does it make? However, other people are worried. 'You think a person is being helpful,' says retail psychologist David 65 Green, 'but that's very different from someone telling us something because they are getting paid for it. You don't know who to trust or who to listen to anymore.' We have already met the stealth marketers and they are just like us. 70

* hauls = large amounts of goods
* stealth = the act of doing something wrongfully or secretly

5 Complete the text with the correct form of the words in exercise 4.

Spend, spend, spend

Every company wants to ¹.............. us that we need their product, so before they ².............. it and present it to the world, they ³.............. their market carefully, so they know how their customers think.

As a result, advertising campaigns appeal to our emotions rather than give us facts – they can even sometimes ⁴.............. us into buying a product with false promises. So, a spot cream will give you a better social life, or a pair of jeans will make everyone think you are 'cool'. They use other tricks too – huge billboards may ⁵.............. celebrities who ⁶.............. products which they've never used before. A magazine advert might show photoshopped models, who look thinner or more youthful than they actually are.

And adverts love to ⁷.............. teenagers and encourage them to spend. Why? Well, they have money and they can ⁸.............. their parents' choices. Companies want to encourage as many people as possible to buy their brand.

V | **insight** Collocations: advertising

6 Study the highlighted collocations in the text. Then replace the phrases in italics in sentences 1–8 with the correct collocations.

1 Many people can't afford *products that are unnecessary and very expensive*, like diamond jewellery.
2 I bought the jeans because they were *cheaper than usual*.
3 The *billboards and magazine advert* for the new trainers were a big success. Lots of people bought them.
4 Most of the models in *weekly fashion publications* are really too thin.
5 Stealth marketers often have *more information about a product than other people*.
6 The *company that develops ideas for adverts* came up with a great idea for a shop window display.
7 Some companies give people *examples of their product that they don't have to pay for*.
8 Nike is a successful sports company with a very strong *idea associated with its name*.

7 **SPEAKING** Work in groups of three. Discuss the statements. Do you agree or disagree with them? Why / why not?

1 'Stealth marketers like Tanya create problems for teens who can't afford designer goods.'
2 'All advertising campaigns are dishonest, not just stealth marketing ones.'

Vocabulary bank | Types of advertising page 139

1 SPEAKING Work in pairs. Look at the photos. What do you think 'fair trade' is? Who does it benefit? Then read the text and check your answers.

[1]Cotton has been grown in Mali for hundreds of years and the crops have been harvested by people like Makandianfing Keita for generations. In the past, life on the cotton plantations was difficult and while [2]big profits were being made by the major companies, the workers were badly paid and the living conditions were very poor. 'In the past, children had to walk 10 km to the nearest school and we had no access to healthcare,' explains Makandianfing. 'But then, in 2005, [3]a co-operative fair-trade farm was established by the farmers in the village. When a farm becomes a fair-trade farm, there is a guarantee that [4]all the farmers will be paid a fair price and [5]part of the profit from selling their products is spent on improving their living conditions.' In Makandianfing's village, this meant that a hospital and a school were built for the workers and their families.

Although [6]efforts to start fair trade had been made after the Second World War, the fair-trade movement really started in 1988 with the launch of the first Fairtrade label. At first, fair-trade goods were available in specialist shops only, but by the 1990s, fair-trade products, like coffee, tea and bananas were being sold in major supermarkets. Now, [7]many different products and clothes with Fairtrade labels are being produced and sold by multinational companies, like Nestlé. This is all great news for people like Makandianfing. 'Fairtrade has really changed the life of my community. I feel as though I have a future, which I didn't before,' he says.

The passive

2 Study sentences a–g. What tense is used in each sentence? Read the text again and match the passive sentences 1–7 in the text to the active sentences a–g.

   a They spend part of the profit from selling their products on improving their living conditions.
   b Multinational companies, like Nestlé, are producing and selling many different products and clothes with Fairtrade labels.
   c They have grown cotton in Mali for hundreds of years.
   d The major companies were making big profits.
   e They had made efforts to start fair trade after the Second World War.
   f The farmers in the village established a co-operative fair-trade farm.
   g They will pay all the farmers a fair price.

3 Study the passive sentences in the text again. Then answer the questions.

   1 When do we use the passive?
   2 How do we form the passive for each tense in exercise 2?
   3 What word do we use when we want to say who or what does the action?

Reference and practice 6.1   Workbook page 114

4 Rewrite the active sentences using the passive.

   1 They are creating farmers' co-operatives to sell the products.
   2 The big companies weren't paying the farmers a decent wage.
   3 Poverty has forced many farmers to leave the land and work in cities.
   4 British supermarkets sold only three fair-trade products in 1994.
   5 They sell over 3,000 fair-trade products today.
   6 Seventy per cent of British households buy fair-trade products.
   7 They didn't produce fair-trade cotton until 2005.
   8 Shops will sell more fair-trade clothing next year.

5 Complete the text with the correct passive form of the verbs in brackets.

Ethical Fashion Show

With fair trade growing in popularity, this year's Ethical Fashion Show in Paris **1**............................... (expect) to be a big success.

The show **2**............................... (hold) every year in Paris since 2000, with the aim of promoting fair-trade clothing. The show **3**............................... (start) after increasing numbers of media reports about poor working conditions in developing countries. Europeans discovered that their clothes **4**............................... (make) by people who **5**............................... (not pay) fairly for working very long hours.

Since then, ethical working methods **6**............................... (introduce) slowly and only clothes that **7**............................... (made) according to fair-trade rules **8**............................... (use) at the show. At first, only a few designers were interested, but now fair-trade clothes **9**............................... (design) by some of the big names in the fashion world. Fair-trade groups hope that more ethical fashion shows **10**............................... (run) in other European cities in the future.

6 SPEAKING Work in pairs. Discuss the questions.

1 Are there many supermarkets or shops that sell fair-trade products in your country?
2 Do you buy fair-trade products? What products do you buy?

7 **2.01** Read *Why buy fair-trade clothes?*. Then listen to a radio interview at a fashion show. Which points from the leaflet are mentioned in the interview?

Why buy fair-trade clothes?

* The designers are being paid a fair salary.
* Cotton is grown on fair-trade farms.
* You can buy beautiful clothes and help people in poorer countries.
* Fair-trade workers are taught to sew.

8 **2.01** Listen again and match 1–6 to a–f. Then use the information to make sentences in the passive.

1 The cotton in the woman's dress
2 On fair-trade farms, the people
3 The cloth
4 Fair-trade clothes
5 When Mahesh was eight years old,
6 Mahesh's life

a sell all over the world
b pay a decent wage
c change by fair trade
d pay a low salary
e grow on fair-trade farms
f cut and sew into a lovely dress

9 SPEAKING Work in pairs. Make a list of the items below. Then discuss questions 1–4.

■ one item of your clothing ■ a food product that you often eat ■ one of your possessions

1 Where was each thing produced?
2 How do you think it was made?
3 Where was it sold?
4 Is it a fair-trade product?

DVD extra Fair trade

1 🔊 **2.02** **SPEAKING** Work in pairs. Discuss the questions. Then listen to part one of a radio programme and compare your ideas.

1 How much money does the average teenager in the UK spend per year?
2 Where do they get their money from?
3 What do teenagers in the UK spend their money on?
4 Do boys and girls spend their money in different ways?
5 Do teenagers in the UK like buying big name brands?

2 **SPEAKING** Work in small groups. Discuss the questions.

1 Do any of the facts from the radio programme surprise you?
2 Do you think teenagers in the UK spend more per year than teenagers in your country?
3 Do you think boys and girls in your country are different in how they spend money?
4 Which brands are popular with teenagers in your country?

STRATEGY

Listening for specific information

Before listening:

1 Think about the type of information that you need. Is it a date, an amount, a measurement, a time, a place, a specific part of speech (noun / verb / adjective / adverb / preposition)?
2 Try to predict the information you will need to complete the gaps.

While listening:

3 Listen for words or phrases that indicate that important information is coming, for example:
   ■ tell us about … .   ■ an interesting fact is … .

---

3 Read the strategy. Then read the notes about teenage spending. What information do you think you will need for each gap in the notes?

4 🔊 **2.03** Listen to part two of the radio interview and complete the notes.

How do teenagers spend their money?

1 Online vs high street
   Shopping online is ¹................. popular.
   People spend ²................. times more on the high street than online.

2 Payment
   Teenagers in the UK must be ³................. years old to get a credit card.
   Teenagers use ⁴................. credit cards or ⁵................. .

3 What do they buy?
   UK teenagers spend more on ⁶................. than other age groups.
   Over ⁷................. % of 16-18-year-olds have a ⁸................. ....
   Don't often ⁹................. .... – usually send texts, check email, post and browse online.
   Spend ¹⁰................. per year on trainers.

5 🔊 **2.03** Listen to part two of the radio programme again. Are the sentences true (T) or false (F)? Correct the false ones.

1 Nina spends a lot of money on fashion and make-up.
2 Nina doesn't think teens are influenced by advertising.
3 Nina buys online and in shops.
4 Cindy says that most people shop online.
5 British teens spend a lot of money on music.
6 Julian only uses his phone to make calls.
7 Julian doesn't spend much money on clothes.

V Describing amounts

6 Study the highlighted phrases in sentences 1–8 from the recording. Then put them into the correct part of the table.

1 Teenagers spend an overwhelming £2,000 per year.
2 I spend a great part of my allowance on clothes.
3 I get a modest £5 a week pocket money.
4 Online shopping represents a tiny minority of total sales.
5 I spend a significant amount of my money on music downloads.
6 A large proportion of my money goes on my mobile.
7 A vast majority, actually, a massive 80% of 16- to 18-year-olds in the UK own a mobile phone.
8 The average UK teenager spends a whopping £250 per year on trainers.

Very small	
Small	
Very big	
Big	

7 **SPEAKING** Work in small groups. Prepare a short survey on your classmates' spending habits. Use the questions below and add your own questions. Then present the results to the rest of the class.

1 Where do you get your money from?
2 What do you spend it on?
3 Do you buy things online or in high street shops?

Talking about photos

8 **SPEAKING** Work in pairs. Look at the photos and discuss the questions.

1 Which shops do you think look interesting / unusual / old-fashioned / expensive / boring?
2 What kinds of people probably visit the different shops?
3 Which of the shops would you most / least like to visit?

9 2.04 Listen to Karen talking about the photos and answer the questions.

1 What does she think about each shop?
2 Where does she normally go shopping?
3 Where would she like to go shopping?
4 Where is she unlikely to go shopping soon?

10 2.04 Listen again and complete the phrases in the box.

Expressing contrast

Making contrasts between two points in the same sentence:

… shoppers have more choice, [1]............... you have to decide … .
… it might be quite expensive, [2]............... the other shops look cheaper.
[3]............... the shop … , I prefer the shops in photo two because … .

Starting sentences or making a contrast with a sentence before:

I shop in places like in the third photo; [4]..............., it's good to … .
[5]..............., if I were buying a present … .
The shops in photo two look quite cheap. In contrast, the shop in photo one looks expensive.

11 **SPEAKING** Work in pairs. Imagine it is your friend's birthday and you want to buy them some music. Look at the photos and select one place where you would buy the present. You have €25 to spend. Explain why you chose this place and why you rejected the other ones.

1 SPEAKING Work in pairs. Which of these festivals do you celebrate in your country? Which is your favourite and why?

■ Christmas ■ Easter ■ Halloween ■ Valentine's Day
■ Mother's / Father's Day

2 Read the text and choose the best title for it. Give reasons for your answer.

A Unwrapped: the origins of popular traditions
B For sale: our traditions!
C Traditions today: will they survive?
D Big business: is it good for our traditions?

3 Read the text again. Are the sentences true (T) or false (F)? Correct the false ones.

1 A prisoner's letter may have started a tradition that has lasted for centuries.
2 In the past, people sent love letters, but not presents.
3 Advertisements for Valentine's Day gifts start appearing on 14 February.
4 The first people to celebrate the beginning of winter were American.
5 A British supermarket wanted to copy the success of American shops.
6 The supermarket advertising campaign increased sales of Halloween products.
7 Christmas trees were first used in pagan celebrations.

4 SPEAKING Work in pairs. Discuss the questions.

1 Which of the traditions mentioned in the text are similar to those in your country?
2 Are there any other festivals that you celebrate in your country? What is their origin?
3 Do any of them encourage people to spend a lot of money?

V Trade

5 Study the highlighted words in the text. Then complete the sentences with the correct form of the words.

1 .... are people who buy things and use services.
2 When you make a ...., you sell something for more money than it cost you to make or buy it.
3 We call the pattern on a product the ....
4 When you .... something, you make it using machines.
5 A person or company who sells goods to people in a shop is called a ....
6 We use the word '............................' to describe companies or events that make a profit.
7 All the businesses that produce goods and services of the same kind form ....
8 A .... is a general change or development.

Big businesses know that popular festivals are a great opportunity for making a **profit**. Some popular celebrations are promoted all over the world. Where do these 'global' celebrations
5 come from and what do they mean to us today?

Valentine's Day

Sixteen-year-old James has been shopping. He's had his hair cut, he's bought a card with a heart-shaped **design** and he's got some chocolates for his girlfriend.
10 Today is 14 February or St Valentine's Day – a day when romance and love is celebrated around the world. Nobody knows exactly who St Valentine was, but according to the legend, he was killed by the Romans because he refused to give up his religion.
15 Thousands of people were killed by the Romans, so why do we remember him more than others? The answer lies in the love letter he wrote to the jailer's daughter on the day of his death, 14 February 269 AD. He signed it, 'from your Valentine'.
20 Whether this story is true or a myth, St Valentine's message of love has become the basis for a multimillion-dollar **industry**. Lovers originally celebrated this day by sending romantic messages to each other, but today, sending a card isn't enough.
25 Businesses advertise flowers, perfume, jewellery and romantic dinners for two in the weeks before 14 February, and millions of gifts are **manufactured**. James may have only spent 12 euros on his chocolates, but globally, **consumers** spend 11 million
30 euros every year!

Halloween

'I'm wearing my costume from last year,' says 'trick or treater' Ellen McDonald. 'It was ripped,' so I got it repaired, but I've bought a new mask.' All over the country, people are spending millions of pounds on one of Britain's newest festivals – Halloween.

The origins of modern-day Halloween can be found in an ancient Celtic celebration of *Samhain* or *Summer's End*, which marked the beginning of winter. The festival was very popular in Ireland and gradually became *All Hallows Eve* (the evening of the dead on 1st November). In the mid-19th century, Irish immigrants made the festival popular in America, helping it become the big commercial event we know as Halloween today.

In Britain, Halloween was hardly celebrated until recently. Most people preferred Bonfire Night* on 5 November. However, one of Britain's biggest supermarkets realised that they could make a lot of money from the event. They decided to go into partnership with an American retailer and together they created a huge advertising campaign. The adverts showed American kids trick or treating and having fun at horror parties. They were a big success and sales of Halloween products rose dramatically. Today, Halloween is the third most popular festival in Britain, after Christmas and Easter.

Christmas

On 1 December in Trafalgar Square in London, hundreds of lights on a huge tree are lit. In high streets and homes across the world, lights on billions of other trees are lit by people, too.

Christmas Day is not until 25 December, but in recent years, customers have started to shop weeks in advance. Because of this trend, people in the UK now start thinking of Christmas presents about eleven weeks before the day! The Christmas tree is often used in advertisements because it's the place where families gather and where presents are left. These decorated trees became popular in England in the mid-19th century, but they originally came from Germany. Other Christmas customs like gift-giving and feasts have their origins in pagan celebrations.

Today, big brands have turned Christmas into a global event, and Christmas products and decorations are made and sold all over the world. In fact no other holiday has the same global influence. Why? Well, Christmas celebrates good will and generosity, and everyone likes to be generous, no matter what their culture or religious beliefs are.

* Bonfire Night = a night of fireworks to celebrate a historic event

6 Choose the correct answers.

1 **Commercials** / **Consumers** spend more at Christmas than at any other time of the year.
2 The factory **manufactures** / **advertises** Halloween costumes. Lots of people from the town work there.
3 The music **industry** / **retailer** is very competitive at Christmas. Lots of pop groups compete to be number one.
4 The greetings card company made a £50 million **profit** / **trend** last year.
5 People aren't spending much this year, so many **consumers** / **retailers** are going out of business.
6 A pink heart surrounded by flowers is a very traditional **trend** / **design** for a Valentine's card.
7 People don't want to make money from the Christmas party. It isn't a **profit** / **commercial** event.
8 Recently, there's been a **trend** / **design** in advertising to use shocking or surprising images.

have / get something done

7 Study the sentences from the text. When do we use *have / get something done*?

1 He's had his hair cut.
2 I got my costume repaired.

Reference and practice 6.2 Workbook page 115

8 Complete the dialogue with the correct form of the words in brackets.

Carl is a manager at Bluewater, one of the biggest shopping centres in the UK. We interviewed him a few weeks before Christmas.

Interviewer Is everything prepared? Have you ¹............... (have / the decorations / put up)?

Carl Yes, we have. We ²............... (have / the shopping centre / decorate) last weekend. There are 15,000 lights and they look fantastic.

Interviewer And the Christmas tree? Have you ³............... (have / it / deliver) yet?

Carl We ⁴............... (have / it / put up) yesterday, and we ⁵............... (get / the lights / switch on) by Father Christmas tomorrow. Children can ⁶............... (have / their photo / take) with him afterwards.

Interviewer And have you ⁷............... (get / a carol concert / organize) for this year?

Carl Yes, there'll be a family concert this weekend.

Interviewer Well, it sounds like Christmas has arrived!

Carl That's true. We ⁸............... (have / lots of posters / put up) recently, advertising special offers, so everyone will be here.

9 SPEAKING Work in pairs. Choose a situation from below and discuss what you will do or what you will need to have done. Use the dialogue in exercise 8 to help you.

■ St Valentine's day ■ a holiday ■ decorating your bedroom ■ a Christmas party

Vocabulary bank Consumerism page 139

1 SPEAKING Work in pairs. Discuss the questions.

1 Have you ever bought something and then returned it?
2 What was the problem?
3 What happened when you returned the item?
4 Did you get your money back?

2 Study the letter extracts. Which are examples from informal letters and which are from formal letters? What features do they have that helped you to decide?

A
Dear Mr Bridges
I am writing to complain about the

B
Hi Sam
I'm really not happy about

C
The guy who came round to fix the TV was a nightmare! He cost loads, too – £50!

D
The computer was not repaired properly and we were very dissatisfied with the attitude of the technician.

E
Furthermore, I was horrified to discover that

F
After trying to transfer the files, which was impossible, the battery ran out

G
My mum washed my favourite jeans and they shrank!! Can you believe it?

H
I would either like to speak to an advisor

I
Anyway – give me a call and let me know what you think ☺.
Speak soon,
Jim

J
I look forward to hearing from you.
Yours sincerely,
James Peachey

STRATEGY

Deciding on register: formal and informal

When we write formal letters, we:

1 address the sender as *Mr / Mrs / Ms +* surname or *Sir / Madam.*
2 often use the passive form.
3 often write longer, more complex sentences.
4 use formal linking words, e.g. *however, furthermore, whereas.*
5 use full forms, e.g. *I am writing … , He has not replied … .*
6 end the letter with *Yours sincerely* (if we know the receiver's name) or *Yours faithfully* (if we don't know the receiver's name) and our full name.

When we write informal letters, we:

7 address the sender by their first name.
8 often use the active form.
9 often write shorter, more simple sentences.
10 use contracted forms (*I'm, He's,* etc.).
11 use colloquial language.
12 use informal punctuation (exclamation marks, emoticons).
13 can use idioms.
14 end the letter with informal phrases, e.g. *Speak soon* and our first name.

3 Read the strategy and check your answers in exercise 2. Then match 1–14 to letter extracts A–J. Sometimes more than one answer may be possible.

---

4 Read the letter of complaint A. Is it a formal or informal letter? Underline the parts of the letter that help you to decide.

5 Read the letter again and match descriptions 1–6 to the parts of the letter a–f.

1 what action is expected
2 a reminder that a reply is expected
3 the date
4 details of the complaint about the product
5 an outline of the complaint
6 details of the complaint about the service

6 Read letter B. Underline the sentences where the writer has used the wrong register. Then rewrite the sentences using the correct register.

A

a — 25 April 2014

Dear Sir / Madam,

b — I am writing to complain about the Dubny MP3 player purchased from your online store last Thursday, 18 April.

c — Although the player was charged for eight hours, as recommended in the instructions, the battery only lasted for half an hour. Furthermore, when the MP3 player was connected to my computer, it was impossible to transfer any audio files across onto the player. I am extremely disappointed with this purchase. It was an expensive item which was advertised as a high-quality product, but in fact, has failed to work properly.

d — In addition, when I called your helpline last Saturday to complain about this item, the helpline advisor was extremely unhelpful and, what is more, didn't even seem to understand how to operate the MP3 player himself.

e — I would either like to speak to an advisor who can advise on how to operate the product properly or receive a full refund.

f — I look forward to hearing from you.

Yours faithfully,

Sarah Chisholm

Sarah Chisholm

V Addition and contrast

7 Study the highlighted words and phrases in both letters. Then put them into the correct part of the table.

Addition	Contrast

8 Rewrite the sentences using the correct words or phrases in brackets.

1 The helpline advisor didn't know how the product worked. He was very rude. (although / besides this)

2 The shop gives out a lot of free samples. I never buy anything because everything is very expensive. (while / what is more)

3 When you shop online, you can't touch the products. You can't try anything on. (in addition / however)

4 When I received the dress it looked nothing like the photo on your website. It was completely the wrong size. (but / to add to this)

5 I enjoy shopping in your store. I will not be returning because the sales assistants are very rude. (although / furthermore)

6 The technician explained how to connect the laptop. He offered to send me a manual. (however / what is more)

B

Dear Mr Smithers,

I'm writing to complain about the jeans that I bought from your store last week.

They were on special offer for £85, reduced from £250 (which was a total bargain!!!) and they were advertised as 'designer'. Anyway, when I put the jeans on at home, I noticed that a button was missing. To add to this, when I washed them, they shrank. I'm a small guy and I like my jeans to fit tightly. However, these are now really small ☹. While I can understand that a button can fall off, I really don't understand how they could get so small!?!? Besides this, I actually don't like them.

I'm really not happy with the poor quality of these jeans, which cost me soooo much money. Could I have my money back?

I look forward to hearing from you.

Speak soon,

Henry Fleder

WRITING GUIDE

■ **Task** Write a letter of complaint about one of these problems:

1 You bought a laptop from a computer shop. When you tried to use it, there were the following problems:
- the battery did not last.
- you could not transfer your old files onto your new laptop.
- you did not like the attitude of the telephone helpline advisor.

2 You ordered an expensive coat from an online clothes store last week. When the coat was delivered, you discovered that:
- two buttons were missing.
- it was dirty inside.
- the coat was not the size that you had ordered.

■ **Ideas** Make notes about:
- Whether you have already contacted the store by phone or in person to complain. If so, how did they respond?
- What you want the recipient of your letter to do.

■ **Plan** Follow the plan:

Paragraph 1: Explain briefly why you are complaining.
Paragraph 2: Give more details about the complaint.
Paragraph 3: State clearly what you expect the store to do about it.

■ **Write** Write a formal letter of complaint. Use the paragraph plan to help you.

■ **Check** Check the following points:
- Have you included all the information from your notes?
- Have you used the correct register?
- Have you checked grammar, vocabulary, spelling and punctuation?

STRATEGY

Collocations

When you learn new vocabulary, it is useful to also learn the most common collocations of that word. Collocations are groups of words which are usually used together.

Example sentences in a dictionary entry show the most common collocations of a word. Some entries also have lists of collocations. Learning collocations will help you to develop your vocabulary and will make you sound more natural.

1 Read the strategy above. Study the dictionary entry for *business*. Then complete the collocations below.

> **business** /ˈbɪznəs/ *noun*
> ➤TRADE **1** [U] buying and selling as a way of earning money: *She's planning to* **set up in business** *as a hairdresser.* ◆ *I'm going to* **go into business** *with my brother.* ◆ *They are very easy to* **do business with**.
> ➤WORK **2** [U] the work that you do as your job: *The manager will be away* **on business** *next week.* ◆ *a* **business trip**
> ➤CUSTOMERS **3** [U] the number of customers that a person or company has had: *Business has been good for the time of year.*
> ➤COMPANY **4** [C] a firm, a shop, a factory, etc. which produces or sells goods or provides a service: *She aims to* **start a business** *of her own.* ◆ *Small businesses are finding it hard to survive at the moment.*

1 set up .... business
2 go .... business
3 do business ....
4 be away .... business
5 start .... business

2 Complete the sentences with the correct forms of the collocations in exercise 1.

1 My dad isn't at home at the moment – he's ....
2 Ron has just .... as an architect.
3 Our company .... other companies from all over the world.
4 My sister had quit her job in a big firm and .... of her own.
5 Kath's decided to .... with her sister and invest some money in it.

3 Study the dictionary entries for the words below. Then complete each line with one of the words.

■ money ■ loss ■ profit ■ launch ■ campaign ■ sample

> **money** /ˈmʌni/ *noun* [U] the means of paying for sth or buying sth (= coins or notes): *Will you* **earn** *more* **money** *in your new job?* ◆ *The new road will* **cost** *a lot of* **money**. ◆ *If we do the work ourselves we will* **save money**. ◆ *The government* **make** *a huge amount of* **money** *out of tobacco tax.* ➔ note at **pay** ➔ look at **pocket money**

> **loss** /lɒs/ *noun* **1** [C,U] (a) loss (of sth) the state of no longer having sth or not having as much as before; the act of losing sth: *loss of blood/sleep*

> **profit¹** /ˈprɒfɪt/ *noun* [C,U] the money that you make when you sell sth for more than it cost you: *Did you* **make a profit on** *your house when you sold it?* ◆ *I'm hoping to sell my shares* **at a profit**. **OPP** loss

> **launch²** /lɔːntʃ/ *noun* [C] **1** [usually sing] the act of **launching** a ship, **spacecraft** (= a vehicle that travels in space), new product, etc: *The official launch date for our newest product is 10 May.* **2** a large motorboat

> **campaign¹** /kæmˈpeɪn/ *noun* [C] **1** a plan to do a number of things in order to achieve a special aim: *to launch an advertising/election campaign* ◆ *a campaign to reduce road accidents*

> **sample** /ˈsɑːmpl/ *noun* [C] **1** a small number or amount of sb/sth that is looked at, tested, examined, etc. to find out what the rest is like: *The interviews were given to a* **random sample** *of shoppers.* ◆ *to take a blood sample* ◆ *a free sample of shampoo* ➔ look at

1 a ship .... / a product ....
2 .... of life / make a .... / a big .... to
3 launch a .... / an advertising .... / an election ....
4 a free .... / a random .... of
5 make a .... / at a ....
6 earn .... / cost .... / save .... / make .... / pocket ....

4 Complete the sentences with the correct forms of the collocations in exercise 3.

1 The company decided to .... the new product before Christmas to .... a bigger profit.
2 A .... sample of students took part in the survey.
3 The advertising .... wasn't successful and the company made a .... of £100,000.
4 When he left, it was a big .... to the agency.
5 The shop was giving away free .... of perfume, but nobody was buying it because it .... a lot of money.
6 She doesn't .... any money because she spends it all on bills, shopping and going out.
7 Students from our school are helping out with the local election ....
8 She buys second-hand products and then sells them at a ....

5 Which of the nouns in exercise 3 (*money, loss, profit, launch, campaign, sample*) have the same verb forms? Use a dictionary to complete the collocations below with these verbs. Then write your own example sentences.

1 to .... from something
2 to .... something onto the market
3 to .... against or for something
4 to .... something

Dictionary entries from *Oxford Wordpower Dictionary*, 4th edition

Vocabulary

1 Complete the sentences with the correct form of the verbs below.

▧ display ▧ launch ▧ persuade ▧ promote ▧ target ▧ trick

1 Toy companies .... adverts at small children.
2 Companies .... their brands on Facebook.
3 Shops .... key products near the entrance.
4 Adverts .... people to buy things they don't need.
5 He signed copies of his book at the ....
6 Advertisers try to .... us with dishonest claims.

Marks .... / 6

2 Match the words in A to the words in B to make compound nouns. Then complete the sentences.

A ▧ advertising ▧ brand ▧ free ▧ insider ▧ luxury
▧ marketing

B ▧ agency ▧ campaign ▧ goods ▧ image ▧ knowledge
▧ samples

Medicines aren't [1]..............., like designer watches or perfume, but they are a multi-million pound business. Each drug company has a [2]............... in charge of promoting their products and developing their [3]............... or reputation. Rather than having a large [4]............... in the media, agencies often sell directly to doctors and they employ medical experts for their [5].............. . They try to persuade doctors with [6]............... and presents. But is it ethical?

Marks .... / 6

3 Complete the sentences with the words below.

▧ majority ▧ modest ▧ proportion ▧ significant ▧ tiny
▧ whopping

Our class survey showed that a large [1]............... of students have part-time jobs. Most earn a [2]............... £10–20 a week, which is considered to be just enough. Students spend the [3]............... of their income on music, books and games (around 60%), and a [4]............... amount on socializing (up to 35%). Only a [5]............... minority of students spend money on cinema tickets, however (2%). One student said, 'Cinema tickets cost a [6]............... £8.50 each! It's too expensive.'

Marks .... / 6

4 Match definitions 1–6 to trade words a–f.

1 to make something using machines
2 a person or company that sells something
3 connected with buying or selling
4 a person that buys something
5 a popular development
6 money from selling something for more than it cost

a profit   c consumer   e manufacture
b retailer   d commercial   f trend

Marks .... / 6

Grammar

5 Complete the text with the correct passive form of the verbs in brackets.

Right now, millions of jeans [1]............... (manufacture), and by the end of tomorrow, thousands [2]............... (sell). Every year, over 450 million pairs [3]............... (purchase) in the USA alone. Fashions come and go, but it seems jeans [4]............... (not forgot) anytime soon.

The first jeans [5]............... (produce) in the USA in the late 19th century. Denim cloth [6]............... (use) since at least the 17th century. In the early 20th century, jeans [7]............... (see) mainly as cheap work clothes. In the 1950s, they [8]............... (buy) by rebellious teenagers and became cool. Now, jeans [9]............... (wear) by everyone, including the rich. It's hard to think of a celebrity who [10]............... (not photograph) in a pair of jeans.

Marks .... / 10

6 Rewrite the sentences without changing the meaning.

1 They'll sell more fair-trade clothes in the future.
More fair-trade ....
2 Factory workers aren't being paid enough.
Manufacturers ....
3 Fair-trade products are promoted by celebrities.
Celebrities ....
4 People have grown coffee in Africa for centuries.
Coffee ....
5 Today, most of the world's coffee is produced in Brazil.
Today, Brazil ....
6 People in Oxford in the UK started the charity 'Oxfam'.
The charity 'Oxfam' ....
7 A century ago, many factories were still employing children.
A century ago, children ....
8 'Unfair trade' hasn't been stopped yet.
We ....

Marks .... / 8

7 Complete the sentences with the correct form of *have / get something done* and the verbs.

▧ cut ▧ dye ▧ paint ▧ repair ▧ send ▧ take ▧ test ▧ wash

1 I can't talk. I .... (have / my photo)!
2 We .... (get / the car) yesterday. It was very dirty.
3 My mum .... (have / eyes) twice a year.
4 I .... (not get / my computer) yet. It still doesn't work.
5 They .... (get / their house) pink last week.
6 I .... (not have / my hair) when I'm older. Grey hair looks good!
7 Right now, I .... (have / my hair) short.
8 I .... (get / my exam results) to my home, because I couldn't collect them from school.

Marks .... / 8

Total .... / 50

Listening

1 You are going to listen to people talking in five different situations. Read the questions and answers a–c. For each question, decide if you need to listen for specific information (S) or general opinions and attitudes (G).

1 Listen to a store manager. In what way is he critical of teenage shoppers?
  a He doesn't think they spend enough.
  b He's worried that they might steal.
  c He thinks that they're too noisy.

2 Listen to a radio caller. Why has Paul phoned the radio station?
  a To complain about the shopping centre.
  b To express support for the shopping centre.
  c To offer suggestions for the shopping centre.

3 Listen to two friends. Katie borrowed an item of clothing from Josie. Why is Katie apologizing?
  a She dropped food on it.
  b She tore it.
  c She lost it.

4 Listen to an announcement. What are shoppers unable to buy in-store today?
  a computer games   b T-shirts   c books

5 Listen to part of a radio discussion. Who does the woman criticize for being lazy?
  a teenagers   b shoppers   c advertisers

2 🔊 **2.05** Now listen to the five recordings. Choose the correct answers in exercise 1.

Speaking

3 Work in pairs. Describe each photo A, B and C and make comparisons.

4 Work in pairs. Imagine it is the last day of your holiday. Decide where you are going to buy your souvenirs: place A, B or C. Give opinions and explain your reasons.

Reading

5 Complete the text *Anti-teen discrimination?* with sentences A–H.

  A But their argument is factually incorrect.
  B Its other, more important duty is to report the truth.
  C But this low figure is one which little interests the media.
  D They frequently describe young people as being lazy, arrogant and stupid.
  E Some go further, and actively seek to restrict their behaviour.
  F That question is even more ridiculous than the previous one.
  G But sadly these aren't the only forms of unfair treatment in society.
  H It's so unpleasant, that most quickly move on!

ANTI-TEEN DISCRIMINATION?

Today, nearly everyone agrees that it is wrong to treat someone differently because of their race or background. [1]............ Prejudice against teenagers is both widespread and largely ignored.

Journalists and news editors have given teenagers a very bad image. [2]............ Many also present teenagers as dangerous! One survey found that over 70% of news articles about young people were critical, and a third of these stories related to crimes.

As a result, it's not surprising that many older people mistrust teenagers. [3]............ For instance, retailers may put up notices saying 'maximum of two students permitted at any one time.' If they wrote 'pensioners' or 'women' instead, they'd be asked to remove the signs immediately!

To justify their actions, shop owners claim that teenagers are more likely to shoplift. [4]............ In reality, around three quarters of shoplifters are adults. Should we ban over-eighteen-year-olds from stores instead?

In some countries, shops and businesses are allowed to use 'mosquitos' in front of their buildings. These are small, electronic gadgets which make a high sound that only young people can hear. [5]............ Fans of the mosquito claim that it reduces anti-social behavior. But why shouldn't teenagers be allowed to talk to their friends? We shouldn't punish people for crimes they haven't committed!

In reality, only around 10–20% of crimes are committed by young offenders. [6]............ Why? Perhaps it's because editors have other numbers to think of, such as profit margins. Bad news sells. Headlines like 'over 40% of teenagers support charities' simply aren't as exciting!

On the other hand, the media is not just a commercial interest. [7]............ Journalists need to raise awareness of different aspects of teenagers' lives – and politicians, businesses, teachers and parents need to listen.

Are all blue-eyed people the same? Of course not. If 10% of blue-eyed people break the law, then should we stop trusting everyone with blue eyes? [8]............ So why do we assume that all young people are 'bad', just because a few misbehave? It's time to start treating teenagers the way they deserve. Not as a 'problem' group, but as individuals.

6 Complete the text. Write one word in each gap.

DIGITAL SHOPLIFTING

While you've been looking at a book, newspaper or glossy [1]............................. in a shop, have you ever taken a photo with your phone [2]............................. that you could look at it later? Perhaps you spotted someone with a stylish haircut, and thought 'I'd like to [3]............................. my hair cut like that. I think I'll show this to my hairdresser next week.' It seems an innocent enough action, but if you are caught, you might be asked to leave the store. What is [4]............................., you might even be arrested [5]............................. the police!

'Digital shoplifting' is a crime, although it's one that few people realize they're committing. Officially, you [6]............................. always get permission before sharing other people's photos. That's the law. But how many of us ever get round [7]............................. doing that?

Many retailers and publishers are now protesting [8]............................. 'digital shoplifting', because they believe it's cheating them out of valuable sales. [9]............................. you go on to buy the publication you've photographed, they won't make any profit. Unfortunately, most of us tend to leave it on the shelf.

So, be careful the next time you think about using your cameraphone in a bookshop or newsagent's. You can never tell – someone [10]............................. be watching you …

7 Your town council is planning to install 'mosquito' devices in the main shopping district. They hope that this will stop groups of teenagers hanging out around shops and other buildings. Write a letter to a local newspaper expressing your views. Think about:

- current concerns about crime and safety.
- possible effects of installing the devices (for retailers and teenagers).
- possible alternatives to installing the device.
- what you think should happen next.

Reading and vocabulary Taste

1 SPEAKING Look at the photos. What are the people doing? Which senses are they using? Which sense do you think is the most important?

2 SPEAKING Work in pairs. Read the statements and decide which ones are true. Then read the text and check your answers.

1 Our taste buds are fully developed when we are born.
2 We can only identify four tastes.
3 Boys like different flavours from girls.
4 Our noses can smell 10,000 different scents.
5 When hot food gets colder, it tastes better.
6 The look and feel of food can make us like it more or less.

STRATEGY

Understanding the purpose of a paragraph

Each paragraph in a text usually deals with a different aspect of the topic.

- The first paragraph normally introduces the general topic or explains the purpose of the text.
- The other paragraphs develop the topic and give more information.
- The final paragraph gives a summary or a conclusion.

3 Read the strategy. Then match paragraphs A–F in the text to purposes 1–6.

1 It provides further information about the four tastes.
2 It explains the connection between smell and taste.
3 It briefly summarizes the argument of the text.
4 It explains the connection between texture and taste.
5 It states the topic of the text and gives some background information.
6 It explains how our mouths work.

4 SPEAKING Work in pairs. Answer the questions.

1 Why do some young people not like vegetables?
2 Where does our love of sweet things originate from?
3 Why does cooked food not taste so good when it is cold?
4 How are smell and taste connected?
5 How does saliva help when we eat?

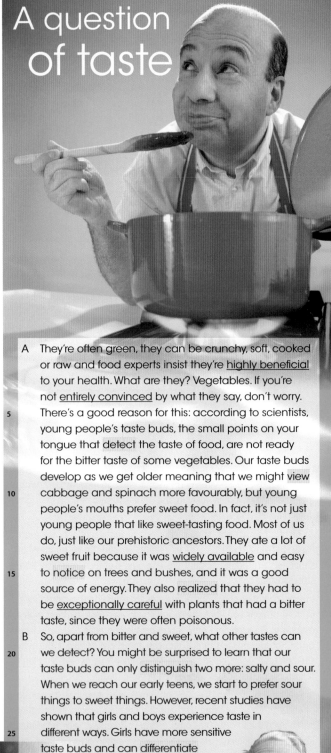

A question of taste

A They're often green, they can be crunchy, soft, cooked or raw and food experts insist they're <u>highly beneficial</u> to your health. What are they? Vegetables. If you're not <u>entirely convinced</u> by what they say, don't worry.
5 There's a good reason for this: according to scientists, young people's taste buds, the small points on your tongue that detect the taste of food, are not ready for the bitter taste of some vegetables. Our taste buds develop as we get older meaning that we might view
10 cabbage and spinach more favourably, but young people's mouths prefer sweet food. In fact, it's not just young people that like sweet-tasting food. Most of us do, just like our prehistoric ancestors. They ate a lot of sweet fruit because it was <u>widely available</u> and easy
15 to notice on trees and bushes, and it was a good source of energy. They also realized that they had to be <u>exceptionally careful</u> with plants that had a bitter taste, since they were often poisonous.

B So, apart from bitter and sweet, what other tastes can
20 we detect? You might be surprised to learn that our taste buds can only distinguish two more: salty and sour. When we reach our early teens, we start to prefer sour things to sweet things. However, recent studies have shown that girls and boys experience taste in different ways. Girls have more sensitive
25 taste buds and can differentiate flavours more easily, especially sweet and sour, while boys prefer stronger, more extreme flavours.

30 C For everyone, though, food has to be wet for it to be tasty. When we smell food, our mouths produce saliva and when we eat it, the saliva transports its taste to our
35 taste buds. Without saliva, some food would have

Vocabulary: perception and observation; adverb-adjective collocations; noun suffixes: *-tion*, *-sion*; approximations and fractions
Grammar: reported statements, questions and commands

Speaking: discussing the role of the senses; interviewing; complaining and asking people to do things
Writing: a report on survey findings

7A

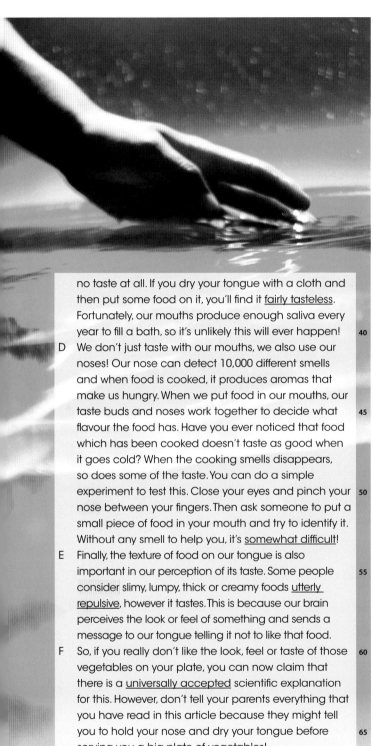

no taste at all. If you dry your tongue with a cloth and then put some food on it, you'll find it <u>fairly tasteless</u>. Fortunately, our mouths produce enough saliva every year to fill a bath, so it's unlikely this will ever happen! 40

D We don't just taste with our mouths, we also use our noses! Our nose can detect 10,000 different smells and when food is cooked, it produces aromas that make us hungry. When we put food in our mouths, our taste buds and noses work together to decide what 45 flavour the food has. Have you ever noticed that food which has been cooked doesn't taste as good when it goes cold? When the cooking smells disappears, so does some of the taste. You can do a simple experiment to test this. Close your eyes and pinch your 50 nose between your fingers. Then ask someone to put a small piece of food in your mouth and try to identify it. Without any smell to help you, it's <u>somewhat difficult</u>!

E Finally, the texture of food on our tongue is also important in our perception of its taste. Some people 55 consider slimy, lumpy, thick or creamy foods <u>utterly repulsive</u>, however it tastes. This is because our brain perceives the look or feel of something and sends a message to our tongue telling it not to like that food.

F So, if you really don't like the look, feel or taste of those 60 vegetables on your plate, you can now claim that there is a <u>universally accepted</u> scientific explanation for this. However, don't tell your parents everything that you have read in this article because they might tell you to hold your nose and dry your tongue before 65 serving you a big plate of vegetables!

5 **Study the highlighted verbs in the text. Match them to definitions 1–7.**

  1 notice or discover something that can be difficult to see or feel
  2 think about something carefully before making a decision
  3 see, hear or recognize with effort
  4 become aware of something
  5 think about something in a particular way
  6 see how things are different
  7 know or understand something that is true

6 **Choose the correct answers.**

  1 I couldn't **detect** / **distinguish** the writing on the board because it was too far away.
  2 A lot of people **consider** / **differentiate** fresh vegetables healthier than frozen ones, but scientists say that there is no difference in nutrition between the two.
  3 A two-week old baby can **differentiate** / **realize** between sweet, sour and bitter tastes, but they can't **view** / **detect** the taste of salt until they reach four months.
  4 He only **considered** / **noticed** that the soup was very hot, once he had a spoonful in his mouth. It's also then that he **distinguished** / **realized** that it was too thick and lumpy.
  5 Many parents **view** / **detect** marketing junk food to children as unethical and feel it shouldn't be allowed.

7 **Study the underlined collocations in the text. Then replace the words in italics with the collocations.**

  1 Processed foods are more *possible to get* in supermarkets now than they were twenty years ago.
  2 It's *not very easy* to taste food if you can't smell it.
  3 You must be *full of extreme care* when you eat wild mushrooms because they might be poisonous.
  4 A lot of food can be *without much taste* without salt.
  5 Five portions of fruit and vegetables a day are *very good for you* for your health.
  6 The connection between sweet things and obesity is *generally believed*.
  7 Some people find the taste of raw fish *very unpleasant*.
  8 A lot of teenagers are not *completely certain* that eating vegetables is good for you.

8 **SPEAKING Work in groups. Discuss the statements.**

  1 Teenagers dislike most vegetables.
  2 Cooked food always tastes better than raw food.
  3 Parents should force children to eat healthy food they do not like.

Vocabulary bank | Food texture page 140

1 **SPEAKING** Look at the photos. What do these dogs have in common? What senses are they using?

2 ◎ **2.06** Listen to a radio news report. What happened? How many people are missing?

3 Read the newspaper article about the avalanche. What happened to Charles Grimaldi?

Dogs to the rescue

■ By Paul Wittens

Charles Grimaldi, the experienced ski instructor who spent an hour buried under tons of snow after this morning's avalanche, is recovering from his injuries at the Sainte Pauline hospital. He spoke to me from his hospital bed earlier and said that he was still feeling very weak and couldn't stand up on his own. He told me that he had worked as an instructor on those slopes for 15 years. He pointed out that he'd set out because the weather reports hadn't shown any indication of avalanches and explained that the weather had been good on the mountain. However, while he was waiting for his group to arrive, he heard a loud rumbling noise and saw a wall of snow heading towards him. Within seconds he was blinded and everything turned white. Then, there was a deafening silence. He admitted that with temperatures well below freezing, he had soon started to panic and added that he had begun to lose the feeling in his arms and legs. After what seemed like hours, he heard barking and realized that the specially-trained mountain rescue dogs had found him using their incredible sense of smell. Charles promised that he would thank the dogs and their handler in person as soon as he was well enough to leave hospital and he agreed that he was a very lucky man.

Reported speech

4 Read the sentences. Underline the parts of the text that match them.

  1 'I'm a very lucky man.'
  2 'I'm still feeling very weak.'
  3 'The weather was good on the mountain.'
  4 'I've worked as an instructor on these slopes for 15 years.'
  5 'The weather reports hadn't shown any indication of avalanches.'
  6 'I can't stand up on my own.'
  7 'I'll thank the dogs and their handler in person.'

5 Compare the sentences in exercise 4 with the parts of the text that you underlined. Then complete the table.

Direct speech	Reported speech
1 present simple	
2 present continuous	
3 past simple	
4 present perfect	
5 past perfect	
6 *can*	
7 *will*	

When you change direct speech to reported speech, remember to also change:

1 pronouns: *I – he / she*; *we – they*, etc.
2 possessive adjectives: *my – his / her*; *our – their*, etc.
3 time expressions: *today – that day*; *last week – the week before*; *yesterday – the day before*; *tomorrow – the next day*, etc.
4 *here – there*; *this – that*; *these – those*

Reference and practice 7.1 Workbook page 116

6 Find more sentences in reported speech in the newspaper article. What reporting verbs are used in the article?

7 Rewrite the sentences in reported speech.

1 'Today has been the worst day of my life,' admitted Ella.
2 'The rescue dogs live here in the winter,' said the rescue team leader.
3 'I spent an hour buried under the snow yesterday,' Gunter told us.
4 'I can't feel my fingers or my toes,' Gunter added.
5 'We'll find your brother,' the rescue team promised.
6 'We're waiting for the rescue dogs to arrive,' explained the search leader.
7 'We had a lucky escape today,' the couple agreed.
8 'Before the avalanche began, we heard a rumbling noise,' the skiers pointed out.

8 Complete the newspaper article with the correct form of the verbs in brackets.

Dolphins save surfer from shark attack

By Emma Wilson

New Zealand teenager, Dan Sibley, owes his life to a group of dolphins after being attacked by a shark. He explained that he ¹................................... (be) still very shocked and that he ²................................... (can't) believe that he ³................................... (survive).

He said that he ⁴................................... (be) in the water for only a few minutes when something ⁵................................... (hit) his board. Then, he ⁶................................... (notice) a huge shark. However, a group of dolphins had sensed the danger and come to his rescue. Dan explained that they ⁷................................... (stay) with him until they were sure he was safe. Dan added that he ⁸................................... (have) a nasty wound on his arm and that his back ⁹................................... (is) still very painful, but that he ¹⁰................................... (get) better.

When I interviewed him, he said that the incident ¹¹................................... (not stop) him from surfing and that he ¹²................................... (plan) his next surf trip – although he admitted that his parents ¹³................................... (not like) that idea.

9 **SPEAKING** Work in pairs, A and B. Student A is Dan Sibley and Student B a news reporter. Interview Dan about the incident. Use the article in exercise 8 to help you.

DVD extra The Blue Cross

1 ◉ **2.07** **SPEAKING** Discuss the questions. Then listen to the first part of a radio interview with two teenagers with hearing and sight impairments and compare your ideas.

1 What do you think blind people can see?
2 What do you think deaf people can hear?

2 ◉ **2.08** Listen to the rest of the interview. Are the sentences true (T), false (F) or not given (NG)?

1 People don't treat Emily any differently when they discover she's deaf.
2 Nick complains that people in the street never help him.
3 Emily often has to remind teachers to face her when they speak.
4 Emily doesn't like being in a large group of people.
5 Blind people are often good linguists.
6 Music is not an important part of Emily's life.
7 Nick enjoys spending time outside.
8 Emily finds being in a laboratory relaxing.

V **insight** Noun suffixes: *-tion*, *-sion*

3 Read the sentences. Who said them, Emily (E) or Nick (N)? What are the verb forms of the highlighted words? Complete rules a–d about forming nouns.

1 I've had similar reactions.
2 Most deaf people can hear something, depending on the situation.
3 I can interpret their feelings from their facial expressions.
4 I haven't made a decision about my future yet.

With some verbs that end in:

a *-t*, add ....
b *-e*, remove the .... and add ....
c *-ss*, add ....
d *-d* or *-de*, remove the .... or .... and add ....

4 Complete the text with the correct forms of the words below. Decide if you need a verb or a noun. There are two words that you do not need.

■ conclude ■ protect ■ express ■ vibrate ■ react ■ impress ■ decide ■ situate

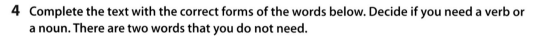

The Deaf Youth Orchestra

Next week sees the start of the Deaf Youth Orchestra's tour. The orchestra helps to empower deaf teenagers and allows them to ¹ .... themselves through music. I met Sophie Wilson, one of the musicians in the orchestra. She is a talented sixteen-year-old and is almost completely deaf. She explained that people's ² .... are very different when she tells them she plays in a deaf orchestra, but most are very surprised. She started to learn the piano at the age of five and realized that she could feel the ³ .... of the notes in her arms and could sense the difference between them. She told me that joining the orchestra had been the best ⁴ .... of her life. I saw the orchestra rehearsing and it was an amazing sight to see the conductor using sign language to communicate with the musicians. I saw the orchestra rehearsing the piece that Sophie will play as the ⁵ .... of their concert. It was amazing, so don't miss the opportunity to see them in action. They're sure to leave a lasting ⁶ ....!

5 **SPEAKING** Discuss the questions.

1 Do you know anyone with a hearing or sight impairment? If so, are their experiences similar to Nick's and Emily's?
2 What have you learned from listening to Nick and Emily? Did anything surprise you?
3 Which do you think is your strongest sense and which is your weakest? Give reasons for your answers.

Complaining and asking people to do things

6 Read complaints 1–5. Where do you think each situation is taking place? In which situation would you complain? Match responses a–e to the complaints.

1 'The people behind me are talking all the time and making a lot of noise.'
2 'It's so loud. I can hear every single thing they're saying and I'm trying to get some sleep.'
3 'I've been waiting here for nearly an hour.'
4 'The chips are cold and some of them are burned.'
5 'I can't read your handwriting on the board.'

a 'I don't think he will be much longer.'
b 'OK, let me change this for you.'
c 'Sorry, I'll turn it down.'
d 'I'll speak to them and see what I can do.'
e 'I'm so sorry. I'll make it bigger.'

7 2.09 Listen to dialogues A–C and match them to one of the situations 1–5 in exercise 6. Then answer the questions.

In which dialogue A, B or C:

1 can the person not wait long?
2 does the person get a replacement?
3 is the person not able to hear the complaint?
4 does the person not know if the situation will be fixed?
5 does the person repeat the complaint?
6 does the person not receive an apology?

8 2.09 Complete the phrases in the table. Then listen to the dialogues again and check.

Complaining	**Asking people to do things**
1 .... to bother you, but	4 .... possibly ... ?
2 .... there's a slight problem.	Do you 5 .... (+ *-ing*) ... ?
3 .... me, I've been waiting	Would you 6 .... (+ *-ing*) ... ?
I'm really not happy about	7 .... you ... ?
I'm not satisfied with	I wonder if you could ... ?

9 2.10 Put the dialogue in the correct order. Listen and check. Then underline two more ways of making complaints and asking people to do things.

.... **Hannah** Well, I'd be grateful if you could tell them to leave if they don't stop. I can't watch the film and I paid £6.40 for my ticket.
.... **Hannah** OK. That sounds good.
.... **Manager** Where are they sitting and what's the problem?
.... **Manager** Oh, dear. I'll go and speak to them.
.... **Manager** Yes, can I help you?
.... **Manager** I'm sorry. Come and show me who they are and I'll speak to them and see what I can do.
.... **Hannah** I'm sitting in row E and the people behind me are talking all the time and making a lot of noise.
.... **Hannah** I'd like to make a complaint about the people sitting near me.

10 SPEAKING Work in pairs. Choose one of the situations below and prepare a dialogue.

1 The classroom next door is really noisy. You are taking a test.
2 You and your friends have been overcharged in a pizzeria.
3 You bought a new phone and it's not working properly. Take it back to the shop.
4 You are at a concert and some people are jumping up and down in front of you. You can't see anything.

1 SPEAKING Discuss the questions.

1 Have you ever been camping or slept outdoors? If so, where did you go? Who did you go with?
2 What noises can you hear when you are outdoors?
3 What kinds of smells do you notice?

2 Look at the cover of *A Walk in the Woods*. What do you think the book is about? Read the information about it and compare your ideas.

3 Read the extract from *A Walk in the Woods*. Then answer the questions.

1 What happened to Bill and Stephen?
2 How would you react if there was a wild animal outside your tent? Would you be more like Bill or more like Stephen?
3 Would you like to read the rest of *A Walk in the Woods*? Why / why not?
4 What do you think happened next?

V Sight and sound

4 Study the highlighted words in the book extract. Which words are connected to sight and which to sound? Match them to definitions 1–6.

1 to look at somebody or something for a long time
2 to look closely or carefully at something when you can't see it clearly
3 to speak very quietly
4 to open and shut your eyes very quickly
5 to breathe noisily while you are asleep
6 to breathe noisily when smelling something (usually in relation to animals)

5 Complete the text with the correct form of the verbs in exercise 4.

Last summer, I went camping with my friend Elka. One evening, after a long day's walk, Elka was so exhausted that she fell asleep straight away and started ¹............................ very loudly as I was trying to cook dinner! She could sleep through anything. Later, after I'd eaten and gone to sleep, a strange noise outside woke me up. Something that sounded like an animal ²............................ noisily around our tent. I ³............................ softly to Elka, but she carried on sleeping, so I pushed her hard. She sat up and just ⁴............................ at me as if she'd never seen me before. Then she ⁵............................ her eyes a few times and went back to sleep. I opened the front of our tent and ⁶............................ out. Imagine my horror when I saw a huge black bull calmly eating the grass in front of our tent. He looked at me, as if to say, 'How dare you disturb my meal!' Then, he turned around slowly and wandered off to the grass in front of the next tent.

Bill Bryson is a famous American author. He has written books about life in the UK, the USA and Australia. This extract is from *A Walk in the Woods* and describes Bill's adventures with his friend Stephen Katz when they hiked along the Appalachian Trail. The trail is 3,540 km long and stretches along the east coast of the USA, passing through some of the most beautiful landscapes in the country.

During their hike, they had lots of experiences, including incidents with wild animals and poisonous plants. In this extract, Bill describes what happened when he heard strange noises outside his tent one night.

It was perfect sleeping weather, cool enough to need a bag, but warm enough to sleep in your underwear, and I was looking forward to having a long night's rest, which is what
5 I was doing when, at some point during the night, I heard a sound nearby that made my eyes fly open. Normally, I slept through everything – through thunderstorms, and through Katz's snoring, so something big
10 enough to wake me was unusual. There was a sound of undergrowth being disturbed – a click of breaking branches, a weighty pushing through low foliage – and then a kind of large, vaguely irritable snuffling noise.
15 Bear!
I sat bolt upright. Instantly, every neuron in my brain was awake and dashing around frantically, like ants when you disturb their nest. I reach instinctively for my knife, then
20 realized I had left it in my pack, just outside the tent. (…)
There was another noise, quite near.
'Stephen, you awake?' I whispered.
'Yup,' he replied in a weary but normal voice.
25 'What was that?'
'How should I know?'
'It sounded big.'
'Everything sounds big in the woods.'
This was true. (…)
30 I shuffled on my knees to the foot of the tent, cautiously unzipped the mesh and peered out, but it was pitch black. (…)
Carefully, very carefully, I climbed from the tent and put on the torch. Something
35 about 15 or 20 feet away looked up at me. I couldn't see anything at all of its shape or size – only two shining eyes. It went silent, whatever it was, and stared back at me.

'Stephen,' I whispered at his tent, 'did you pack a knife?' 40

'No.'

'Have you got anything sharp at all?'

He thought for a moment. 'Nail clippers.' (...)

I nervously threw a stick at the animal, and 45 it didn't move, whatever it was. A deer would have bolted. This thing just blinked once and kept staring.

I reported this to Katz.

'Probably a buck. They're not that timid. 50 Try shouting at it.'

I cautiously shouted at it: 'Hey! You there!' The creature blinked again, singularly unmoved. 'You shout,' I said.

'Oh, you brute, go away!' Katz shouted in 55 merciless imitation. (...)

I peered and peered, but I couldn't see anything but those two wide-set eyes staring from the near distance like eyes in a cartoon. (...) 60

'What are you doing, Bryson? Just leave it alone and it will go away.'

'How can you be so calm?'

'What do you want me to do? You're hysterical enough for both of us. (...) 65

'Well, I'm going back to sleep,' Katz announced.

'What are you talking about? You can't go to sleep.'

'Sure I can. I've done it lots of times.' There 70 was the sound of him rolling over and a series of snuffling noises, not unlike those of the creature outside.

'Stephen, you can't go to sleep,' I ordered. But he could and he did, with amazing 75 rapidity.

The creature – creatures, now – resumed drinking with heavy lapping noises. I couldn't find any replacement batteries, so I flung the torch aside and put my miner's lamp on my 80 head, made sure it worked, then switched it off. Then I sat for ages on my knees, facing the front of the tent, listening keenly, gripping my walking stick like a club, ready to beat back an attack, and with my knife 85 open and at hand as a last line of defence. The bears – animals, whatever they were – drank for perhaps twenty minutes more, then quietly departed the way they had come. It was a joyous moment – but I knew from my 90 reading that they would be likely to return. I listened and listened, but the forest returned to silence and stayed there.

Reported questions and commands

6 Which sentences 1–5 are reported questions and which are reported commands? Underline the parts of the text that match them.

1 Bill asked Stephen whether he had packed a knife.
2 Bill asked Stephen if he had anything sharp at all.
3 Stephen told the bear to go away.
4 Stephen told Bill to just leave it alone.
5 Bill asked Stephen how he could be so calm.

7 Choose the correct answers in rules 1–3. Then find more questions and commands in the text and rewrite them as reported questions and commands.

1 When we report yes / no questions, we use if or *that* / *whether*.
2 In reported questions, the subject comes **before** / **after** the verb.
3 When we report commands, we use reporting verb + **object** / **subject** + *to* + infinitive.

4 When we report negative commands, we use verb + object + *not* + *to* + infinitive.

Reference and practice 7.2 | Workbook page 117

8 You are going on a night hike with your teacher. Report the teacher's questions and commands.

1 'Is anyone really frightened of the dark?'
2 'What sights and sounds do you think you'll see?'
3 'Put your torches away. You don't need them.'
4 'Don't speak or whisper because you'll frighten the wildlife.'
5 'Go to your tents when I ask you to.'
6 'Don't wander off alone.'
7 'Does anyone recognize the smell? It's a fox.'
8 'Did you hear the owl hooting?'

9 SPEAKING Work in pairs. Imagine you are walking in the woods with a friend. Prepare a dialogue that you have with your friend. Include statements, questions and commands. Talk about: the noises, the smells, how you feel, what you decide to do. Then report your conversation to another pair.

Vocabulary bank | Ways of speaking page 140

1 SPEAKING Are there any problems with noise at your school? Do the survey in pairs. Compare your results with another pair.

Noise at school

1 Do you like the sound of the school bell?   YES / NO / I DON'T NOTICE IT

2 Is the canteen too noisy?   YES / NO

3 Should there be a separate quiet room for eating?   YES / NO

4 Would you like to have background music in the library?   YES / NO

5 Can you always hear what your teacher is saying in class?   YES / NO

6 Does the noise from the playground and sports fields distract you during lessons?   YES / NO

2 Read the report and put paragraphs A–E in the correct order. Are the findings similar or different to your answers to the survey in exercise 1?

An analysis of noise at school

A ....

Moving on to the second question about the noise in the canteen, well over a quarter of the students thought it was too noisy and would like a separate quiet room. However, just over half of the students said they didn't mind the noise. The other students had no strong feelings on the matter.

With regard to music or silence in the library, well under half of the students said they would prefer background music in the library, while approximately a third of students said they preferred to work in silence. The remaining students expressed no opinion at all on this question.

B ....

In conclusion, it appears that there are some noise issues in the school. Most students complain about the sound of the school bell and I therefore recommend that the school should change it. Additionally, it is not clear whether students would prefer to have background music in the library, so I suggest we try it out for a period of one month.

C ....

The purpose of this report is to present the findings of a survey into students' views on noise in school due to recent complaints from some students. The survey was conducted among sixty students in Years 10 and 11.

D ....

Regarding noise in the classroom, just under three quarters of students agreed that they had no problems hearing what their teacher was saying, while about a quarter of students admitted that they would prefer their teacher to use a microphone. Turning to the final question, well over three quarters of the students replied that they were not distracted by noise from the playground and sports fields, but just under 20% of the students said it did bother them.

E ....

As far as the first question about the sound of the school bell is concerned, nearly all the students said they disliked the loud ring and would prefer a different noise. Some of them said that they would like popular mobile phone ringtones instead of a bell. Only two students said they didn't notice the bell.

3 Match headings 1–6 to paragraphs A–E. There is one heading that you do not need.

1 Noise inside the school
2 The aim of the report
3 Noise in the playground
4 Conclusion and recommendations
5 The bell
6 Noise during lessons

STRATEGY

Making your writing flow

When you write a report, use phrases to make your report flow smoothly and to make it easier for the reader to follow your points. The most common phrases used in reports are:

- *As far as … is concerned, … .*
- *As for … .*
- *Regarding … .*
- *Moving on to … .*

4 Read the strategy. Find more phrases that make your writing flow smoothly in the model report.

V **Approximations and fractions**

5 Study the highlighted words in the report. Match them to meanings and percentages 1–9.

1	a bit more than	6	31%
2	a bit less than	7	74%
3	a lot more than	8	81%
4	a lot less than	9	99%
5	24%		

6 Study the information in the pie chart. Are the sentences true (T) or false (F)? Correct the false ones.

1 Just under half of students in Year 9 like sweet things.
2 Just over a third of the students like the taste of spicy food.
3 Well over half of students like sour tastes.
4 Around a third of the students like the taste of sweet things.
5 Almost everyone likes the taste of bitter food.
6 Approximately a quarter of the students enjoy salty tastes.

Year 9 taste preferences

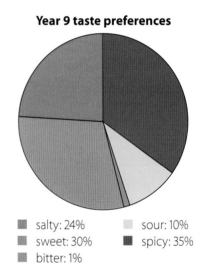

- salty: 24%
- sweet: 30%
- bitter: 1%
- sour: 10%
- spicy: 35%

WRITING GUIDE

- **Task** Do a survey and write a report on the findings.

- **Ideas** Think about your survey:
  1 Decide what your survey will be about. Use the ideas below or your own ideas.
     - food and tastes people like / do not like
     - music and sounds people like / do not like
  2 Make notes about:
     - who the survey is aimed at.
     - what you want to find out by doing the survey.
     - the number and type of questions you want to ask.

- **Plan** Follow the plan:
  1 Prepare your survey.
  2 Do your survey.
  3 Collect and analyze the results.
  4 Write your report.

- **Write** Write a report on your survey results.

- **Check** Check the following points:
  - Have you explained the purpose of the survey?
  - Have you grouped similar ideas in the same paragraph?
  - Have you used a variety of phrases to help your writing flow?
  - Have you used approximations and fractions?
  - Have you written a conclusion and made a recommendation?
  - Have you checked grammar, vocabulary, spelling and punctuation?

STRATEGY

Homonyms

Homonyms are words that have the same spelling and pronunciation, but different meanings. In the *Oxford Wordpower Dictionary*, the different meanings are numbered within the entry. For example, *view* has two meanings:

> **view²** /vjuː/ *verb* [T] **1** view sb/sth (as sth) to think about sb/sth in a particular way: *She viewed holidays as a waste of time.* **2** to watch or look at sth: *Viewed from this angle, the building looks much taller than it really is.*

Sometimes, if a word has more than one part of speech, there will be a small number next to the headword:

> **view¹** /vjuː/ *noun* **1** [C] a view (about/on sth) an

1 Read the strategy above. Study the dictionary entries for *view* and answer the questions.

> **view¹** /vjuː/ *noun* **1** [C] a view (about/on sth) an opinion or a particular way of thinking about sth: *He expressed the view that standards were falling.* ♦ *In my view, she has done nothing wrong.* ♦ *She has strong views on the subject.* **2** [U,sing] the ability to see sth or to be seen from a particular place: *The garden was hidden from view behind a high wall.* ♦ *to come into view* ♦ *to disappear from view* **3** [C] what you can see from a particular place: *There are breathtaking views from the top of the mountain.* ♦ *a room with a sea view* ⊃ note at **scenery**

> **view²** /vjuː/ *verb* [T] **1** view sb/sth (as sth) to think about sb/sth in a particular way: *She viewed holidays as a waste of time.* **2** to watch or look at sth: *Viewed from this angle, the building looks much taller than it really is.*

1 How many entries are there for *view*?
2 How many different parts of speech are there?
3 How many meanings are there of the noun *view*?
4 How many meanings are there of the verb *view*?

2 Study the dictionary entries in exercise 1 again. Write the entry number and the meaning number of the underlined words in the sentences.

1 <u>Viewed</u> from the top of the hill, the boats looked tiny.
....

2 She <u>viewed</u> health foods as very expensive.
....

3 As soon as we turned the corner, the palace came to <u>view</u>. ....
4 We booked a room with a sea <u>view</u>. ....
5 In my <u>view</u>, vegetables are horrible. ....

3 Choose the correct meaning of the underlined words. Use a dictionary to help you.

1 I didn't <u>realize</u> that you were such a good cook.
   a to know and understand that something is true
   b to make something that you imagined become reality
2 He <u>realized</u> his dream and became a famous author.
   a to know and understand that something is true
   b to make something that you imagined become reality

3 The <u>notice</u> on the door said that the restaurant had been closed.
   a to see and become conscious of something
   b a piece of paper or a sign giving information, a warning, etc.
4 I didn't <u>notice</u> you the other day.
   a to see and become conscious of something
   b a piece of paper or a sign giving information, a warning, etc.
5 It was very foggy, so we couldn't <u>distinguish</u> the writing on the sign.
   a to recognize the difference between two things or people
   b to see, hear, or recognize with effort
6 She can't <u>distinguish</u> between the twins.
   a to recognize the difference between two things or people
   b to see, hear, or recognize with effort

STRATEGY

Homophones

Homophones are words that have the same pronunciation, but different meanings. They can be spelled the same way (so are then also homonyms), or they can have different spellings.

4 Read the strategy above. Then study the dictionary entries for *peer* and *pier*. Are the sentences true (T) or false (F)?

> **peer¹** /pɪə(r)/ *noun* [C] **1** a person who is of the same age or position in society as you: *Children hate to look stupid in front of their peers.* **2** (in Britain) a member of the **nobility** (= people of the highest social class, who have special titles)

> **peer²** /pɪə(r)/ *verb* [I] peer (at sb/sth) to look closely or carefully at sb/sth, for example because you cannot see very well: *He peered at the photo, but it was blurred.*

> **pier** /pɪə(r)/ *noun* [C] **1** a large wooden or metal structure that is built out into the sea in holiday towns, where people can walk **2** a large wooden or metal structure that is built out into the sea from the land. Boats can stop at **piers** so that people or goods can be taken on or off.

1 *Peer* and *pier* are homonyms.
2 *Peer* and *pier* are homophones.
3 The noun and verb forms of *peer* are homonyms.
4 The noun and verb forms of *peer* are homophones.

5 Use a dictionary to find homonyms or homophones of the words below. Then write your own example sentence with each word.

■ stare ■ bear ■ blink ■ glare

1 ....
2 ....
3 ....
4 ....

Dictionary entries from *Oxford Wordpower Dictionary*, 4th edition

Vocabulary

1 Replace the words in italics with the correct form of the verbs below.

▨ differentiate ▨ detect ▨ view ▨ realize ▨ notice
▨ distinguish

1 This is tasty! I didn't .... (*know*) you could cook.
2 I've always .... (*thought of*) health food as boring, but this has changed my mind.
3 The students were listening carefully, but they couldn't .... (*hear properly*) what the teacher was saying.
4 Humans .... (*discover*) different tastes with taste buds on their tongues.
5 I never .... (*was aware of*) the different flavours in this dish until I cooked it myself.
6 Our school doesn't .... (*treat differently*) between any groups of students. We treat everyone the same.

Marks .... / 6

2 Complete the text using the correct adjective or adverb form of the words below.

▨ care ▨ difficulty ▨ entire ▨ taste ▨ utter ▨ wide

Eating in the dark makes food tastier! If you aren't ¹............... convinced, try it! 'Dining in the dark' experiences are now ²............... available in many cities. You need to be exceptionally ³............... with your knife and fork, to avoid accidents! At first, eating can be somewhat ⁴..............., but after a while, you'll notice that even fairly ⁵..............., boring foods become more interesting. Unfortunately, foods you don't like may seem ⁶............... repulsive!

Marks .... / 6

3 Complete the text with the correct form of the verbs in brackets.

When a baby elephant is in a dangerous ¹............... (situate), the mother's first ²............... (react) is to stamp her feet. People used to think this was an ³............... (express) of anger, to frighten enemies and give the baby ⁴............... (protect). But scientists have come to the ⁵............... (conclude) that foot-stamping is a warning signal. ⁶............... (vibrate) from the mother's feet can travel for miles, alerting other elephants to danger.

Marks .... / 6

4 Complete the sentences with the correct form of the verbs below.

▨ peer ▨ snuffle ▨ snore ▨ stare ▨ blink ▨ whisper

1 Sleeping on your side can help to reduce ....
2 During my presentation, most students were ....
3 We could hear some animals .... outside our hut.
4 I .... at my friend's notes, but couldn't read his handwriting.
5 I had something in my eye and couldn't stop ....
6 The animals .... at me for a very long time and didn't want to move.

Marks .... / 6

Grammar

5 Complete the text with the correct reported speech form of the verbs below.

▨ can ▨ feel ▨ not find ▨ have ▨ investigate ▨ smell
▨ wake ▨ will

After the fire, Ada said that she ¹............... lucky to be alive. She told reporters that her cat ²............... her up after he ³............... the smoke. She explained that cats ⁴............... a powerful sense of smell, adding that they ⁵............... smell ten times better than humans. She also said that her cat ⁶............... sleep in her room in future! The police said that they ⁷............... the cause of the fire. They told us that they ⁸............... any evidence yet.

Marks .... / 8

6 Complete sentence b so that it has a similar meaning to sentence a.

1 a 'I've never been so frightened,' Ada admitted.
  b Ada admitted ....
2 a 'I'm proud of my cat,' she told reporters.
  b She told reporters ....
3 a She explained that her cat had smelled the fire.
  b '...............,' she explained.
4 a She added that she didn't feel safe there.
  b '...............,' she added.
5 a 'I'll sleep in a hotel tonight,' she told us.
  b She told us ....
6 a The police said they were interviewing witnesses.
  b '...............,' the police said.
7 a A girl said she had seen a man outside.
  b '...............,' said a girl.
8 a 'We can't say if it's important yet,' the police warned.
  b The police warned that ....

Marks .... / 8

7 Rewrite questions and commands 1–10 in reported speech.

Ben: '¹Stop!' Anna: '²Why have we stopped?' Ben: '³Look ahead. ⁴Can you see the bear?' Anna: '⁵Don't be stupid.' Ben: '⁶Will you just trust me, for once? ⁷Don't argue with me.' Anna: 'Ow! ⁸Let go of my arm! ⁹Why are you pulling me back?' Ben: '¹⁰Do you want to go ahead and get eaten?'

1 Ben told ....
2 Anna asked Ben ....
3 Ben told ....
4 He asked ....
5 Anna told ....
6 Ben asked ...., for once.
7 He told ....
8 Anna said 'Ow!' Then she told ....
9 She asked ....
10 Ben asked ....

Marks .... / 10

Total .... / 50

1 SPEAKING Think about your future job and put the ideas below in order of importance. Compare your list with other people in the class. Then read the text. Which ideas are mentioned?

- have the same job for a long time ■ make a lot of money
- work outside ■ do many different things every day
- do the same thing every day ■ help other people
- make your own decisions ■ work with a variety of people

2 Read the text again. Are the sentences true (T), false (F) or not given (NG)?

1 Children are more sure about their passions than adults.
2 Sean earned money for the jobs he did.
3 His first job was with a national newspaper.
4 Sean found out that he was a good communicator.
5 The yoga class taught Sean the value of making excuses.
6 The teachers in Idaho enjoyed teaching their students.
7 Sean's experiences have helped him to find a career he enjoys.
8 He believes that most jobs are for life.

3 SPEAKING Answer the questions.

1 The text mentions ten of the jobs Sean tried. Do any of them appeal to you? Why / why not?
2 What are your talents? What is your passion?

V Describing jobs

4 Study the highlighted adjectives in the text. Then match them to job descriptions 1–9.

1 I left because there was no chance of moving to a higher position.
2 It requires a lot of training or practice.
3 So many things were new and difficult. It forced me to make a lot of effort.
4 It's extremely well paid and offers plenty of chances for promotion.
5 It's a lot more exciting or attractive than ordinary jobs.
6 It's not that difficult – the same tasks are repeated many times.
7 You will need to be able to cope well under pressure.
8 It's an enjoyable and interesting career and well worth the effort.
9 Every day is different, dealing with different tasks and different people.

The big question

What do you want to be when you grow up? An actor? An astronaut? A famous sportsperson? Most children know the answer to this question, and so did a schoolboy called Sean Aiken. He wanted to be a famous basketball player. But then
5 he grew up and, all of a sudden, like many adults, he didn't know the answer any more.
His dad said, 'Sean, it doesn't matter what you do, just make sure it is something you are passionate about.' The problem was that Sean didn't know what he was passionate about and
10 he was scared of making the wrong choice, so he decided to go on a journey and gain some experience. His journey took him across Canada and America, trying out fifty-two different jobs in as many weeks: from a highly-skilled tattoo artist to a high-flying stockbroker, and from a glamorous fashion buyer
15 to a not-so-glamorous cat tail picker*! In the process, he learned some valuable lessons.

#1 Create opportunity

'It's okay not to know what you want to do, but it's not okay to do nothing,' says Sean. Doing fifty-two jobs in a year
20 and writing a blog about them was his plan of action. An interview with a national newspaper <u>started the ball rolling</u>, and the one-week job offers began to arrive. Sean <u>had a lot on his plate</u> – doing different jobs meant developing different skills. It was hard work, but it also created opportunities for
25 Sean to find his natural talent.

#2 Find your natural talent

There were plenty of jobs Sean liked and plenty he hated. Working in an office was boring and repetitive – a real dead-end job, he thought. Selling T-shirts at the Toronto film festival
30 was more varied with different tasks, but it was stressful, too. He had three different bosses and no time to <u>put his feet up</u> and relax. But there were other things he loved. 'The dairy farm was cool,' he said, because he enjoyed working outside. As Sean went from job to job, good or bad, a pattern started to
35 emerge. He discovered he was great with people – he could get on with almost anyone. Perhaps this was his natural talent?

Vocabulary: describing jobs; idioms: work; decisions and ideas; conflict; action verbs
Grammar: third conditional; *I wish* and *If only*; speculating about the past

Speaking: discussing ambitions and decisions; expressing regrets; giving presentations
Writing: a covering letter

8A

#3 Be flexible and have the right attitude

You have to be flexible to be a yoga instructor. You also need the right attitude. When Sean was asked to teach a yoga class, he felt he'd been <u>thrown in at the deep end</u>. 'I'd never even stepped inside a yoga studio before, so I immediately began to think of excuses (not to teach),' he admitted. Luckily for Sean, an instructor took time out to <u>show him the ropes</u>. That and his positive attitude helped him to <u>rise to the challenge</u> and within a few days, he was ready to teach the class.

#4 Find your passion

Sean didn't find his perfect job, but he did find his 'passion'. In Idaho, he spent a week as a pre-school teacher, which taught him the value of helping others. A week as a fund-raiser for cancer research confirmed this. For Sean, <u>the bottom line</u> was doing something meaningful and worthwhile, something that made a difference to other people's lives. Fifty-two weeks later … Sean's journey has turned into his career. He has written a book about career choice and spoken to college students about where their talents lie. He's realized his passion to help others, but he also knows that people's passions and talents change. No job is forever and what is challenging and new today might not be so interesting in five years' time. 'The reality is that I'm going to have five or six different careers in my life,' says Sean, 'but instead of being bothered by that, now I'm excited by it.'

* cat tail picker = agricultural worker who collects cat tails (a type of plant you can eat) in swamps and wetlands.

5 Complete the text with adjectives in exercise 4.

Follow your dream …

Matt didn't hate school, but he found the lessons boring and ¹_____, often learning the same old things over and over again. He loved drawing, though, so he constantly drew cartoons. It kept him out of trouble.

Matt was very imaginative, so every picture was different – the subjects were ²_____ and often funny. But drawing wasn't easy; it was a ³_____ activity which required practice. Matt did practise and soon he became so good that he could draw without looking (and pretend he was paying attention in class!). It made all the effort ⁴_____.

When Matt decided to become a cartoonist, his parents and teachers discouraged him. They thought it was a ⁵_____ career, going nowhere. It was much better to work as a well-paid company executive. That was their idea of a glamorous, ⁶_____ job. But Matt wasn't interested in that type of job. He knew the constant pressure would be challenging and ⁷_____ 'I knew it wasn't going to work for me. I knew I was going to be drawing cartoons forever.'

Luckily, Matt didn't listen to his parents or teachers, because if he had, he wouldn't have realized his dream. Today, Matt Groening has one of the most exciting jobs in TV – he's the creator of *The Simpsons*!

V insight **Idioms: work**

6 Study the underlined idioms in the text. Then match them to definitions 1–7.

1 take a break and relax
2 begin a project or start an idea
3 teach someone new how to do something correctly
4 put in a new and difficult situation without any help
5 have a lot of work and responsibilities
6 the most important reason for something
7 try your best to do something difficult and be successful

7 SPEAKING Work in small groups. Discuss the statements.

1 Many people want a high-flying job that pays lots of money. But if you love what you do, money isn't important.
2 You should listen to your parents and your teachers. They have experience and can show you the ropes.

Vocabulary bank Gender-neutral job titles page 141

1 SPEAKING **You are going to read a text about how a goat changed a girl's life. Before you read, discuss the questions.**

1 How do you think the goat changed the girl's life?
2 In which country do you think this took place?
3 What do you think the girl does now?

2 **Read the text and compare your ideas in exercise 1.**

If they hadn't owned a goat …

When we think about who has had the biggest impact on our lives so far, many of us would probably say parents, friends or teachers. For Beatrice Biira it is … a goat.

Beatrice, her mother and her seven brothers and sisters lived in a small village in Uganda. They were very poor and basic necessities were a luxury. [1]If her family had had $20, they would have paid for Beatrice to go to school, but they didn't have this kind of money. When Beatrice was nine, a life-changing event happened to them. The family was given a goat by a small charity called Heifer International. Within three months of receiving the goat, Beatrice and her family had raised enough money from the sale of the goat's milk to send Beatrice to school. Although she was much older than the other children in her class, she did well, studied hard and soon won a scholarship to a school in Massachusetts, USA. From there, she went on to Connecticut College and then finally studied for a Master's Degree.

Beatrice has many people to thank for their support and encouragement along the way. But most of all, she's grateful to that first goat. [2]If they hadn't received the goat, they wouldn't have had the money to allow Beatrice to get an education. [3]If she had stayed in the village, her life would have been completely different.

Beatrice now works as an ambassador for Heifer. It's a very meaningful and worthwhile job – she is happy to help other children like her and to return the gift of hope that Heifer gave her when she was nine years old.

3 **Read sentences 1–3 from the text and choose the correct answers in a–b.**

1 If her family had had $20, they would have paid for Beatrice to go to school.
   a The family **had / didn't have** $20.
   b They **paid / didn't pay** for Beatrice to go to school.
2 If they hadn't received the goat, they wouldn't have had the money to allow Beatrice to get an education.
   a They **received / didn't receive** the goat.
   b They **had / didn't have** enough money to allow Beatrice to get an education.
3 If she had stayed in the village, her life would have been completely different.
   a Her life **was / wasn't** completely different.
   b She **stayed / didn't stay** in the village.

Third conditional

4 **Study the sentences and the answers in exercise 3 and choose the correct answers.**

The third conditional:

a refers to events in the **future / past**.
b talks about **real / imaginary** events.
c talks about **possible / impossible** conditions.
d talks about **possible / impossible** results.

We form the third conditional with:
If + subject + past perfect, subject + *would / could / might* + *have* + past participle.

Reference and practice 8.1 | Workbook page 118

5 **Complete the sentences with the correct form of the verbs in brackets. Use the third conditional.**

1 If Beatrice's family .... (have) $20, they .... (can afford) to pay her school fees.
2 They .... (be) too poor to send her to school if they .... (not earn) money from the goat's milk.
3 If Beatrice .... (not look after) the goat, it .... (might not produce) so much milk.
4 Beatrice .... (not get) a degree from an American college if she .... (stay) in her village.
5 She .... (not learn) skills to help other people if Heifer .... (not help) her when she was young.
6 Her life .... (might be) completely different if her parents .... (not be) so poor.

6 🔊 **2.11** Listen to a story about another family who were helped by Heifer. Match sentences 1–5 to a–e. Then make sentences using the third conditional.

1 They didn't have much money.
2 They drank the milk.
3 They earned some money from the milk sales.
4 They used the milk money to buy materials.
5 Someone gave them a cow.

a Their situation wasn't difficult.
b They could rebuild their house.
c Their lives changed.
d They became strong and healthy.
e They couldn't afford much food.

7 SPEAKING **Work in pairs. Discuss the questions.**

1 Heifer's policy of 'Passing the gift on' encourages people who benefit from a gift of a cow or a goat to pass on the benefits. How did Beatrice and Daniel do this?
2 Heifer donates cows and goats to people in poor areas. Do you think this is more helpful than donating food or money? Why / why not?
3 Can you think of other useful, life-changing things which charities like Heifer could donate?

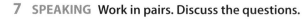

I wish and If only

8 🔊 **2.12** Listen to three people talking about their regrets. Match speakers 1–3 to regrets a–c.

a accepting a job offer   **b** listening to parents   **c** leaving a team

9 Study the sentences from the listening. For each sentence choose the correct answer a or b. Then complete the rules.

1 I wish I was there with him.
   a I'm there with him now.
   b I'm not there with him now.
2 If only I hadn't left Susie.
   a I left Susie.
   b I didn't leave Susie.

Which sentence refers to the past and which to the present?

We use *I wish* and *If only* + ... to express wishes about the present.
We use *I wish* and *If only* + ... to express regrets about the past.

Reference and practice 8.2 | Workbook page 118

10 🔊 **2.12** Listen again. Are the sentences true (T) or false (F)? Rewrite the sentences to express wishes and regrets.

1 Speaker 1 followed his teacher's advice.
2 He decided to do more athletics.
3 He's still in contact with his friend.
4 Speaker 2 missed a great opportunity.
5 She needed to make money.
6 She'd like to be working with Susie now.
7 Speaker 3 experienced problems at school.
8 He had a serious disagreement with his parents.

11 SPEAKING **Work in pairs. Tell your partner about:**

▪ three decisions which you made, but now regret.
▪ three things you want to change about your life.

Popular culture quiz

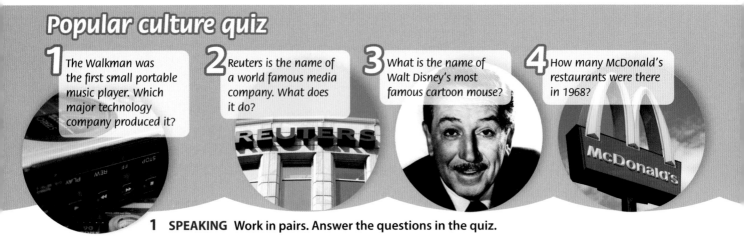

1 The Walkman was the first small portable music player. Which major technology company produced it?

2 Reuters is the name of a world famous media company. What does it do?

3 What is the name of Walt Disney's most famous cartoon mouse?

4 How many McDonald's restaurants were there in 1968?

1 SPEAKING Work in pairs. Answer the questions in the quiz.

STRATEGY

Dealing with unknown words while listening

When you listen to a text, you might not understand every word that you hear.

■ Do not panic! You do not have to understand every word in order to make sense of the text.

■ Use the words that you do know to create a framework – a basic understanding of the text.

■ Do not try to translate the text into your own language.

■ If possible, listen once for general understanding and again to find out the details.

2 ◉ 2.13 Read the strategy. Then listen to a short extract from a talk and follow the steps below.

1 While you listen, write down the key words that you understand.

2 Work in pairs. Compare your notes and try to retell the listening text.

3 What is the main idea of the text?

4 Did you have to understand every word in order to understand the text?

---

3 ◉ 2.14 Listen to the whole talk and check your answers to the quiz in exercise 1.

4 ◉ 2.14 Listen again and choose the correct answers.

1 What kind of market research did Akio Morita do for the Walkman?
   a None.
   b He asked lots of young people for their opinions.
   c He talked to people in his company about the idea.

2 When did the first Walkman come onto the market?
   a 1978   b 1979   c 1995

3 Where was Julius Reuter originally from?
   a England   b Belgium   c Germany

4 Reuter pioneered the use of carrier pigeons to transport news
   a from one country to another.
   b around the country very quickly.
   c to the financial markets.

5 What job was Ray Kroc doing in the 1950s?
   a paper cup salesman   b restaurant manager   c milkshake machine agent

6 Why did Kroc decide to visit the restaurant in California?
   a Because it had ordered a lot of milkshake machines.
   b Because he wanted to pick up some milkshake machines from them.
   c Because he was impressed by their cheap, fast food.

V Decisions and ideas

5 Study the phrases from the listening text. Put them into the correct category.

create something   decide something   think again about something

   ■ come up with a scheme ■ change your mind ■ conceive an idea ■ make a decision
   ■ go ahead with a plan ■ reconsider a decision ■ have second thoughts ■ make up one's mind
   ■ dream up an idea

6 Choose the correct answers.

1 I've **dreamed up** / **come up** an idea for a new type of mobile phone.
2 The judges liked your plan originally, but they've now **reconsidered** / **changed** their mind.
3 My brother has **come up** / **made up** with a scheme for making a lot money.
4 My parents have **made** / **conceived** a decision. We are moving to France.
5 I like your plan, so now I think you should **dream up** / **go ahead** with it.
6 Charlie's not sure which university to go to. He can't **make up** / **have second thoughts** his mind.

7 SPEAKING Which decision in the listening do you think was the most important? What are the most important decisions that you have made in your life?

Giving presentations

8 🔊 **2.15 SPEAKING** Work in pairs. Complete the tips with *Do* or *Don't*. Then listen to eight speakers. Match each speaker 1–8 to a tip a–j. There are two tips that you do not need.

How to give a **successful** presentation

a .... **tell** the listeners at the beginning what you are going to talk about.

b .... **read** your talk out from a prepared script.

c .... speak very **fast.**

d .... make and follow a **plan** for your talk.

e .... **allow time** for questions at the end of the talk.

f .... use humour or personal anecdotes to make your talk more **interesting**.

g .... use some **visual aids,** for example, pictures, graphs or slides.

h .... talk in a flat, monotonous **voice.**

i .... **remind** people what you have told them at the end of the presentation.

j .... hand out lots of **information** at the beginning of the talk.

9 🔊 **2.16** Read the speaker's plan and then listen to the presentation. Which two things in the plan does the speaker not mention?

introduce topic / give an outline of the talk
personal experience

Health benefits
• good exercise, doesn't put too much stress on body
• good way to lose weight
• works all the muscles
• develops stamina

Social benefits
• meet different types of new people
• competing is an opportunity to travel
• fun activity for holidays

Conclusion: benefits. Encourage audience to join local pool.

10 🔊 **2.16** Listen to the presentation again and complete the phrases in the box.

Introducing a topic
I'd like ¹................... about ... .
I'm going ²................... briefly at ... .
In this presentation, my subject will be ... .

Giving an example
To ⁵................... example ... .
To illustrate this point ... .
A good example of this is ... .

Sequencing events
I'll ³................... telling you ... .
⁴................... on to ... .
Let's begin by ... .
Now let's look at ... .

Concluding
So, to ⁶..................., ...
Finally, to sum up ... .
In conclusion ... .

11 SPEAKING Prepare and give a presentation on the following topic: 'What is your passion in life?'

1 SPEAKING Work in pairs. What would you do if the things below became the law in your country? How would you feel?

1 Teenage boys and girls must travel on separate buses.
2 The minimum age for having a mobile phone is eighteen.
3 All clothes worn by teenagers must be approved by parents.
4 Under-eighteens may only use the internet for study purposes.

2 Read the article about Rosa Parks. What happened to her? What did she do?

3 Read the article again. In which paragraph A–F is information 1–7 stated? There is one statement that you do not need.

1 What would have happened if Rosa hadn't protested.
2 Where African Americans could sit on buses.
3 How Martin Luther King reacted to violence.
4 How the driver on Rosa's bus felt.
5 Why Rosa admired Martin Luther King.
6 How Rosa's actions improved everyday life for African Americans.
7 How people showed their support for Rosa.

4 SPEAKING Work in pairs. Discuss the questions.

1 If you had been in the same situation as Rosa Parks on that bus, what would you have said and done?
2 Which present-day issues would you like to protest about? Why? What would you do?

V Conflict

5 Read the text. Then replace the words and phrases in italics with the correct form of the highlighted words in the article about Rosa Parks.

Martin Luther King was an American clergyman, Nobel Peace Prize winner and one of the most famous leaders of the civil rights movement. Dr King first achieved national fame when he helped people organize a ¹*refusal to use a product or service* in Montgomery in 1955. People refused to use the buses in support of Rosa Parks. After his success in Montgomery, he went on to organize a ²*public protest against something* in Birmingham, Alabama, where there was violent ³*resistance to the black civil rights movement*. Civil rights protesters received ⁴*warnings of an intention to hurt someone* and some were attacked. Dr King was arrested, although the protest was non-violent.
Dr King carried on the ⁵*difficult fight* against ⁶*the treatment of one group of people worse than others because they are different* and joined a huge civil rights ⁷*walk to protest against something* in Washington. It was there, in August 1963, that he delivered his famous 'I have a dream' speech. In his speech, he predicted a day when social ⁸*unfairness* would end, and freedom and equality would become a reality for everyone in America. Unfortunately, he didn't live to see that day. On 4 April 1968, Martin Luther King was assassinated during a visit to Memphis, Tennessee.

A BUS RIDE TO FREEDOM

A On 1 December 1955, Rosa Parks had just finished work at a department store in Montgomery, Alabama. She had a job as a seamstress there, and was making her way home to help with a NAACP* youth meeting.
5 There were a lot of people at the bus stop that evening, so Rosa did some shopping, then caught the next bus home. Luckily, she found a seat at the back, but after a few stops, more passengers got on, so the driver told Rosa to stand up. Why? Because the new
10 passengers were white and Rosa was black. African Americans could only sit on the back seats of the bus and when the bus was full, they had to give up their seats to white people.

B In the 1950s, African Americans were treated like
15 second-class citizens. Segregation laws separated people of different races and meant that inequality was present everywhere – on buses, in restaurants, in cinemas and in shops. Even schools were divided up according to the colour of people's skin. Back
20 on the bus, the driver shouted at Rosa to stand up again. She wasn't tired and her feet didn't hurt, but she didn't move. By now, the driver was furious and told Rosa he would get the police. 'You may go and do so,' she calmly replied. The police arrived and
25 Rosa was arrested. ¹She must have felt humiliated as she was driven to jail, but she didn't back down. She didn't know it at the time, but her simple act of opposition would change the course of history and end segregation in America.

C The next day, news of Rosa's arrest spread rapidly 30
through the city. People decided to boycott the buses
and use other means of transport. They wanted
the bus company to stop discrimination against
black passengers. In fact, 75% of the bus company's
passengers were African Americans, so surely they 35
would listen? They didn't, so on Monday 5 December,
thousands of people walked, shared cars, rode bicycles
and even rode mules to get to work. ²It can't have been
easy, but everyone was united in a common struggle.

D In the end, the boycott lasted 381 days. During that 40
time, protestors received threatening phone calls and
homes were vandalized. A young pastor at the local
church called Martin Luther King led the boycott and
his home was attacked, too. People were ready to
fight back, but Dr King made them stop and think. 45
'We cannot solve this problem with violence,' he
said. 'We must meet violence with non-violence.' The
attacks and threats failed to scare off supporters. In
fact, they united people and taught everyone the
value of peaceful opposition. 50

E Then, finally, on 13 November 1956, the Supreme Court
ruled that segregation on buses in Alabama was illegal.
The next day, Rosa Parks, along with Martin Luther
King, got on a city bus. Proudly, she took a seat right at
the front. Rosa had shown how one person's decision 55
could make a huge difference. She showed that civil
disobedience was a powerful way to protest and she
inspired the civil rights movement. Across America, more
and more people took part in public demonstrations
and went on marches. Now they were fighting against 60
segregation and injustice in all areas of society.

F 'When I declined to give up my seat, it was not
because of that day or bus in particular,' Rosa said
later. 'I just wanted to be free, like everybody else.'
But what would have happened if Rosa Parks hadn't 65
refused to stand up on the bus that day? ³Another
African American passenger might have done the
same soon afterwards. On the other hand, they might
not have. Without Rosa's brave protest, ⁴segregation
could have lasted for longer than it did. 70

* NAACP = The National Association for the Advancement
of Colored People, founded in 1909

Speculating about the past

6 Study sentences 1–4 in the article about Rosa Parks.
Then answer questions 1–3 and complete rules a–c.

1 Which sentence talks about things we are certain
happened in the past?

2 Which sentence talks about things we are certain did
not happen in the past?

3 Which sentences talk about things we are not sure
happened in the past?

> **a** We use .... + *have* + past
> participle to talk about things we are certain
> happened in the past.
>
> **b** We use .... + *have* + past
> participle to talk about things that we are certain
> did not happen in the past.
>
> **c** We use .... or ....
> + *have* + past participle to talk about things we are
> not sure happened in the past.

Reference and practice 8.3 Workbook page 119

7 Look at the photo. Then answer the questions using
the modal verbs in exercise 6.

1 Do you think this took place recently? Why / why not?

2 In which country did this happen? How do you
know?

3 What could have happened to cause this situation?

4 How do you think the students must have felt?

5 What might have happened afterwards? Why?

8 2.17 Listen to the recording and compare your
ideas in exercise 7.

9 **SPEAKING** Work in pairs. Discuss the questions.

1 Could you have done what the Little Rock Nine did?
Why / why not?

2 At that time, what could teenagers have done to help
to end segregation and discrimination? Discuss the
ideas below and your own ideas.
▪ boycott school ▪ marches ▪ demonstrations
▪ civil disobedience (school sit-ins)

3 Do you think a situation like the one in Little Rock
could ever have happened in your country? Why /
why not?

Vocabulary bank Conflict: phrasal verbs page 141

DVD extra Suffragettes

SUMMER CAMP COUNSELLOR

National Summer Camp is looking for young, enthusiastic people to help with teaching, food preparation and evening entertainment at our summer camps for seven- to fourteen-year-olds.

We are looking for people who:
★ enjoy working with children
★ have experience in teaching sports, arts and crafts or music.

LIBRARY ASSISTANT

Guildford Library has a summer vacancy for a hard-working student who has excellent IT skills and is organized and efficient. Daily tasks will include:

- sorting books
- dealing with customer enquiries and helping to promote the library
- scanning and filing documents.

1 SPEAKING Read the job advertisements and answer the questions.

1 Which job:
   a requires computer skills?
   b expects candidates to help in educational activities?
   c will probably be mainly outdoors?
   d will probably be mainly indoors?

2 Which job would you prefer to do?

STRATEGY

Avoiding general statements

A covering letter for a job application should include detailed information which is relevant to the employer and the job.

1 Use facts, dates and numbers.
   I've got a tennis coaching qualification.
   → In July 2012, I received a Level 2 tennis coaching certificate.

2 Avoid quantifiers, like *some, a lot of, many ...* .
   I did some work in a shop.
   → I worked for Hegarty's Pie Place for three months in 2011.

3 Give specific examples of how your experience and skills match the employer's requirements.
   I'm hard-working and reliable.
   → I had the opportunity to develop my customer service skills during my work experience with Rocket Records in August.

---

2 Read the strategy and the covering letter. Find examples of 1–3 in the strategy in the covering letter.

3 Rewrite the general sentences using your own ideas. Add details and specific examples.

1 I worked for a children's after-school club.
2 I'm efficient and organized.
3 I like working with animals.
4 I've got a swimming qualification.
5 Last year I did a computer course.
6 I passed a few exams at school.

4 Read the covering letter again. Then match headings 1–5 to parts of the letter A–E.

1 Achievements
2 Why you are writing
3 Experience

4 Signing off formally
5 What you are doing now

Dear Ms Frank,

Re: Library Assistant position

A   I am writing to apply for the above post, which was advertised in yesterday's *Daily Review*. Please find my CV enclosed.

B   I am currently studying English and Drama at Walworth Sixth Form and feel that my love of books and literature would make me a very good candidate for this job.

C   As you will see from my CV, I achieved excellent grades in my GCSE exams, and also received the ECDL computer certificate in May 2013. Furthermore, for the last two years, I have held the role of library assistant at my school and have gained some useful experience in sorting books. In this role, I have also developed an online catalogue and coordinated training for the students.

D   Last year, as part of my work experience at the local sports centre, I advised customers about the services there and assisted with filing and scanning documents. I also designed a new leaflet for the centre advertising its tennis coaching scheme, and arranged an Open Day for new customers. This experience has given me a good understanding of dealing with customers and helping to promote services.

E   I am available for interview immediately and look forward to hearing from you.

Yours sincerely,

Jonathan Bartholomew

V **Action verbs**

5 **Study the highlighted verbs in the covering letter. Match them to meanings 1–3.**

1   helped: .... , ...
2   created: .... , ...
3   organized: .... , ...

6 **Choose the correct answers.**

1   During the holidays, I **organized / developed** several activities for children in the local park.
2   Last summer, I **helped / coordinated** the manager with handing out leaflets around town.
3   We **created / assisted** customers with enquiries about the course.
4   As part of my coursework, I **designed / advised** a new scheme for attracting tourists to the shop.
5   While I was at school, I **assisted / developed** an international exchange programme between our school and a school in Spain.
6   In the past, I **advised / arranged** several training sessions for students at my school.

WRITING GUIDE

■ **Task** Write a covering letter in response to the advert for a Summer Camp Counsellor.

■ **Ideas** Make notes about:
- the qualifications you have.
- the experience you can offer.
- why you want this job.

■ **Plan** Follow the plan:

Paragraph 1: Explain where you saw the job advertisement and mention that you are attaching your CV.

Paragraph 2: Give reasons for your interest in this job / company.

Paragraph 3: Refer the employer to specific information in your CV and show how this relates to the job.

Paragraph 4: Mention any other experience from school, part-time work or voluntary work which might be relevant to the job.

Paragraph 5: Request an interview and say when you are available.

■ **Write** Write your covering letter. Use the paragraph plan to help you.

■ **Check** Check the following points:
- Have you used a clear paragraph structure and register?
- Have you used a variety of action verbs and avoided general statements?
- Have you checked grammar, vocabulary, spelling and punctuation?

Vocabulary insight 8   Using a dictionary: idioms

1 Work in pairs. Study the highlighted idioms in the extract from the text on page 95. Are they the same in your own language?

> Luckily for Sean, an instructor took time out to show him the ropes. That and his positive attitude helped him to rise to the challenge and by Friday, he was ready to teach the class.

STRATEGY

Finding idioms in a dictionary

An idiom is a phrase with an overall meaning that is different from the meanings of the individual words in it.

Dictionaries do not always put idioms in the same place, so you need to read the introduction to your dictionary to find out where they are. In the *Oxford Wordpower Dictionary*, idioms are explained after the symbol **IDM**.

When you want to find an idiom in a dictionary, search for it under the first <u>meaningful</u> word in the idiom (verb, noun, adjective, etc.). If there is a very common verb in the idiom (*be*, *have*, *go*, *start*, etc.), you might have to search for it under the second meaningful word.

2 Read the strategy above. Which word in each idiom in exercise 1 would you look up in a dictionary to find the meaning of the idiom? Use a dictionary to check your answers.

3 Read the idioms below. Underline the word that you would look up in a dictionary to find the meaning of each idiom.

1 be rushed off your feet
2 fall / land on your feet
3 get off on the wrong foot (with somebody)
4 put your feet up
5 put your foot down
6 stand on your own two feet
7 under your feet

4 Study the dictionary entries for idioms with *foot*. Are the sentences true (T) or false (F)? Correct the false ones.

> **foot**[1] /fʊt/ *noun* (*pl* feet /fiːt/)
>
> **IDM** **be rushed/run off your feet** to be extremely busy; to have too many things to do: *Over Christmas we were rushed off our feet at work.*
> **fall/land on your feet** to be lucky in finding yourself in a good situation, or in getting out of a difficult situation: *I really landed on my feet getting such a good job with so little experience.*
>
> **get/start off on the right/wrong foot (with sb)** (*informal*) to start a relationship well/badly: *I seem to have got off on the wrong foot with the new boss.*
>
> **put your feet up** to sit down and relax, especially with your feet off the floor and supported: *I'm so tired that I just want to go home and put my feet up.*
> **put your foot down** (*informal*) to say firmly that sth must (not) happen: *I put my foot down and told Andy he couldn't use our car any more.*

> **stand on your own (two) feet** to take care of yourself without help; to be independent
> **under your feet** in the way; stopping you from working, etc: *Would somebody get these children out from under my feet and take them to the park?*

1 If you have something **under your feet**, there's something in your way.
2 When you **put your foot down**, you relax.
3 If you **get off on the right foot** with somebody, you start your relationship in a good way.
4 When you **stand on your own two feet**, you're healthy.
5 When you're **rushed off your feet**, you're very busy.
6 If you **land on your feet**, you get yourself out of a difficult situation.
7 When you **put your feet up**, you say that something shouldn't happen.

5 Complete the sentences with the correct forms of the idioms in exercise 3.

1 I was so tired when I got home, I just wanted to
....
2 After looking for a job for so long, I finally
.... when I got this one.
3 I don't think my boss likes me – we didn't
.... when I first joined the company.
4 I'm really .... these days. There's so much to do – I have no time to sit down and relax.
5 It's time you moved out of your parents' house and
.... You need to be more independent.
6 Our boss has .... and says we can't make personal phone calls at work.

6 Find the idioms below in a dictionary. Then use the idioms to rewrite the underlined parts of the sentences. Make any other changes if necessary.

▪ on end ▪ at a loose end ▪ make ends meet
▪ come to an end ▪ in the end ▪ at the end of your tether

1 I've been waiting so long to hear if I got the scholarship – <u>I can't deal with it any more</u>.
....
2 She keeps talking about her new job <u>all the time</u>.
....
3 When my grandparents were young, they didn't have much money and found it difficult to <u>buy the things they needed</u>.
....
4 I regret not going to university after school. I now <u>have nothing to do</u>.
....
5 After applying to many colleges, she <u>finally</u> got a place in the one she wanted to attend the most.
....
6 Her career as a singer is <u>about to finish</u>.
....

Dictionary entries from *Oxford Wordpower Dictionary*, 4th edition

Vocabulary

1 Complete the text with the correct adjective form of the words below.

▨ fly ▨ glamour ▨ challenge ▨ stress ▨ repetition ▨ vary

In my dream future, I'd love to be either a
¹............... Hollywood actress, or a wealthy, high-
²............... businesswoman. I want to do ³...............
work, trying different things every week. A job
that's quite ⁴............... is OK, but not so difficult
that it becomes ⁵............... But on the other hand,
I also don't want to do anything that's so
⁶............... it's boring. Sounds easy, doesn't it?

Marks .... / 6

2 Complete the idioms with one word in each gap.

1 'Is it your first day in the office? Wow, you've been thrown in at the .... end, haven't you?'
2 'Don't worry, I'll .... you the ropes and explain what to do.'
3 'Let's start the .... rolling. You organize these files, while I make coffee.'
4 'More work. I know it's hard, but I'm sure you'll .... to the challenge.'
5 'I've got a .... on my plate at the moment. Could you do my paperwork, too?'
6 'I'm going to .... my feet up for a break. Training you has tired me out!'

Marks .... / 6

3 Complete the text with one word in each gap.

My mid-morning coffee can be very inspiring! At 11
a.m. today I ¹............... up with a brilliant scheme to
raise more money for the charity, but then I had second
²............... and changed my ³............... I then dreamed
⁴............... several more great ideas, but it was so hard to
choose. I couldn't ⁵............... up my mind! My boss liked
my original plan best, so now we're going ⁶............... with
that. And now I need another coffee ...

Marks .... / 6

4 Complete the sentences with the words below.

▨ boycott ▨ demonstration ▨ discrimination ▨ march
▨ struggle ▨ threat

1 We must end prejudice and racial ....
2 Protesters held a noisy .... inside the town hall.
3 'You'll be arrested!' 'Is that a ....?'
4 We took part in a .... of the unethical supermarket.
5 The animal rights .... was four kilometres long.
6 We're fighting for equal rights, but it's a ....

Marks .... / 6

Grammar

5 Rewrite the sentences using the third conditional.

1 Mark Zuckerberg did well at school, so he went to university.
If ...., he .... to university.
2 The university didn't have a social networking site, so Mark invented one.
Mark .... a social networking site
if .... one.
3 Facemash wasn't a success because the university didn't approve of it.
If .... of it, Facemash .... a success.
4 Mark invented Thefacebook because he wasn't happy with the university's decision.
Mark .... Thefacebook if .... the university's decision.
5 Thefacebook became so popular that thousands of Harvard students joined it.
If ...., thousands of Harvard students .... it.
6 Facebook opened to the public in 2006, becoming the biggest social networking site in the world.
If .... in 2006, it .... the biggest social networking site in the world

Marks .... / 6

6 Imagine you are Mark Zuckerberg's former college friend. Express the ideas in brackets as wishes or regrets using *I wish* or *If only*.

1 (I didn't invent Facebook.) I ....
2 (I don't have as much money as Mark.) If ....
3 (I work in a boring office job.) If ....
4 (I didn't work hard at university.) I ....
5 (I spent most of my time socializing.) If ....
6 (I'm not a computer genius.) I ....
7 (I thought programming was boring.) If ....
8 (I laughed at Mark.) If ....
9 (Mark and I aren't friends today.) I ....
10 (I'm addicted to Facebook now!) If ....

Marks .... / 10

7 Complete the sentences with one of the modal verbs in brackets and the correct form of the verbs below.

▨ feel ▨ have ▨ know ▨ miss ▨ see

1 She .... terrible when she failed her exam, that's for sure. (must / may)
2 'Why is she late?' 'She .... the bus.' (can't / might)
3 'I saw him yesterday.' 'You .... him. He's still in Tokyo!' (must / can't)
4 You .... the time of your life in Africa. I'm jealous! (might / must)
5 'Why didn't he come to my party?' 'He .... about it. He never misses a party!' (can't / must)

Marks .... / 10

Total .... / 50

Listening

1 ○ **2.18** **Read the advertisement. Then listen to four extracts from job interviews. Make short notes of all the key words and ideas you hear.**

> **Scope**, the biggest disability charity in the UK, is looking for volunteers to raise funds, help to organize campaigns and deal with enquiries. Could this be you?

2 ○ **2.18** **Listen again. Match speakers 1–4 to options A–E. There is one option that you do not need.**

Which speaker:

A has a disability? ....

B enjoys telephone work? ....

C had second thoughts about applying? ....

D has had previous experience of volunteering? ....

E hopes that the work won't be repetitive? ....

Speaking

3 **Work in pairs. Tell each other what your dream job is and why.**

4 **In pairs, take it in turns to interview each other for your dream job. The interviewer should ask at least three questions. Use the ideas below or your own ideas.**

Student A: interviewer
- Let's begin by …
- I'd like to ask you about …
- Would you mind telling me … ?

Student B: job applicant
- I would describe myself as …
- A good example of this is …
- As far as I'm concerned, I'd be the ideal candidate for this job because …

Reading

5 **Read the blog and choose the correct answers.**

1 What does Mellie tell us about disabled museum visitors in the first paragraph?
- **a** Many people find the appearance of disabled visitors in museums shocking.
- **b** Access to museums is still very poor for people with all kinds of disabilities.
- **c** Access is generally excellent for people with hearing problems.
- **d** People who can't see well are now visiting museums more frequently.

2 What happened when Mellie went into a museum in Los Angeles?
- **a** The employees were alarmed.
- **b** She got lost.
- **c** Assistants refused to help her.
- **d** She was asked to leave.

3 Why was Mellie a concern for museum staff?
- **a** She tried to touch the exhibits.
- **b** Staff didn't trust her to obey the rules.
- **c** Other visitors tried to copy her behaviour.
- **d** She took part in an organized protest.

4 What does Mellie tell us about the New York museum?
- **a** It has copied ideas from other museums.
- **b** It doesn't offer any printed literature for the blind.
- **c** There's a special exhibition featuring touch and sound.
- **d** Visitors may touch any object in the museum.

5 What do we learn about Art Education for the Blind?
- **a** Its main focus is to organize protests.
- **b** It teaches blind people how to paint.
- **c** Volunteers cooperate with museum staff.
- **d** It doesn't give any money to others.

www.blindsight.co.uk/mellie

About Me: Mellie Vickers is a history-lover, artist and blogger. She also happens to be partially-sighted.

Monday 11 April

Museums for the blind

🔊 listen now

The greater part of the population may view, enjoy, or even be shocked by museum exhibits whenever they choose. For disabled visitors, it can be more difficult. Nevertheless, facilities for wheelchair users have greatly improved in recent years, and tours for the deaf are now more widely available (although we still have some way to go). However, the treatment of blind and partially-sighted people lags far behind, despite growing admission figures from this minority group.

Last Saturday I visited a museum in Los Angeles. I sensed an air of panic among the staff as soon as they noticed my white stick. One even asked me if I was lost! Don't get me wrong, the curators couldn't have been more courteous in assisting me with directions, but I got the impression that I shouldn't really have been there. I wasn't so much a valued guest as a potential problem.

I'm not unsympathetic to their concerns. After all, the first law of most museums is 'Don't Touch'! I can barely see more than a few centimetres in front of me, so I have to peer closely at displays. But each time I did so, an assistant waited anxiously behind me, terrified that I might commit an act of disobedience, or perhaps set some sort of bad example to other museum-goers (neither happened!). I soon felt so uncomfortable that I left – boycotting the gift shop in an ineffectual protest!

It doesn't have to be this way. I wish more museums could be like the Metropolitan Museum of Art in New York. Not only is there a choice of Braille guides to read, but there's an utterly unmissable 'Touch Collection'. This allows you to explore objects using your fingers, while simultaneously listening to detailed descriptions. Of course, more fragile items have to be excluded from the programme, but even so, the range is astonishing.

I'd like to visit *more* museums like this! Do any of my blog visitors have any recommendations?

Comments

Thanks for an interesting post, Mellie. I'm sorry to hear about your experience in Los Angeles You might be interested in a charity I volunteer for: Art Education for the Blind. Rather than protesting against discrimination, we usually try to work with museums to develop educational programmes for people with sight disabilities. We also support visually-impaired artists who want to exhibit, although we're unable to offer as much financial aid as we'd like. If you're interested, I'll send details!

Bruno Daviz, 12 April

6 Complete the second sentence so that it has a similar meaning to the first sentence. Write between three and five words, including the given word. Do not change the given word.

1 Welcoming disabled visitors would be a good idea for all museums. (ought)
All museums .... disabled visitors.

2 'What skills can you offer us?' they asked me. (I)
They asked me what skills ....

3 I regret not volunteering last year. (wish)
I .... last year.

4 Giving up was an option I chose not to take. (could)
I .... , but I chose not to.

5 Thousands of people visit the museum every year. (visited)
.... thousands of people every year.

6 I started volunteering in 2011. (volunteer)
I've .... 2011.

7 I leave college at the end of July. (will)
By August, ... college.

8 'You've shown lots of commitment,' my employer said to me. (I)
My employer told .... lots of commitment.

9 I'm passionate about transforming people's lives. (difference)
I really want .... to people's lives.

10 I hope to hear from you soon. (look)
I .... from you soon.

7 Read the job advertisement. Then write a covering letter in response to the advertisement.

The British Museum, London

We are looking for summer volunteers to welcome and assist international visitors. We will provide free accommodation. Please apply to the manager, Mr Bolton, including the following information:

- Why are you interested in applying?
- Do you have any useful experience?
- What languages have you studied? Do you have any other useful skills?
- When will you be available in the summer?

9 Digital humans

Reading and vocabulary   A day in the life

1 SPEAKING Imagine you are sitting next to a stranger on a train. Discuss the things you might show them or talk to them about.

- personal photos ▪ personal text messages
- your age ▪ where you live ▪ who your friends are
- what you are interested in ▪ what you were doing last weekend

2 SPEAKING Discuss the questions. Then read the article from a science magazine and compare your answers.

1 What are the advantages and disadvantages of sharing information on a social media website?

2 Is it easier to be mean to people in the digital world?

3 Complete the article with sentences A–G. There is one sentence that you do not need.

A I didn't know one of them, but that's why Facebook is so exciting.

B Issy enjoys being part of a community.

C I talked to my friend about the nasty comment and she apologized.

D However, friends can compromise this image by tagging you in photos, saying where you've been or what you've said.

E He left his mobile in class today and I found it.

F Issy did the right thing when she deleted the comment.

G I looked absolutely awful so I clicked 'untag'.

V insight Phrasal verbs: relationships

4 Study the highlighted phrasal verbs in the text. Then replace the phrases in italics with the correct form of the phrasal verbs.

1 John hasn't *returned to his usual self after* our argument. He refuses to *be friends with* me.

2 Whenever Peter was bullied at school, he usually *lost control of his feelings* and cried.

3 I called an old friend today and we *brought each other up-to-date on* our news. We hadn't spoken to each other for a while.

4 We *unexpectedly met* our teacher while we were walking around the museum.

5 Isabel is very shy. She doesn't usually *talk freely* about her feelings.

6 You should always *support and defend* your friends when someone is mean to them.

7 When Ciaran met my sister, they *liked each other* immediately. They were both obsessed with World of Warcraft.

8 People who *are horrible or nasty to* other people are called bullies.

A DAY IN THE LIFE OF A DIGITAL HUMAN

As part of our week on digital humans, we asked teenager Issy Tyler to keep a 'digital' diary. Psychologist Mia Graham analysed the results.

7.30 a.m.
I'm usually on Facebook first thing and today was no different. I actually logged in while I was still in bed, just to see what my friends had posted the night before and to catch up with the gossip. Over breakfast, I did a status update and within thirty minutes, I had five likes and two comments. Nothing special about that – it was just another ordinary day.

Mia: It's natural and human to share experiences and open up to people. ¹............. . She likes it when people from this community comment on her status.

8.45 a.m.
On the school bus, I noticed that I'd been tagged in a picture. ²............. . It's stressed me out, so I'm currently checking the latest updates again. Hopefully, no one realized it was me!

Mia: On Facebook, Issy is always on display and she feels the pressure to consistently 'look good'. In a recent survey, 41% of teens said their online image was extremely important, consequently, they made an effort to look 'cooler than they really are'. ³............. . You might not like it, but you can't stop friends sharing information about you.

Vocabulary: phrasal verbs: relationships; words often confused; describing gadgets; words with more than one meaning
Grammar: defining and non-defining relative clauses; introductory *It*

Speaking: discussing social media; analyzing real life and online life; asking for instructions, explanations and clarification
Writing: a for and against essay

9A

12.30 p.m.

At lunchtime, a friend posted quite a nasty comment about another friend on my profile. The two girls recently had a row, but they need to get over it and make up with each other. I deleted the comment because I don't want to get involved.

Mia: It's easy to pick on people in the digital world. Cyberbullies can post an unflattering picture or a nasty comment and reach a wide audience. And in an online world, you can't see people break down in tears. As a result, you're less sympathetic and less likely to stick up for them. ⁴.................

5.30 p.m.

At home, I wrote a post about a boy I quite like. ⁵................. It was nice to talk to him, he was friendly and we had a lot in common – we really hit it off!

Mia: Like so many of us, Issy shares intimate details of her life online. The problem is, these details stay on the web forever and are easy to dig up again. In a recent survey, 40% of teens said they were concerned about who was viewing their online activities. They also worried about how these activities might eventually be perceived by parents, teachers, future employers or their peers. They are right to be concerned about who is watching. The internet never forgets, so Issy needs to think before she posts.

11.00 p.m.

My last status update before I go to bed and I had two friend requests, which I accepted. ⁶................. You can chat with people who you possibly wouldn't run into in your everyday life and you can contact people who you haven't seen for years ...

Mia: Issy's right – it's good to talk, but she needs to be extremely careful about who she talks to. The average teen has 237 'friends', however, they have talked to only a fraction of these people in real life. Essentially, it's a question of trust, so before you accept a friend request, consider this: who is this person and do I really want them to read my posts? Don't forget, there are people behind the machines.

30
35
40
45
50
55
60
65

V insight Words often confused

5 Study the underlined words in the text. Then match each word in 1–5 to definitions a–b.

1 actually / currently
  a really, in fact
  b at the present time, at the moment
2 latest / last
  a final, coming after all others
  b the most recent
3 consequently / consistently
  a as a result, because of this
  b regularly, constantly
4 sympathetic / friendly
  a happily communicating with someone
  b showing that you understand people's feelings and feeling sorry for them
5 eventually / possibly
  a perhaps, maybe
  b in the end, finally

6 Choose the correct answers.

1 It took a long time, but I **eventually / possibly** uploaded a video on my Facebook page.
2 Issy had a new friend request today. She didn't **actually / currently** know who the person was.
3 I know how the victims of cyberbullies feel. I was bullied myself at school, so I am totally **sympathetic / friendly**.
4 We waited a long time for Max. He was the **last / latest** person to arrive.
5 Beth did **consequently / consistently** well in class, so everyone was surprised when she failed her exam.
6 Last week, we learned about computer programming and we are **actually / currently** studying the problems of privacy on Facebook.
7 I get the **last / latest** stories in my newsfeed on Facebook.
8 My sister forgot to post the party invitation on Facebook. **Consequently / Consistently**, no one turned up.
9 Troy was **sympathetic / friendly** and pleasant, but he wasn't a good friend when it really mattered.
10 Are you playing football this weekend? **Eventually / Possibly**, unless it rains.

7 SPEAKING Discuss the questions.

1 Have you got a social media account? How often do you use it? What do you actually use it for?
2 Do you think everyone will eventually have a social media account? Why / why not?
3 In the future, will we possibly be interacting more with machines than with people? What effect might this have?

Vocabulary bank Technology page 142

1 **SPEAKING** **Look at the photo of two friends, Maggie and Tessa. Answer the questions. Then read the text and check your answers.**

1 Where are the women from?
2 How did they meet?
3 How long have they known each other?
4 How do they usually communicate?

Maggie and Tessa: a lasting friendship

We live in a world where instant communication is possible. With access to the internet, we can make friendships with people thousands of miles away. But Maggie and Tessa, now both in their seventies, formed their long-distance friendship nearly sixty years ago, using only pen and paper.

[1]Maggie was an English girl who lived in a small house in east London. [2]Tessa was an American girl who lived on a ranch in Colorado. They first started writing to each other when they were twelve years old. 'It was in 1955 when I got my first letter from Tessa,' explains Maggie. 'I joined a pen pal club which was set up to encourage friendships between children from different countries.' [3]Maggie has still got the first letter which Tessa sent her. 'It was so exciting,' says Maggie. 'I had never travelled abroad, and now I was writing to a girl whose family lived nearly five thousand miles away!'

Maggie and Tessa wrote to each other for twenty-five years before they met. Then, in 1980, Tessa came to England on a family holiday and met up with Maggie at Paddington Station in London. 'I recognized Maggie from her photograph,' says Tessa. 'I saw this tall, blonde woman whose eyes were bright blue and I knew immediately that I was looking at the girl that I'd been writing to for twenty-five years.' Maggie and Tessa hit it off in person, just as they had on paper; now their grandchildren have also become friends. 'They all get on very well with each other, but of course, they don't write proper letters!' laughs Tessa. 'They keep in touch on Facebook.'

Defining relative clauses

2 **Study sentences 1–3 and the highlighted relative pronouns in the text. Complete rules a–e.**

The underlined clauses are defining relative clauses. They come immediately after a noun and they give essential information about the noun. Relative pronouns introduce the clause.
We use:

a .... or *that* for people.
b .... or .... for things.
c .... for possessions.
d .... for places.
e .... for time.

3 **Study sentences 1 and 3 in the text again and answer the questions.**

1 In which sentence is the relative pronoun the subject of the verb in the relative clause and in which is it the object of the verb?
2 In which sentence can we leave out the relative pronoun? Why?

Reference and practice 9.1 Workbook page 120

4 **Read the text again and find more examples of defining relative clauses.**

5 **Complete the text with relative pronouns.**

Although many people use email to communicate long distance, there are still some traditional penfriend organizations **1**............. are popular around the world. One of the biggest and best known is the Student Letter Exchange, which was started in 1936. The Exchange is a programme **2**............. links 500,000 students in over 100 countries. It was first started **3**............. a teacher wanted to encourage his students to learn more about other countries and cultures. It has a database of students **4**............. have registered with the organization because they want to find penfriends. Any English-speaking student **5**............. is aged between eight and twenty-three years old can join. Teachers **6**............. students are interested in the programme can register their class on the database. Students **7**............. apply for details of possible penfriends also receive a guide **8**............. shows them how to write letters and also gives advice and ideas, penfriend projects and postage rates.

6 **Combine the sentences to make one sentence. Use a defining relative clause. Use a pronoun only where necessary.**

1 Steph is my friend. Her family moved to another country.
Steph is my friend ....
2 It was last year. Her dad got a new job and they all left.
It was last year ....
3 In primary school in London. We met there ten years ago.
It was in primary school ....
4 We were both six years old. Our teacher introduced us.
They were both six years old ....
5 These are the emails. We write them to each other.
These are the emails ....
6 Email is the main form of communication. It helps us to stay in touch.
Email is the main form of communication ....

7 🔊 **2.19** **Listen to a radio programme and match 1–8 to a–h. Then make full sentences with *who, whose, which, that* or *where.***

1 Can we trust the people
2 Julia Price is a psychologist
3 *Screen Friends* is a novel
4 Are we losing the friends
5 We have another place
6 I can find three or four websites
7 Now I'm talking to people
8 That's something

a are specifically about corn snakes.
b interests are the same as mine.
c we can meet new people.
d would be very difficult to do in real life.
e has just written *Screen Friends*.
f we know in real life?
g is about an online friendship.
h we meet online?

8 **SPEAKING** **Work in groups. Discuss the questions.**

1 How many online friends have you got? How did you meet them?
2 How many real friends have you got? How did you meet them?
3 Do your online friends know you as well as your real friends?
4 Is your personality the same when you are online and when you talk to friends face-to-face? Why / why not?

1 SPEAKING Look at the photos and put them in order from 1–5 (1 = most important in your life, 5 = least important). Then work in small groups and compare your ideas.

2 🔊 **2.20** Listen to four people talking about their favourite gadgets. Match the speakers to the gadgets A–E in exercise 1. Which gadget is not mentioned?

3 🔊 **2.20** Listen again and answer the questions.

1 Who uses a gadget when driving?	Speaker	....
2 Who talks about a friend who broke his gadget?	Speaker	....
3 Who talks about the size of a gadget?	Speakers	..........., ...
4 Who says that a gadget is not very new?	Speaker	....
5 Who uses a gadget to help with their coursework?	Speaker	....
6 Who makes calls with a gadget?	Speakers	..........., ...
7 Who talks about accessories for a gadget?	Speakers	..........., ..., ...
8 Who talks about the cost of a gadget?	Speaker	....

V Describing gadgets

4 Which gadgets in exercise 1 are sentences 1–7 about? What other gadgets could they describe?

1 It's extremely convenient and easy to use.
2 It was very expensive, actually, so I'm careful with it.
3 I used to have a walkman, but that's so out-of-date now.
4 It's a really old car, with just an inexpensive radio.
5 My favourite gadget is so efficient – it does everything and it's really fast.
6 It's a bit fragile, but I bought a durable cover, so I'm not worried that something will happen to it.
7 It's not very reliable now and there are all sorts of problems with it.

5 SPEAKING Work in pairs. Think of a gadget and describe it to your partner. Use the highlighted words in exercise 4. Your partner needs to guess the gadget that you are describing.

DVD extra | Inventors

Asking for instructions, explanations and clarification

6 SPEAKING Work in pairs. Do you always read the instructions for a new gadget before you use it? Read opinions 1–4. Which opinions do you agree / disagree with?

1 'I never read instructions! I prefer to experiment and try out lots of different things. If you're careful, you won't do any damage and you'll learn a lot about your new gadget.'

2 'I usually read the most basic instructions – the 'Quick Set-up' page that comes with most new gadgets. After that, I work stuff out for myself.'

3 'If I have a problem, I don't read the manual; I usually go online and do a search. It's quicker!'

4 'I always read all the instructions before I start to use something. It takes time, but afterwards I know exactly what I'm doing!'

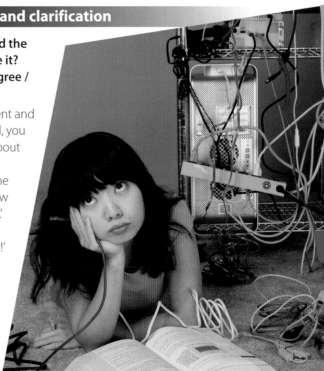

7 ⊙ 2.21   Listen to the dialogue and answer the questions.

1   Why is the woman phoning the helpline?
2   Which button does the woman press first?
3   What does the 'home' button look like?
4   What does the helpline advisor tell the woman to do with the icons on the screen?
5   Why is there nothing on the phone screen?

8 ⊙ 2.21   Complete the phrases from the dialogue. Then listen again and check.

Asking for instructions
How do I ¹.................................?
How does it work?
What do I do next?

Giving instructions
Could you ²................................., please?
Now ³................................. the 'settings' option.
First, switch it on.
Then, choose ... .

Asking for repetition or clarification
Sorry, ⁴................................. again, please?
I don't ⁵................................. you.
I'm not quite sure ... .
I'm sorry, I didn't quite catch that.

Giving clarification
Let me ⁶..................................
What I mean is ... .

Checking that the listener understands
Do you see ⁷.................................?
Is everything clear so far?

Confirming understanding
I ⁸................................. you, but ... .
Right, I've got that.

9 ⊙ 2.22   Complete the dialogue with phrases in exercise 8. Then listen and check.

Customer   I like this camera, but it does look quite complicated. ¹.................................?
Assistant   It's simple. ².................................. That's the 'on' button there. Then choose 'automatic' or 'manual'.
Customer   ³................................. how to do that.
Assistant   It's this button here. Just turn it to 'automatic' or to 'manual'.
Customer   ⁴.................................. I've selected 'manual'.
Assistant   Now press the 'AV' button for the picture exposure.
Customer   ⁵..................................
Assistant   You press the 'AV' button for the picture exposure.
Customer   Picture exposure?
Assistant   Yes. ⁶................................. you press the 'AV' button to make the picture lighter or darker. ⁷.................................?
Customer   Yes, that's quite clear, thanks. ⁸.................................?
Assistant   Point the camera and press the black button on the top.
Customer   Well, that's easy. Thank you.

10   Read the dialogue in exercise 9 again and find three more phrases to add to the table in exercise 8.

11   SPEAKING   Work in pairs. Choose one of the situations and prepare a dialogue.

Situation 1: Games console
Student A (customer)
You have bought a new games console, but
• you can't see a picture on the TV screen.
• the controller doesn't work.
Student B (helpline advisor)
Check that the customer
• has connected the games console to the TV.
• has put batteries in the controller.

Situation 2: MP3 player
Student A (customer)
You are trying to use your MP3 player, but
• the screen won't come on.
• there's no sound.
Student B (helpline advisor)
Check that the customer
• has switched the machine on.
• has connected the player to the speakers.

1 ◎ **2.23** **SPEAKING** Use the ideas below to discusss the ways you communicate with friends. Then read and listen to a 'slam' poem. Which ideas does the author mention?

- ■ text message ■ posting on Facebook ■ Twitter
- ■ face-to-face talking ■ instant messaging
- ■ talking on the phone ■ sending an email

2 ◎ **2.23** **SPEAKING** Read and listen to the poem again. Then discuss the questions.

1 Who is the Apple iPerson? What does the poet think has happened to people?

2 Why does he spend time on Facebook rather than reading or meeting friends?

3 How many friends has he got in the digital world and in the real world?

4 Does the poet think we have evolved? Why / why not?

5 In line 42, the poet says 'it's scary'. What is he referring to?

6 What is the poet's hope for the future?

Touchscreen
by Marshall Soulful Jones

STRATEGY

Understanding poetry

When you read a poem, notice the techniques the poet uses.

1 Repeating a key word or a phrase.
2 Rhyming words.
3 Using words with more than one meaning.

3 Read the strategy. Then find examples of 1–3 in the poem. Some words and phrases may be used more than once.

V **insight** Words with more than one meaning

4 Study the highlighted words in the poem. Complete the gaps in 1–3 with the meanings below. Then think of two meanings for the other highlighted words. What effect does this word play have?

- ■ a round, flat object you put into a computer
- ■ to make an arrangement ■ the front part of your head

1 face
  a ....
  b to be opposite something, looking at it
2 book
  a a written work on printed pages
  b ....
3 disc
  a ....
  b a thing between the bones in your back

5 **SPEAKING** What type of poetry is popular with young people in your country?

Introducing the new Apple iPerson complete with multitouch
doesn't it feel good to touch?
doesn't it feel good to touch?

compatible with your iPod and your iPad
doesn't it feel good to touch?   5
doesn't it feel good to touch?
no friends, there's an app for that
no life, there's an app for that
you're a complete loser, there's an app for that
doesn't it feel good to touch?   10
doesn't it feel good to touch?
doesn't it feel good to touch?

my world, my world has become so digital
I have forgotten what that feels like

It was difficult to connect when friends formed cliques*   15
now it's even more difficult to connect
now that clicks form friends

But who am I to judge
I face Facebook more than books face me
hoping to book face-to-faces   20
I update my status 420 spaces
to prove I'm still breathing
failure to do this daily
means my whole web wide world will forget that I exist
but with 3,000 friends online   25
and only five I can count in real life
why wouldn't I spend more time in a world where there are
more people that 'like' me
Wouldn't you?

You would need Blueray to read what is really me   30
but I'm not that focused ten tabs open hoping

my problems are resolved with a 1500 by 1600 resolution
provin' we might have missed a step in this evolution
doubled over we used to sit in treetops
till we swung down to stand upright   35
then someone slipped a disc
now we're doubled over at desktops from the garden of Eden
to the branches of Macintosh
apple picking has always come at a great cost
iPod iMac iPhone iChat   40
I can do all of these things without making eye contact
We used to sprint* to pick and store blackberries
now we run to the Sprint store* and pick Blackberries
it's scary
can't hear the sound of mother nature speaking over all this   45
tweeting
and our ability to feel along with it is fleeting

so when my phone goes off in my hip iTouch and iTouch
and iTouch and iTouch and iTouch because in a world
Where laughter is never heard   50
And voices are only read
we are so desperate to feel
that we hope our Technologic can reverse* the universe
until the screen touches us back
and maybe one day it will   55
when our technology is advanced enough …
to make us human again.

*cliques = small groups of people with the same interests
*sprint = to run a short distance very quickly
*Sprint store = a mobile phone shop
*reverse = to return to what existed before

Non-defining relative clauses

6 Read the text. What is the difference between slam poetry and rap music?

Slam poetry became popular in Chicago in 1986. The first slam poems were performed in a club called the Greenmill Lounge, [1]where jazz musicians usually played. This poetry, [2]which can be performed by anyone, provided a new way for people to get their message across. It encouraged ordinary people, [3]who weren't used to expressing themselves publicly, to tell their stories or talk about social issues. In fact, slam poetry is very similar to rap. Both are examples of performance poetry, [4]whose aim is to tell a story. The difference is that rap uses music, whereas slam poetry relies on the power of the spoken word.

7 Study non-defining relative clauses 1–4 in the text in exercise 6. Then answer the questions.

1 Does the text make sense without the clauses?
2 Do the clauses add essential or extra information?
3 Where can the clauses go in a sentence?
4 Which words are used at the beginning of the clauses?
5 Can the clauses begin with *that* instead of *which*?

Non-defining relative clauses always start with a comma.

Reference and practice 9.2 | Workbook page 121

8 Combine the sentences to make one sentence. Use a non-defining relative clause.

1 Marshall Soulful Jones came second in the National Poetry Slam in Boston. His poem was about technology.
2 I posted a photo of my dog on Facebook. It was very funny.
3 My computer broke down. It had all my friends' contact details in it.
4 My brother Seth wants to be a famous jazz musician. He plays the saxophone.
5 We sometimes go to Jamaica. My grandparents live there.
6 That's Café Europa. I often meet my friends there.
7 My friend Jade writes rap songs. Her sister is in my class.

Vocabulary bank | Poetry page 142

1 SPEAKING Work in pairs. Answer the questions.

1 When was the last time that you did the things below?
   ▨ checked your emails ▨ wrote a letter ▨ bought something online ▨ bought something at a shop
   ▨ looked for information online ▨ looked for information in a book ▨ read the news online
   ▨ read a newspaper

2 Do you switch your phone off when you go to bed?

3 How soon after you wake up in the morning do you go online or check your text messages?

2 Read the statement. Think of two advantages and two disadvantages of constant connection. Then read the model essay and see if any of your ideas are mentioned.

> With modern technology, we can be connected to the web 24 hours a day. The advantages of constant connection are greater than the disadvantages. Discuss.

The advantages and disadvantages of constant connection

A With smartphones and computers, [1]it is often said that we are rarely more than a few minutes away from our emails, updates from friends or global and local news. However, [2]it could be claimed that we have become too reliant on technology. Does this make our lives better or more stressful? In this essay, I will discuss the advantages and disadvantages of being constantly connected.

B One advantage is that people can find important information very quickly and they don't have to go to the library or read books for research. Another point is that people can buy many things online. This is useful for people who have mobility problems. [3]It may also be argued that people are safer because they know that they can instantly get help if there is an emergency. Furthermore, photographs, videos and news can be shared online, so people can always catch up with friends who live on the other side of the world.

C However, there are also some disadvantages to constant connection. Firstly, although people can access a lot of information online, some claim that the information is often misleading or inaccurate. Anyone can put information onto a webpage and, as a result, it can be difficult to check the source. Secondly, [4]it seems evident that some shops on the high street are now struggling due to the rise in online shopping. Many shops are being closed down. Thirdly, although there are people who feel safer because of mobile phones, others would argue that there are new dangers like cyberbullying. [5]It is true that constant connection helps us to keep in touch with friends, but it can be very stressful when people expect instant responses.

D In conclusion, I believe that although there are many advantages to constant connection, we should also switch off our phones sometimes, walk away from our computers and talk to some real people.

3 Match the descriptions to paragraphs A–D.

1 Conclusion and statement of writer's own opinion
2 Introduction of topic
3 Arguments against the statement
4 Arguments for the statement

4 Answer the questions.

1 According to the writer, who can benefit from shopping online?
2 How can we maintain contact with friends who live far away?
3 Why can there be problems with using online information?
4 What can make people feel stressed?
5 What advice does the author give at the end?

Introductory *It*

5 Study sentences 1–5 in the model essay. Then put them into the correct part of the table.

It + the passive	
It + the passive (with modal verbs)	
It + *is* / *seems* + adjective	

6 Rewrite the sentences using the introductory *It* and the words in brackets.

    1 There is no real privacy in today's world. (said)
    2 Computers are getting smaller, faster and cheaper. (could argue)
    3 People have forgotten how to think for themselves. (may claim)
    4 The internet has changed the way that we do our research. (obvious)
    5 Students are able to access more information about their subject. (clear)
    6 Constant connection is a normal part of our lives. (seems evident)

STRATEGY

Making your writing neutral

When you write a for and against essay, you should avoid using phrases, like *I believe* or *I think* until the conclusion. You should use impersonal language to express different opinions.

The most common impersonal structures are:

1 Introductory *It*
2 The passive
3 *Some / Other people*:
    Some people claim / believe / say … .
    There are those who say that … .
    Other people (would) argue that … .

7 Read the strategy. Underline examples of impersonal structures in the model essay.

8 Use the strategy to make the sentences more neutral. Use as many different structures as you can.

    1 I think that children should read books rather than play computer games.
    2 In my view children's attention spans are getting shorter.
    3 I think we need to change our teaching methods.
    4 In my opinion computer games develop important skills.
    5 I believe that young people's brains are developing differently.
    6 The internet is a very important tool in language development.

WRITING GUIDE

■ **Task** Choose one of the statements and write a for and against essay about it.

1 We are losing our social skills in real life due to the amount of time we spend online. Discuss.
2 Modern technology has made life much better for most people in the developed world. Discuss.

■ **Ideas** Make notes about:

Essay 1

■ the importance of body language and facial expressions.
■ telling the truth online.
■ ways of sharing our interests with people.
■ ways of finding out about different cultures and beliefs.

Essay 2

■ how modern technology can help people with poor mobility.
■ the amount of free time we have now.
■ the amount of stress in our lives.
■ how modern technology develops our skills.

■ **Plan** Follow the plan:

Paragraph 1: Write an introduction with a clear outline of the topic.
Paragraph 2: Present the arguments in favour of the statement.
Paragraph 3: Present the arguments against the statement.
Paragraph 4: Write a conclusion to the essay. Include your own opinion.

■ **Write** Write your essay. Use the paragraph plan to help you.

■ **Check** Check the following points:

■ Have you used a clear paragraph structure?
■ Have you included all your points for and against the statement?
■ Have you used neutral language?
■ Have you checked grammar, vocabulary, spelling and punctuation?

STRATEGY

Understanding new words

New words appear frequently in English, often to describe new technology. Recognizing how words are formed will help you to understand a new word. Ways of forming new words include:

1 Blending – putting two existing words (or parts of existing words) together to make a new word.
2 Loaning – borrowing a word from another language.
3 Conversion – forming a word from an existing identical word (for example, using a noun as a verb).

1 **Read the strategy above. Study the dictionary entries below and match them to ways of forming new words 1–3 in the strategy.**

> **text²** /tekst/ (also 'text-message) *verb* [T,I] to send sb a written message using a mobile phone: *I texted him to say we were home.* ➲ look at **SMS** ➲ note at **mobile phone**

> **'snail mail** *noun* [U] (*informal*) used by people who use email to describe the system of sending letters by ordinary post

> **karaoke** /ˌkæri'əʊki/ *noun* [U] a type of entertainment in which a machine plays only the music of popular songs so that people can sing the words themselves

2 **Match the underlined words in sentences 1–8 to definitions a–h.**

1 My mum hates walking around shops, so she buys most things from the <u>teleshopping</u> channel.
2 During my trip around Asia, I wrote a <u>travelogue</u>.
3 Many of my friends comment on posts on my <u>blog</u>.
4 When we go on holiday, we usually take our <u>camcorder</u> to film all the wonderful places we visit.
5 My dad is a huge <u>technophobe</u> – he hates everything digital.
6 We rarely talk to each other – all communication is done by <u>email</u>.
7 The program that I downloaded online came with a lot of <u>malware</u>.
8 Many people are rude on message boards – they don't know the <u>netiquette</u>.

a a book, film or lecture about places visited by a traveller
b buying products advertised on a television shopping channel
c an electronic device used for recording videos and audio
d messages sent electronically
e computer programs designed to damage a computer system
f the rules people should use when they are posting on forums or chatting on the internet
g a person who does not like or use technology
h an online personal journal

3 **Match the words in A to the words in B to make the underlined new words in exercise 2.**

A ▪ website ▪ electronic ▪ camera ▪ internet ▪ technology ▪ television ▪ travel ▪ malicious
B ▪ mail ▪ etiquette ▪ recorder ▪ software ▪ monologue ▪ shopping ▪ log ▪ phobia

1 ....
2 ....
3 ....
4 ....
5 ....
6 ....
7 ....
8 ....

4 **Match the words in A to the words in B to make new words for definitions 1–5. Use a dictionary to help you.**

A ▪ emote ▪ free ▪ wireless ▪ teen ▪ user
B ▪ ware ▪ friendly ▪ between ▪ icon ▪ fidelity

1 a machine that is easy to use ....
2 a person between 8–12 years old ....
3 a symbol of a facial expression ....
4 software that you do not have to pay for
....
5 technology that allows you to go online wirelessly
....

5 **Complete the sentences with words in exercises 3 and 4.**

1 I didn't have any problems with this machine – it's very ....
2 Many .... came to the Carly Rae Jepsen concert.
3 A big publisher wants to publish my .... about my experiences in South America.
4 I don't like .... channels, but I don't mind buying things online.
5 You need to protect your computer against .... as it can do a lot of damage.
6 You can get online anywhere in the city centre now because there is free .... everywhere.
7 I hate when people use lots of .... instead of words in their emails.
8 Many computer magazines add CDs with ....

6 **Work in pairs. Invent a new word using each of the ways below. Write a definition and an example sentence.**

▪ blending ▪ loaning ▪ conversion

1 ....
....
2 ....
....
3 ....
....

Dictionary entries from *Oxford Wordpower Dictionary*, 4th edition

Vocabulary

1 Complete the phrasal verbs with one word.

I met Tom at a party and we hit it ¹................................. immediately. I then ran ²................................. him in the park the next day! After that, we met often. He was the first person I ever really ³................................. up to – I used to tell him everything. When he moved to New York, I almost broke ⁴................................., I was so upset! I ⁵................................. over it, of course, and we're still friends. We ⁶................................. up with news over Skype now.

Marks .... / 6

2 Complete the sentences with the words below.

▪ actually ▪ currently ▪ friendly ▪ latest ▪ sympathetic ▪ last

1 I used to date Zoe, but I'm .... single.
2 He's a ...., sociable person, and talks a lot!
3 When I was ill, Fay was very .... and kind.
4 You're late! You're the .... person to arrive.
5 It looks warm outside, but it's .... cold.
6 He always buys the .... gadgets.

Marks .... / 6

3 Complete the sentences about six gadgets. There is one adjective that you do not need.

▪ durable ▪ efficient ▪ expensive ▪ fragile ▪ inexpensive ▪ out-of-date ▪ reliable

1 This radio is strong and ....
2 These batteries are good value. They're quite ....
3 Don't drop my camera. It's rather ....
4 This watch is always correct – it's ....
5 The camping stove cooks food quickly. It's ....
6 This satnav is .... The maps are old.

Marks .... / 6

4 Write one word that matches both definitions.

1 .... is a noise that birds make AND the activity of posting messages on Twitter.
2 .... is a computer brand AND a fruit.
3 .... means (*noun*) the front part of your head OR (*verb*) be in front of something or someone.
4 .... means (*verb*) make an arrangement OR (*noun*) pages of writing joined inside a cover.
5 A .... is something that you have between the bones in your back OR a round, flat object that you can use to record, read or play material in a computer.
6 A .... is a brand of mobile phone OR a small, soft black fruit.

Marks .... / 6

Grammar

5 Complete the sentences with *who, which, when, where* or *whose*.

1 Xing is a friend .... I met online.
2 We met .... we were playing *TERA*.
3 He's the only friend .... gaming skills are even better than mine!
4 Gamers .... play *TERA* live all over the world.
5 Xing's showed me photos of the town .... he lives in China.
6 It's a country .... I'd love to visit.

Marks .... / 6

6 Read the sentences in exercise 5 again. In which sentences could you:

1 replace the relative pronoun or adverb with *that*? ...., ... and ....
2 omit the relative pronoun or adverb? .... and ....

Marks .... / 5

7 Combine the key information in the sentences using a defining relative clause.

1 Galileo was the astronomer. He invented the word 'telescope' (but not the instrument!).

2 Alexander Graham Bell is the Scot. His invention connected the world.

3 The USA was the place. Credit cards were first used here.

4 Space Invaders was the computer game. It first made gaming really popular.

5 1978 was the year. GPS made navigation easier.

Marks .... / 5

8 Combine sentences 1–5 and the sentences below. Use a non-defining relative clause.

▪ Her dad is a games programmer. ▪ It's bright.
▪ She hasn't got a mobile. ▪ I bought it a few years ago.
▪ Many software millionaires live there.

1 My grandmother hates technology.

2 In summer I can't see my computer screen.

3 Life is expensive in 'Silicon Valley'.

4 My laptop is quite old now.

5 Isla's dad is famous.

Marks .... / 10

Total .... / 50

1 **SPEAKING Answer the questions.**

1 Which artists do the photos show? What were they famous for?

2 Which artist's work might appear
- on a T-shirt? ■ as a ringtone? ■ on a postcard?

STRATEGY

Summarizing what you read

When you summarize a text, it is important to focus on the main ideas and describe them in your own words.

To summarize a text:
- underline the main ideas or facts (dates, people, places, etc.) in the paragraph.
- paraphrase the information that you have chosen, using your own words. Try to use synonyms.
- use linking words to connect the information.

2 **Read the strategy. Work in pairs. Student A read about Picasso and student B read about Mozart. Underline the main ideas, then complete the chart. Tell your partner about the person you read about.**

When / Where born	
When first created art	
What created	
Childhood activities	
Greatest achievements	
Most surprising fact	

3 **Read about the other artist and answer the questions.**

According to the texts, which artist:
1 surprised people when he was born?
2 could create new work while he was doing something else?
3 didn't mind being punished at school?
4 travelled a lot when he was very young?
5 offended people with their work?
6 experienced financial problems?
7 was interrogated about a crime?
8 didn't complete his final work?

4 **SPEAKING Answer the questions.**

1 What are the similarities and differences between Mozart and Picasso?
2 How do you think their teachers and classmates felt about them?
3 What do you think are the advantages and disadvantages of being a child genius?

The stories behind

You might see a Picasso painting printed on a T-shirt or hear Mozart's *Piano Sonata* music played as a ringtone on a phone, but how much do you know about these artists? Picasso and Mozart were both
5 child geniuses, but with very different stories …

Pablo Picasso (1881–1973)

When Picasso was born in Malaga, Spain in 1881, the midwife thought he was
10 stillborn. Luckily the doctor, who was smoking a cigar, blew some smoke into the baby's face and Pablo started screaming. Picasso was alive
15 and well, to everyone's relief!

Pablo Picasso was a born artist and to prove it, his first word was *piz*, short for *lápiz* (*pencil* in Spanish). His father Ruiz, who was an art professor, recognized his son's talent and taught him from the age of seven.
20 Picasso completed his first painting when he was nine (*Le Picador*).

Between 1892 and 1897, Picasso studied art in Madrid and Barcelona. His work showed a brilliance and maturity that was years ahead of his classmates, but
25 Picasso was not a good student. He was sick and tired of school, so he didn't listen to his teachers. As punishment he was put in a room on his own. 'I took along a sketch pad and drew …,' said Picasso later. 'I could have stayed there forever, drawing without stopping.'
30 Eventually Picasso left art school and went to Paris, where he met a painter and sculptor called Georges Braque. Picasso began to experiment and through trial and error produced many different styles. One of these styles was *Cubism*, which grew into an art movement
35 founded by Picasso and Braque. Braque and Picasso used squares and triangles in their paintings and showed the front and side view of people at the same time. Picasso used this technique in his most famous works, such as *Les Demoiselles d'Avignon* (1907) and
40 *Guernica* (1937). Many people found the style shocking and controversial, but others recognized his genius.

While he was in Paris, Picasso also made friends with the poet Apollinaire, who sometimes bought stolen paintings. In 1911, when the *Mona Lisa* was stolen
45 from the Louvre, the police arrested Apollinaire and questioned Picasso. Fortunately, both were released, and the *Mona Lisa* turned up in Italy two years later.

Picasso enjoyed much success in his life and could pick and choose what he painted, but he never stopped
50 experimenting. That's why he is known as *El Maestro* (or the master) of Modern Art.

Vocabulary: abstract nouns: talent; phrases with *and*; describing art; compound adjectives: describing events; synonyms: evaluative adjectives

Grammar: participle clauses; determiners
Speaking: discussing art; summarizing the main points of a film; debating
Writing: a review of an event

10A

the names

Wolfgang Amadeus Mozart (1756–1791)

Like Picasso, Mozart was a child genius – he wrote musical notes before he could write words and began composing music when he was only four years old. One day, his father came home from church and found Wolfgang at his desk. There were bits and pieces of paper everywhere and at first his father was angry. Then he realized that the child had written a sonata for the piano. When he commented that it was difficult to play, little Wolfgang replied, 'not with some practice,' and began to play the piece himself. Mozart went on to write his first symphony at the age of nine.

The Mozart family were very talented and his sister, Maria Anna, was also a brilliant musician. The family lived in Austria, but the two children and their father toured Europe several times, travelling far and wide. Unfortunately, the children often fell ill. But thanks to his travels, Mozart learned fifteen different languages.

During Mozart's life, many people admired the beauty and originality of his music. Young Mozart could compose anything, anywhere – during meals, while talking to friends, or while travelling on a coach. He composed very quickly and wrote huge amounts of music – more than 600 pieces in all, including symphonies, piano concertos and *Eine Kleine Nachtmusik*. He also gave music lessons and played at concerts. But despite this hard work and dedication his life had many ups and downs. Mozart spent money faster than he made it. He loved the high life, including fancy clothes and servants and was often anxious about his finances.

In July 1791, a stranger wearing dark clothes and a hood came to Mozart's house, asking him to compose a Requiem or a Mass for the Dead. Mozart was ill, but needed the money, so he agreed to do the work. As Mozart composed the piece, he had a vision that he was writing music for his own funeral. In fact, he died before the Requiem was finished. Mozart was 35 years old and had so little money that he was buried in an unmarked grave.

DVD extra | Art is everywhere

V Abstract nouns: talent

5 Study the highlighted words in the text. Then match them to definitions 1–8.

1 the quality of being new and interesting
2 a picture in your imagination
3 doing well and becoming rich and famous
4 very great and unusual intelligence or ability
5 the way something is done or made
6 being fully developed
7 a quality that gives pleasure to the senses
8 giving all of your time and energy to something

6 Complete the sentences with the words in exercise 5.

1 Although Mozart was very young, he showed a lot of .... when he performed in front of princes and kings.
2 There is much .... in Picasso's paintings. His ideas were often exciting and new.
3 I was impressed by the .... and charm of Leonardo da Vinci's *Mona Lisa*. She was a very attractive lady.
4 Michelango showed a lot of .... when he painted the *Sistine Chapel*. He worked 16–18 hours a day for four years!
5 Michelangelo's *Last Judgement* shows the artist's .... of heaven and hell.
6 The artist Andy Warhol founded *Pop Art*, a .... of art popular in the 1960s.
7 Albert Einstein was a natural .... in mathematics. It helped him develop the *Theory of Relativity*.
8 The Harry Potter series has been a great .... More than 500,000 books have been sold.

V insight Phrases with *and*

7 Match the words in A to the words in B. Check your answers in the text.

A ▪ alive ▪ sick ▪ trial ▪ pick ▪ ups ▪ far
B ▪ downs ▪ well ▪ wide ▪ tired ▪ choose ▪ error

8 Replace the words in italics with phrases in exercise 7.

1 At university you can *freely select* which subjects you'd like to study.
2 My grandparents are both *still living and healthy*.
3 I'm *fed up with* the weather. It's always raining!
4 I managed to find the right key to the door through *trying repeatedly for success*.
5 Dave had his *good times and bad times*, but despite this he was happy with his life.
6 We looked *everywhere* for our lost cat, but we couldn't find it.

9 SPEAKING Work in small groups. Imagine you could choose to be the best in one skill or ability. Which one would you choose and why?

▪ singing ▪ acting ▪ painting ▪ composing
▪ playing an instrument ▪ solving mathematical problems
▪ playing chess ▪ playing a sport ▪ inventing

Vocabulary bank | The arts page 143

1 SPEAKING **Look at the photos and answer the questions. Then read the text and compare your answers to questions 1 and 2.**

1 What is happening in the photos?
2 Why are they doing this?
3 What are the most popular dances in your country?
4 Do you enjoy dancing? Are you good at it?

Dancing badly around the world

In 2003, Matt Harding, a video game designer working in Australia, decided to leave his job and travel around Southeast Asia with his friend Brad. Like most people travelling from place to place, they took photos and filmed short video clips of the places they visited. One day in Hanoi, Brad suggested that Matt did a silly dance in front of the camera. Matt, thinking the idea was great fun, agreed and from there, the idea grew. Matt made a video showing his silly dances all around the world and put it onto his blog. Gradually, more and more people began to talk about him. Matt's 'bad dancing' video, watched by millions of people, became an internet sensation. Matt was contacted by a chewing gum company. They loved his clips and wanted him to make a video for them. In 2006, Matt made a round-the-world tour sponsored by the company. But this time, something changed. Matt performed his silly dance in Rwanda. He inspired some Rwandan orphans watching him to dance, too. Suddenly, Matt had a new mission. He didn't want to dance around the world, he wanted to dance with the world. Matt's new videos, made in 2008 and 2012, have a sense of joy and community. They show crowds of people dancing and laughing together. In each place, he tried to learn new dances and persuade people to join in with him. Matt says, 'It helps to remind people that we're all the same and we don't need to be so afraid of each other.'

2 SPEAKING **What do you think about Matt Harding's 'bad dancing' project? Discuss the quotes. Which do you agree / disagree with?**

1 'It's just a really silly idea and a waste of time. He should get a proper job.'
2 'The videos are fun, but he's never going to change the world.'
3 'Projects like this are great because they make us more aware of the different cultures and people around the world.'

Participle clauses

3 **Underline sentences in the text that have a similar meaning to sentences 1–6.**

1 Matt Harding, a video game designer who was working in Australia, decided to leave his job.
2 Matt's 'bad dancing' video, which was watched by millions of people, became an internet sensation.
3 Like most people who travel from place to place they took photos and filmed short video clips of the places they visited.
4 Matt, who thought the idea was great fun, agreed and from there, the idea grew.
5 Matt inspired some Rwandan orphans who were watching him to dance, too.
6 They show crowds of people who are dancing and laughing together.

4 **Compare sentences 1–6 in exercise 3 with the sentences in the text. Then choose the correct answers.**

1 We use the present participle (-*ing* form) to replace relative clauses containing **active** / **passive** verbs.
2 We use the past participle (-*ed* form) to replace relative clauses containing **active** / **passive** verbs.

Reference and practice 10.1 Workbook page 122

5 Rewrite the phrases in brackets using participle clauses.

Diversity, a street dance troupe from London [1] .... (*which was formed*) in 2006, is now one of the most successful dance groups in the UK. The eleven young men, [2] .... (*who perform*) as *Diversity* are a mix of ages, heights, and backgrounds, but they all share a passion for street dance. Their dance routines, [3] .... (*which show*) their incredible skills, became famous when they won *Britain's Got Talent* in 2009. The show, [4] .... (*which was watched*) by over 17 million viewers, had an almost instant effect. Suddenly everyone wanted to learn street dance. The month after *Diversity's* win, 850 extra students applied to take street dance classes [5] .... (*which are run*) by *Pineapple Dance Studios* in London. So what is street dance? It started on the streets of New York and Los Angeles in the 1970s and included moves [6] .... (*which were improvised*) by the dancers as they performed. Recent television advertisements [7] .... (*which use*) street dance moves have helped to popularize street dance, while making the advertised products seem cool and desirable. Now many schools in the UK run street dance classes, [8] .... (*which encourage*) young people to exercise and stay healthy.

6 ⊕ **2.24** Look at the photo from a famous film. What type of film do you think it is? Listen to an interview and compare your answer.

7 ⊕ **2.24** Make participle clauses with the verbs in A and phrases in B below. Then listen and check your answers.

A ▪ choreograph ▪ perform ▪ pour ▪ born
▪ play ▪ know ▪ worry

B ▪ from the sky ▪ about Kelly ▪ fifty or sixty years
▪ the role of ▪ the dance ▪ that the scene
▪ by Gene Kelly

1 Even people .... after this film was made would probably know the song.
2 Gene Kelly is the actor ....
3 The director, ... because he was ill, didn't want to shoot the scene.
4 Kelly, ... had taken a long time to prepare, didn't want to stop.
5 In this famous scene, we see Kelly .... Don Lockwood.
6 The dance, ..., is one of the most iconic dances in movie history.
7 The rain, ..., was made from milk mixed with water.

8 SPEAKING Work in pairs. Read the notes about a famous classic film *Red Shoes*. Use the information to describe the film using participle clauses.

* **Red Shoes: a classic film made in 1948**
* stars Moira Shearer as Victoria Page
* **famous dance sequence lasts 15 minutes**
* story is based on fairy tale by Hans Christian Andersen
* **ballet dancer wears red ballet shoes**

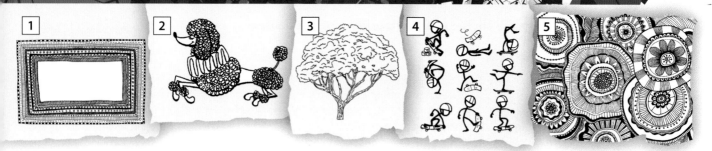

1 **SPEAKING** Look at the doodles. What sort of people do you think drew each one? Think about age, personality and profession.

2 ⊙ **2.25** Listen to an expert talking about doodles. Match the personality descriptions a–e with doodles 1–5.

- **a** is emotional and perhaps romantic
- **b** has physical or creative energy
- **c** wants to develop as a person
- **d** is practical and needs security
- **e** likes to play and have fun

V Describing art

3 Match the words below with meanings 1–8. Then use the words to describe doodles 1–5.

■ original ■ flowing ■ elaborate ■ romantic ■ comical ■ lifelike ■ dramatic ■ moving

1 complicated and detailed
2 appearing to be real
3 smooth and continuous
4 full of action and movement
5 making you feel very sad or sympathetic
6 funny in a strange or silly way
7 making you feel strong emotions of love
8 new and interesting

4 Complete the sentences with words in exercise 3.

1 Sylvia paints very .... pictures, but mine are much simpler.
2 Picasso's powerful and .... *Guernica* shows the horrors of war.
3 It's a highly .... piece of work. Nobody has created anything like that before.
4 .... paintings can be of couples in love, or lovely natural scenes.
5 A .... style of drawing has confident, unbroken lines.
6 It's meant to be a serious work of art, but many people find it ....
7 The photo is very .... and it makes many people cry.
8 It was such a .... sculpture that one tourist said 'have a nice day' to it.

5 ⊙ **2.26** Listen to an interview with an art therapist. Then choose the best description of an art therapist's job.

- **a** Art therapists teach people how to understand their own drawings, sculptures and paintings.
- **b** Art therapists analyze people's drawings and encourage people to express their feelings through art.
- **c** Art therapists look at famous works of art and use them to discuss feelings and emotions with people.

6 ⊙ **2.26** Listen again. Are the sentences true (T), false (F) or not given (NG)?

1 Art therapists only work with children or sick people.
2 It's important to look at all the small details in a doodle, not just at the main picture.
3 Frank usually asks people to talk about their doodles.
4 Some patients don't want to talk about their drawings.
5 Drawing or doodling is a good way of using both the left and the right sides of the brain.
6 Frank thinks it's important to help people improve their technique.
7 *Doodles of Happiness* includes many examples of different types of doodles.
8 Frank thinks it's useful to know when and where people drew their doodles.

7 **SPEAKING** Answer the questions.

1 When do you doodle? Why?
2 What kind of doodles do you do?
3 What might your doodles say about you?

Debating

8 SPEAKING. You are going to listen to a debate on: *Art classes are an important part of the school curriculum*. Read the arguments below. Add two more ideas for and against art classes.

> Art classes are an important part of the school curriculum
>
> For
>
> Teach important skills,
> e.g. perception,
> co-ordination, planning
>
> Help us to understand other
> people's view of the world
>
> Encourage creativity and
> self-expression
>
> Against
>
> Require expensive materials
>
> Too personal – can't be
> taught at school
>
> Not useful for getting a job

9 🔊 **2.27** Listen to the debate. Number the arguments in exercise 8 in the order you hear them.

10 🔊 **2.27** Listen again and complete the phrases in the box.

Agreeing	Interrupting
I think (Jessica) is [1]................................ right.	Could I [5]...................................?
I agree with (Jessica).	Can I [6].. here?
That's a [2]............................... .	Sorry to interrupt, but … .
That's so true.	
	Encouraging
Disagreeing	Tracy, [7]............................ add anything?
That's not always [3]............................... .	Do you have anything to say about this?
I [4]........................ with Tracy about … .	
I'd say the exact opposite.	
Not necessarily.	

11 SPEAKING Work in small groups and hold a debate on: *Students should be able to choose the subjects they study at school. No subjects should be obligatory*. Follow the instructions.

- Select a chairperson for the debate. This person will introduce the debate and make sure that everyone gets an opportunity to speak.
- Make a list of arguments for and against the statement.
- Hold the debate. Try to mention all the arguments in your list and use the phrases in exercise 10.

FAMOUS FESTIVALS

Sundance

1 **SPEAKING** Look at the photos and discuss the questions. Then read the article and compare your ideas.

1 What kinds of festivals are they?
2 Why do people go there?

2 Read the article again and choose the correct answers.

1 The main purpose of *The Utah Film Festival* was to
  a attract Hollywood stars.
  b show popular Hollywood films.
  c encourage people to visit Utah.
  d show films by new film makers.

2 The main purpose of *The Sundance Festival* is to
  a make money for big companies.
  b attract celebrity endorsements.
  c support and encourage independent film-makers.
  d screen popular, well-known films.

3 People mainly go back to the festival every year because
  a they might see a famous person.
  b they enjoy the stories that the film-makers tell.
  c they only want to watch 'classic' movies.
  d they want to enter their own film.

4 WOMAD gives people the opportunity to
  a get to know music from their own culture.
  b listen to well-known bands.
  c enjoy traditional music from other countries.
  d record their own music.

5 Peter Gabriel created WOMAD in order to
  a teach people about other cultures and ways of life.
  b provide entertainment for families.
  c help unknown musicians make money.
  d find new musicians for a record label.

6 WOMAD festivals <u>don't</u> include
  a educational classes.
  b entertainment for children.
  c open-air cinema.
  d places to try new food.

3 **SPEAKING** Answer the questions.

1 Do any of the festivals appeal to you? Why / why not?
2 What type of festivals do people hold in your country? What do they celebrate?
3 What can you learn about another culture through its music?

What have Steven Soderbergh (*Ocean's Eleven*) and Quentin Tarantino (*Pulp Fiction*) got in common? Well, they're both world-famous directors, but they're also
5 independent film-makers who got their 'big break' at the *Sundance Film Festival*.
When the film festival first started in 1978, its aim was to attract tourists to Utah, a little-known state in Midwest America. Back then, the festival was
10 called *The Utah Film Festival* and it showed mostly retrospectives of old films. It wasn't a popular event and as a result made little money. Then, in 1981, Hollywood star Robert Redford got involved and founded the *Sundance Institute*. The purpose of the
15 festival changed and a competition for independent film-makers became the main focus. Redford wanted to bring exciting new films, made outside the Hollywood system, to a wider audience.
During the 1980s and 1990s the event grew in size
20 and film studios became interested. Unfortunately, celebrity actors and paparazzi started to appear on the scene, too. Big companies began paying a few of the celebrities to endorse products that had nothing to do with film, taking attention away from the independent
25 directors. Festival organizers responded with a *Focus on Film* campaign, urging people to remember the real purpose of *Sundance*. 'It was never intended to be commercial. It was intended to be a place of discovery,' said Redford. Luckily, the campaign worked and today
30 most of the 50,000 festival-goers come to see the new directors, rather than famous film stars.
Today, *Sundance* is one of the most eagerly-awaited film festivals in America. The competition includes feature-length films, short films, thought-provoking
35 documentaries and drama, but there are few famous names, because most entries are from first-time directors. Some of these films may be controversial and cutting-edge, but they all tell a good story. 'Storytellers broaden our minds,' says Robert Redford. 'They
40 engage, provoke, inspire, and ultimately, connect us.' And it's that inspiration that keeps people going to *Sundance*, year after year.

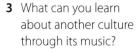

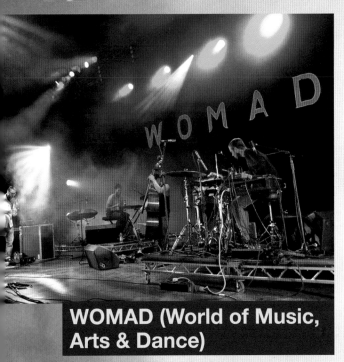

WOMAD (World of Music, Arts & Dance)

In 1982, the world was a very different place. Bands like *The Rolling Stones* or *Aerosmith* dominated the music scene, and people didn't know much about traditional musicians from other cultures. No one had heard of the *Drummers of Burundi* or Youssou N'Dour from Senegal, but then *WOMAD* came along and things started to change. These artists now had an international stage where they could show off their talent ... and their culture.

WOMAD was originally the vision of a British rock star called Peter Gabriel, who wanted to bring traditional music to the world. As well as a festival, he founded a record label called *Real World*, so artists could reach audiences in other countries. In 1982, when the first *WOMAD* took place in England, many of the performers were unknown, but the festival was still a huge success. 'Music is a universal language that brings people together,' said Gabriel later, 'and each festival allows many different audiences to gain an insight into cultures other than their own.' That was the purpose of *WOMAD* – it championed diversity and difference, while at the same time celebrating everyone's common humanity. People were united through music.

Since then, *WOMAD* has held more than 160 festivals in 27 different countries. Most of the festivals are open-air events with a little of everything – live music, ethnic markets with some traditional food and artefacts, and family-oriented zones with a few workshops teaching dance, music and art. *WOMADelaide* in Australia is a good example. It's the most talked-about music festival in the country and brings together some of the best traditional artists in the world. *WOMADelaide* proves that the purpose of the festival is still going strong. 'If the world was just like a big version of *WOMADelaide*,' commented one performer, 'it would be a better place.'

45
50
55
60
65
70
75
80

1 **SPEAKING** Look at the photo and answer the questions.

1 What kind of festival do you think this is?
2 What kinds of events do you think there might be at this festival?
3 Have you ever met any of your favourite authors?
4 Would you like to listen to your favourite author talk about their books?

2 Read the review of the Hay-on-Wye Literary Festival and answer the questions.

1 Did the writer enjoy the festival? Which words tell you?
2 Which of these art forms is <u>not</u> mentioned in the review: film, illustration, dance, music, comedy, poetry?
3 Why do you think the writer included a quote from Sir Terry Pratchett in the review?

3 Which of these things are mentioned in the review? Put them in the correct order.

a information about the organizers
b detailed information about what happened at the event
c summary and recommendation
d technical details about the event
e background information (name of the event, where and when it was organized, etc.)
f description of what the author liked most

Hay-on-Wye Literary Festival

Every summer, the eagerly-awaited Hay-on-Wye Literary Festival welcomes internationally acclaimed writers, comedians, poets and actors for a week of discussion, readings and performances in a muddy field in Wales.

This year, it was such an amazing festival that book lovers of all ages had plenty to entertain them. For the youngest book fans, illustrator Axel Scheffler drew pictures and told stories from his new book for 3–5-year-olds, *Pip and Posy*. It was so captivating that even the three-year-olds were interested. Comedian Bill Bailey gave a hilarious talk in which he covered a range of topics, from politics to social media, popular fiction and the end of the world.

What is fascinating about the Hay-on-Wye Literary Festival is that it's not just about books. There were concerts from folk singers, hip hop artists, jazz bands and string quartets. Poetry recitals, screenings of Bollywood films, cartoons, and interviews with designers, actors, sportspeople and politicians were also on offer.

What made the biggest impression on me was the appearance of Sir Terry Pratchett on the final day. The renowned author of more than 50 comic fantasy novels collected his Wodehouse Comic Fiction award. 'How do you write fantasy?' asked one fan. 'Don't sit around listening to me,' replied an amusing Sir Terry, 'you should be at home typing!'

Seeing such remarkable artists and experiencing everything that the literary world has to offer in one place, made this an unforgettable experience. The whole festival was organized so well that I can only recommend it to all the literature fans out there.

V insight Synonyms: evaluative adjectives

4 Study the highlighted adjectives in the review. Who or what do they describe? Match two adjectives to each of the words below.

1 wonderful
2 interesting
3 famous
4 funny

STRATEGY

Creating emphasis

When you write a review of an event, you may want to put emphasis on particular information to indicate what is most important or to show how you feel.

Ways of creating emphasis:

1 Nominal clauses
   - *What* + clause + *be*
     The appearance of Sir Terry Pratchett made the biggest impression on me.
     What made the biggest impression on me was the appearance of Sir Terry Pratchett.

2 *so* and *such*
   - *be* + *so* + adjective
     It was so captivating that …
   - *so* + adverb
     The whole festival was organized so well that …
   - *such* + adjective + plural noun / uncountable noun
     Seeing such remarkable artists … .
   - *such* + *a* / *an* + adjective + noun
     This year, it was such an amazing festival.

5 **Read the strategy and study the underlined examples in the review. Then complete the second sentence so that it has a similar meaning to the first sentence.**

1 It was such an expensive festival that many people couldn't afford to buy tickets.
   The festival .... that many people couldn't afford to buy tickets.

2 I really liked that the festival was family-oriented.
   What .... that the festival was family-oriented.

3 They were such wonderful dancers and gave a moving performance.
   The dancers .... and gave a moving performance.

4 Her sculptures are so elaborate that it's not surprising that she won the award.
   She makes .... that it's not surprising that she won the award.

5 The children's orchestra moved me the most.
   What .... the children's orchestra.

6 The talk was so boring that I left early.
   It .... that I left early.

WRITING GUIDE

- **Task** Write a review of an event for a popular entertainment magazine.

- **Ideas** Make notes about:
  - the name of the event, type of event, where and when it is organized.
  - details about what happened at the event, who performed.
  - comments about the quality of the performances.
  - what you enjoyed / did not enjoy the most.
  - any quotes you would like to include.
  - would you recommend the event to others?

- **Plan** Follow the plan:

  Paragraph 1: Give the background details about the event: type of event, where and when it was.

  Paragraph 2: Give details about the performances and include any quotes.

  Paragraph 3: Write what you enjoyed / did not enjoy most.

  Paragraph 4: Finish your review with a summary or a recommendation.

- **Write** Write your review. Use the paragraph plan to help you.

- **Check** Check the following points:
  - Have you used a clear paragraph structure and the correct register?
  - Have you used a variety of evaluative adjectives and emphasis?
  - Have you checked grammar, vocabulary, spelling and punctuation?

Vocabulary insight 10 Fixed phrases with two key words

Fixed phrases with *and*

There are a lot of fixed phrases in English that consist of two words joined with *and*, for example, *alive and well*. The order of these words cannot be changed. There are three main types of phrases with *and*:

1 Words that have a similar meaning.
2 Words that are opposites.
3 Words that often go together.

To find these phrases in the dictionary, find the first word in the phrase. They can often be found in the idioms section near the end of the entry.

1 Read the strategy above. Complete the phrases with the words below. Then match them to types 1–3 in the strategy. Use a dictionary to help you.

■ early ■ sound ■ error ■ cons ■ chips ■ tired ■ white ■ quiet

1 sick and ....
2 trial and ....
3 black and ....
4 fish and ....
5 bright and ....
6 peace and ....
7 pros and ....
8 safe and ....

2 Match the phrases in exercise 1 to definitions 1–8.

1 positive and negative sides ....
2 trying repeatedly for success ....
3 fed up with ....
4 in writing ....
5 early in the morning ....
6 not hurt ....
7 a typical English dish ....
8 a calm and silent environment ....

3 Complete the sentences with the phrases in exercise 1.

1 I'm not going to believe you until I see the agreement in ....
2 Before we decide what to do, we need to look at the .... of each possible solution.
3 Inventing the machine involved some ....
4 Our train leaves at 7 a.m., so we need to get up ....
5 When I got to Paris I phoned my parents to let them know I was ....
6 I don't like the noise of the city, but really enjoy the .... of the countryside.
7 Go and tidy your room now! I'm .... of having to ask you.
8 When we were in England, we had .... several times.

Fixed phrases with *by*, *for* and *or*

Some fixed phrases with two key words in English can be joined by other words, for example, *by*, *for* and *or*. You can find them in a dictionary in the same way as phrases with *and*.

4 Read the strategy above. Study the entries below. Then replace the words in italics in sentences 1–4 with the fixed phrases in the entries.

> **word for word 1** repeating sth exactly: *Sharon repeated word for word what he had told her.*

> **sooner or later** at some time in the future; one day

> **IDM more or less** approximately; almost: *We are more or less the same age.*

> **step by step** (used for talking about a series of actions) moving slowly and gradually from one action or stage to the next: *clear step-by-step instructions*

1 The journey to the festival will take *approximately* an hour.
2 If you follow the instructions *slowly and carefully*, you won't have any problems making the plane.
3 Jodie repeated *every single thing* what I had told her.
4 If you work very hard, you'll win the championships *one day*.

5 Find fixed phrases with the words below in a dictionary. Then complete the sentences.

■ back ■ bit ■ bits ■ neat ■ pins

1 .... by .... , she managed to finish her sculpture in time for the exhibition.
2 After sitting on the plane for nine hours, I had .... and .... in my legs.
3 We forgot some .... and .... when we went camping, but we managed to get everything in the local shop.
4 Walking .... and .... to school every day takes me about an hour.
5 His room is always .... and .... Everything has its own place.

6 Write your own example sentences with the fixed phrases in exercise 5.

1 ....
2 ....
3 ....
4 ....
5 ....

Vocabulary

1 Complete the sentences about six talented people.

▨ beauty ▨ dedication ▨ maturity ▨ style ▨ success
▨ vision

1 Sergey Karjakin achieved .... aged twelve, becoming a chess Grandmaster.
2 Cleopatra, who was famous for her glamorous ...., became queen as a teenager.
3 H.P. Lovecraft, whose dramatic .... of horror writing is still popular, learnt to read aged two.
4 Steffi Graf began playing tennis aged 4. Her .... made her famous.
5 Doctor Akrit Jaswal started treating patients aged seven, displaying the .... of someone much older.
6 Before he became famous for his .... of equality, Martin Luther King excelled at school.

Marks .... / 6

2 Complete the phrases with one word.

Study tips

1 Pick and .... your best subjects.
2 Solve problems through trial and ....
3 Search far and .... for information.
4 Don't get .... and tired of studying!
5 There will be times of ups and .... Don't let this demotivate you.
6 Stay healthy and alive and ....!

Marks .... / 6

3 Complete the sentences. Replace the definitions in italics with six of the adjectives.

▨ comical ▨ dramatic ▨ flowing ▨ lifelike ▨ moving
▨ original ▨ romantic

1 Albrecht Dürer's art is often very .... (*realistic*).
2 Buñuel's films were very .... (*new and interesting*).
3 Charlie Chaplin's films are .... (*funny*), but also often sad and .... (*emotionally affecting*).
4 The .... (*smooth and continuous*) lines in Van Gogh's art also have a .... (*strong, exciting*) effect.

Marks .... / 6

4 Match the words in A to the words in B to make compound adjectives. Then complete the text.

A ▨ cutting ▨ family ▨ little ▨ open ▨ talked ▨ world

B ▨ -about ▨ -air ▨ -edge ▨ -famous ▨ -known ▨ -oriented

The Edinburgh Festival Fringe is perhaps the most [1] .... cultural event in Britain. Acts include successful, [2] .... stars, as well as [3] .... performers hoping for success. Visitors can see new, [4] .... comedy acts and plays. There are indoor shows and [5] .... events, and many [6] .... performances for children.

Marks .... / 12

Grammar

5 Rewrite the phrases in brackets as participle clauses.

1 Cannes is a film festival .... (*which is held*) in France.
2 It's an international festival, ... (*which celebrates*) all cultures.
3 Films .... (*which are shown*) here often become famous.
4 The Palme d'Or is the most famous prize, ... (*which is given*) to the best film.
5 In 1960, the Film Market opened, ... (*which grew*) rapidly in the following years.
6 Thousands arrive every year, ... (*which triples*) Cannes' population.
7 Wealthy guests .... (*who arrive*) in yachts are a frequent sight.
8 Last year, they used 2 km of red carpet .... (*which was changed*) three times a day.
9 Unfortunately, film fans .... (*who hope*) to attend may be disappointed.
10 Tickets .... (*which are sent*) out in advance, are to selected guests only.

Marks .... / 10

6 Complete the text. Use the words below.

▨ any ▨ all ▨ each ▨ few ▨ little ▨ many ▨ most ▨ much
▨ none ▨ some

The Metropolitan Museum of Art (MOMA) has [1] .... famous works of art. I go there [2] .... time I'm in New York and I still haven't seen [3] .... of it! I usually spend [4] .... time (hours and hours!) looking at the paintings upstairs. I also try to spend a [5] .... time in the garden, where there are a [6] .... sculptures. I don't spend [7] .... time in the photography section – I like [8] .... photos, but I prefer paintings. [9] .... of the other paintings are as interesting as Van Gogh's *Starry Night* – it doesn't have [10] .... rivals for the best painting of all.

Marks .... / 10

Total .... / 50

Listening

1 🔘 **2.28** **Listen to part of a radio programme about superheroes. Choose the correct answers.**

1 According to the speaker, how are the earliest comics similar to today's comics?
  a They shared similar concerns about the world.
  b The appearance of the heroes hasn't changed much.
  c Their scientific background remains relevant today.
  d They both primarily reflect American interests.

2 What was life like in 1930s America?
  a Many people were enjoying wealthier lifestyles.
  b Few people were interested in superheroes.
  c People wanted to forget about their troubles.
  d The government had lots of support.

3 What do we learn about the popularity of superhero films?
  a They have made comic book superheroes unpopular.
  b They are not as popular as comedies.
  c They are mainly popular with young people.
  d They are not taken very seriously.

4 In the speaker's opinion, why do people like Batman?
  a He has a more stylish image.
  b He seems more similar to us.
  c He is stronger than other heroes.
  d He is perfect in every way.

5 What criticism does the speaker make of CGI (computer-generated images)?
  a They don't look realistic.
  b They are quite expensive.
  c They aren't used often enough.
  d They don't surprise us.

6 What does the speaker think about the future of superhero films?
  a They'll grow in popularity.
  b They'll disappear forever.
  c They'll be more innovative.
  d They'll change completely.

Speaking

2 **Read the sentences from the radio programme. What do *you* think? Think of two or three ideas to support your opinion.**

1 Technology is getting out of control.
2 When life is hard, people turn to fantasy.
3 We treat heroes with respect.
4 Batman is better than Superman.
5 There's too much violence in films.
6 Teenagers get bored very easily.

3 **Work in pairs and discuss each of the sentences in exercise 2. Do you agree or disagree with each other?**

Reading

4 **Read the text about *Comic-Con International*. Then complete the summary. Use the clues to help you.**

Comic-Con is an **1**............................ *(how often?)* event held every **2**............................ *(what time of year?)* in **3**............................ *(city?)*, **4**............................ *(country?)*. Over **5**............................ *(how many?)* people attended this year, of whom around **6**............................ *(what percentage?)* were female. Tickets will cost **7**............................ *(how much?)*. In this article, **8**............................ *(how many?)* people give their opinions of the event, which celebrates comic books, fantasy films and related popular culture.

WELCOME TO COMIC-CON INTERNATIONAL!
COSTUMES OPTIONAL.

Some of this year's attendees give their views … and criticisms.

THE FAN

The Tokyo comic convention is bigger, but San Diego hosts the largest American event, which is probably how they get away with robbing us with whopping ticket prices each summer. I stay to the end to justify the cost, but really three days would be enough. I love the film previews and 'meet and greets', but let's have fewer academic lectures, please! Despite writers' attempts to give us dramatic 'messages', comics are hardly works of philosophy, are they? That isn't to say I'm not a huge fan of larger-than-life heroes. I've even come dressed as Storm from the *X-Men*! If any of the cast are here, it'll absolutely make my day. Normally, people would stare at my outfit. That's what I love about Comic-Con, though. Here everyone's paying more attention to having fun.

THE ARTIST

Thursday to Sunday is a short time in which to pack a lot in. But if it were extended, I'd probably go slightly mad! Around 1,000,000 people try to get tickets every year, and over 130,000 are successful. Amongst those crowds, smaller artists like me struggle to get noticed. My modest profit makes my attendance worthwhile, however, despite not making a fortune. Movie actors are the main draw, although that's not an enthusiasm I particularly share. I once imagined that graphic novels would be the art of our times, offering new visions. I still think they could be. So it's a shame

that, rather than rising to that challenge, most of today's comic artists still choose to restrict themselves to crime-fighters in costume. I know – I need to get over it!

THE TECHNICIAN

I put on special effects at the events – robots, lights, the works. No one could claim they aren't getting a lot for their $175. As a female technician, I seem to be something of an attraction myself. About four in ten ticket-holders are women, and they're often keen to chat. And some men imagine I'd be an ideal geek girlfriend! I meet a lot of renowned stars day-to-day on film sets, so that's less of a big deal for me. It's the atmosphere at Comic-Con that I love. People are so friendly that the end always comes too soon. I have a confession, though. Although I don't mind *Spiderman* and *Batman*, it's romantic classics like *Casablanca* which really speak to my heart. But don't breathe a word to anyone …

5 Read the text again and answer the questions.

Who:
1 would like to stay longer at the festival?
2 is excited about meeting film stars?
3 gets a lot of attention at the event?
4 is critical of superheroes?
5 believes that comics can say something important?
6 isn't sure that the event is good value?

Grammar and vocabulary

6 Choose the correct answers.

What's in a name? Well, having the right name can [1]............... quite a lot, in some cases!

To [2]............... an example, consider graphic novels. When they [3]............... as 'comics', they received little respect. The greater [4]............... of the adult population used to question the maturity of comics, claiming that they were just picture books for children. Nowadays, these 'picture books' are [5]............... available in libraries. So why did the comic-book critics [6]............... their minds?

In the 1970s and 1980s, some longer comics were published under the description 'graphic novels', which sounded much more respectable. Art Spiegelman, [7]............... graphic novel *Maus* won the 1986 Pulitzer Prize, also popularized the term. This was a huge boost to the genre's credibility. One critic said that *Maus* was the best work about the Holocaust she [8]............... in *any* genre.

Today, fans of the genre argue that graphic novels ideally [9]............... to be taught in schools and universities as part of literature courses. If the genre hadn't changed its name, this recent development [10]................

1 a matter b experience c depend d argue
2 a present b argue c give d put
3 a described b describe c were described
   d have been described
4 a lot b part c amount d many
5 a exceptionally b utterly c widely d highly
6 a transform b move c consider d change
7 a who b who's c that d whose
8 a had read b reads c has read d was reading
9 a must b should c ought d can
10 a will not happen b might not have happened
   c had not happened d did not happen

Writing

7 Choose one of the statements below and write a for and against essay about it. Use the paragraph plan to help you.

1 To encourage teenagers to read more, we should teach graphic novels instead of classic literature in schools.
2 We do not need superheroes today.
   Paragraph 1: Give a general introduction to the topic
   Paragraph 2: Give arguments *for* the topic.
   Paragraph 3: Give arguments *against* the topic.
   Paragraph 4: Give a conclusion, including your own opinion.

Vocabulary bank 1

Describing hair

1 Label the photos with the words below.

■ a bob ■ a bun ■ cropped hair ■ curly hair ■ dreadlocks ■ dyed hair ■ a plait ■ a ponytail ■ a shaved head ■ spiky hair ■ straight hair ■ wavy hair

1 .... 2 .... 3 ....

4 .... 5 .... 6 ....

7 .... 8 .... 9 ....

10 .... 11 .... 12 ....

2 Complete the sentences with the hairstyles in exercise 1.

1 Her hair is quite short and is the same length all around. She's got ....

2 His hair is in sharp points all over his head. He's got ....

3 She divides her hair into three parts and joins them together. She's got ....

4 His hair is bright blue with green stripes! He's got ....

5 His hair isn't very easy to control. He's got ....

6 She hasn't got any curls. She's got ....

7 His hair is twisted into long thick pieces which hang down from his head. He's got ....

8 All of her hair is together at the back of her head. She's got ....

9 The hairdresser cut his hair very short with a machine. He's got ....

10 She wears her long hair in a ball on top of her head. She's got ....

11 The hairdresser cut his hair very short with a pair of scissors. He's got ....

12 Her hair is slightly curly. She's got ....

3 SPEAKING Work in pairs. Think of people you know with the hairstyles in exercise 1.

Clothes

1 Match the words below to definitions 1–12.

■ Bermudas ■ camisole top ■ cardigan ■ combat trousers ■ fleece ■ hoody ■ leggings ■ maxi dress ■ mini skirt ■ polo shirt ■ vest ■ tracksuit bottoms

1 a sweatshirt with a hood
2 a very short skirt
3 a sleeveless top for men
4 a long dress which reaches the ankles
5 a long-sleeved top made of soft warm material
6 an informal pair of trousers often worn for sports practice
7 loose informal trousers with large pockets on the legs
8 shorts that come down to just above the knees
9 a summer top for women which is held up by straps
10 an informal T-shirt with a collar
11 women's trousers that fit tightly around the legs
12 a top made of wool with buttons down the front

2 Label items 1–12 with words in exercise 1.

1 .... 7 ....
2 .... 8 ....
3 .... 9 ....
4 .... 10 ....
5 .... 11 ....
6 .... 12 ....

3 SPEAKING Work in pairs. Which clothes do you usually wear in warm weather? Which clothes do you usually wear in cool weather?

Types of holiday

1 Match the types of holiday to sentences 1–12.

■ adventure holiday ■ backpacking holiday ■ city break ■ coach tour ■ DIY holiday ■ honeymoon ■ house swap ■ package holiday ■ self-catering holiday ■ sightseeing holiday ■ staycation ■ working holiday

1 'We travelled around Europe carrying our clothes and our sleeping bags with us.'
2 'We spent the weekend exploring Paris.'
3 'We spent a fortnight in Mexico after our wedding.'
4 'The journey from one place to the next took ages and we were sitting down all the time.'
5 'We got a fixed price for the flight, the hotel and all our meals.'
6 'There were lots of different extreme sports to try.'
7 'They took us to see all the monuments in Rome.'
8 'We spent a month cleaning a polluted river.'
9 'We organized our own holiday last year.'
10 'We lent our flat to an American family while we stayed at their place in New York.'
11 'We didn't go away, but we did some day trips.'
12 'We cooked all our own meals.'

2 Complete the text with the types of holiday in exercise 1.

People choose a particular type of holiday for different reasons. A ¹............................. is for those who prefer to have everything organized and paid for before they leave. Those who book a ²............................. want to be taken in a comfortable bus to visit a number of different places. Time is also an important factor. Busy executives often book a ³............................. to Amsterdam or Berlin for the weekend, while students have the summer to spend three months on a ⁴............................. . Couples who have just got married can have two weeks to enjoy their ⁵............................. . Then, there are holidays that offer different activities. A ⁶............................. is for those who enjoy visiting landmarks, while those who prefer more action can book an ⁷............................. . There are even people who go on a ⁸............................. because they want to make a difference to the world. But the most important question is often money. Some people save money by planning their own ⁹............................. on the internet. Others book a ¹⁰............................. to save on food while even bigger savings can be made on accommodation if you do a ¹¹............................. and stay in somebody else's house while they live in yours. A ¹²............................. where you stay at home is another option for a nice, cheap holiday.

3 SPEAKING Work in pairs. Which types of holiday would you like to go on? Which ones wouldn't you like to go on?

Travel and transport

1 Complete the mind map with the words below. Some can be used more than once.

nouns ■ aisle ■ buffet car ■ cabin ■ carriage ■ crossing ■ cruise ■ deck ■ flight ■ gate ■ hold ■ luggage rack ■ motorway ■ overhead locker ■ pier ■ platform ■ runway ■ seat belt ■ stand ■ tracks ■ voyage

verbs ■ get on ■ get off ■ go ashore ■ land ■ set sail ■ slow down ■ speed up ■ take off

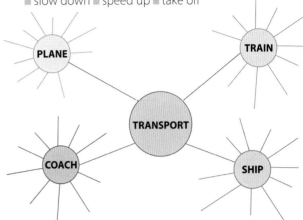

2 Complete the texts with the correct form of the words in exercise 1.

A There was no one left on the ¹............................. when the train left the station. There were a lot of passengers without seats, and some of them were standing in the ²............................. of our ³............................. . We put our bags in the ⁴............................. and I went to the ⁵............................. to get some sandwiches. After we came back, the train began to ⁶............................. . Eventually it stopped, and we had to wait for someone to clean the leaves off the ⁷............................. .

B I'd never been on a ¹............................. before, so I was really excited when we got to the ²............................. and saw the ship. We went out on the ³............................. when we ⁴............................., so we saw the land slowly disappear from view. The ⁵............................. from Southampton to Dublin was very rough because of a storm. I was desperate to ⁶............................. when we reached Ireland and I had no idea how I was going to survive the rest of the ⁷............................. !

C The coach was already at the ¹............................. when we arrived, so we put our luggage in the ²............................. and ³............................. . I had only just put my ⁴............................. on when the driver started the engine and we set off. Some of the cars on the ⁵............................. were going very slowly, so the driver ⁶............................. to overtake them. We arrived very early, so there was nobody waiting for us when we ⁷............................. .

D We didn't have to wait long at the ¹............................. for our ²............................. to be announced. I only had a small suitcase, so I took it in the ³............................. of the plane with me and put it in the ⁴............................. . Then we sat on the ⁵............................. for nearly an hour before we ⁶............................. . We ⁷............................. very late, so I went straight home to bed.

3 SPEAKING Work in pairs. Tell your partner about the last long journey you went on.

Vocabulary bank 3

Feelings

1 Complete the table with the feelings below. Which word is the strongest in each category?

■ surprise ■ shock ■ fear ■ happiness ■ sadness ■ anger

1	2	3 ....
annoyed	delighted	devastated
cross	pleased	upset
furious	excited	unhappy

4	5	6 ....
frightened	appalled	amazed
petrified	disgusted	astonished
scared	shocked	surprised

2 Which adjectives in exercise 1 can go with *a bit / very* and which with *absolutely*? Complete 1 and 2 with the words in each category.

1 a bit / very ....
....
....

2 absolutely ....
....
....

3 Complete the sentences with adjectives in exercise 1. Sometimes more than one answer is possible.

1 She was absolutely .... when she failed her exams. She really wanted to go to university.

2 They were a bit .... by the joke because they felt it was inappropriate.

3 He was absolutely .... when he found out that he had won. He couldn't believe it!

4 My sister's absolutely .... of spiders. She can't be in the same room as one.

5 I was a bit .... that you didn't call, but I understood when you told me why.

6 I'm absolutely .... with my new tablet. It's exactly what I wanted!

4 SPEAKING Work in pairs. Ask and answer questions about the feelings in exercise 1.

> What makes you feel annoyed?

> I feel annoyed when my friends are late.

Health problems

1 Complete the table with the symptoms below.

■ a headache ■ numb ■ painful ■ a rash ■ a runny nose
■ sick ■ a stomach ache ■ swollen ■ unwell ■ weak
■ backache

I'm feeling ...	dizzy, shivery, ..., ..., ...
I've got ...	a cough, chest pains, ..., ..., ..., ..., ...
My (x) is ...	bruised, itchy, sore, ..., ..., ...

2 Complete the dialogues with words in exercise 1.

Doctor   Hello, what's the matter?

Patient   I've got a terrible ¹........................ I think it could be something I ate.

Doctor   How long has it been hurting?

Patient   Since yesterday. I had some seafood for lunch and it started right after that. I also have a ²........................ on my neck and shoulders. And now it's spreading down to my back. It's really ³........................ I can't stop scratching.

Doctor   Have you taken anything for this?

Patient   No, nothing.

Doctor   OK, let's take a closer look ... This could be a food allergy, I'm going to prescribe an antihistamine. You should also have some tests done ...

Doctor   Good morning. What's the problem?

Patient   I was playing basketball this morning and I fell and did something to my ankle.

Doctor   Oh, yes, I can see. It's very ⁴........................ .

Patient   Yes, it's twice the size of my other ankle.

Doctor   Does it hurt when you walk?

Patient   Yes, it's very ⁵........................ and I can't feel my toes – they're completely ⁶........................ .

Doctor   OK, this looks very serious. We'll have to take an X-ray ...

3 Work in pairs A and B. Student A is a doctor and Student B is a patient. Use the phrases in exercise 1 and the dialogues in exercise 2 to act out your own dialogue at the doctor's. Then change roles.

Global issues

1 Label the photos with the words below.

- climate change - deforestation - disease - drought
- earthquakes - famine - floods - pollution - poverty
- unemployment - urbanization - volcanic eruptions

1 .... 2 .... 3 ....

4 .... 5 .... 6 ....

7 .... 8 .... 9 ....

10 .... 11 .... 12 ....

2 Match the global issues in exercise 1 to the headlines.

1 **Village under water**

2 **Extreme weather continues**

3 **Millions with no money for food**

4 *Thousands of people flocking to the city*

5 **Ash cloud stops flights**

6 **Buildings fall as ground moves**

7 **CROPS FAIL ONCE AGAIN**

8 **Jobless rate highest in 20 years**

9 **NO RAIN FOR MONTHS**

10 **Massive oil spill off the coast**

11 **Amazon trees used for packaging**

12 **CHOLERA EPIDEMIC HITS COUNTRY**

Charities

1 Complete the table with the verb forms. Which two verbs have the same noun form?

Verbs	People
1	campaigner
2	organizer
3 .... for charity	(charity) worker
4	participant
5	competitor
6	promoter
7	distributor
8	sponsor
9	donor
10	supporter
11 .... funds	fund-raiser
12	volunteer

2 Complete the definitions with the nouns in exercise 1.

1 A .... makes a gift of money to a charity.

2 An .... arranges for something to happen.

3 A .... does a job in an organization that helps other people.

4 A .... tries to persuade others about the importance of something.

5 A .... takes part in a sporting event, like a race.

6 A .... collects money for a charity or an organization.

7 A .... takes part in an activity.

8 A .... gives somebody money for charity if that person succeeds in completing a particular activity.

9 A .... does work without being paid for it.

10 A .... leads or takes part in a campaign.

11 A .... shows that they agree with an organization.

12 A .... supplies products to different areas.

3 Complete the text with the correct forms of the verbs or nouns in exercise 1.

The charity Oxfam has been around for over seventy years now. Oxfam GB employs a number of paid
[1] ...., but most of its helpers are unpaid
[2] .... [3] .... of Oxfam help
the organization in many ways. Some of them
[4] .... money regularly to the charity while
others [5] .... fund-raising events, such
as sponsored head shaves. This is a fun activity for
everyone who [6] ...., from the person who
has their head shaved to the [7] .... who
give their money. On a larger scale is the London
Marathon. Many [8] .... do this race to
[9] .... money for charity. Oxfam uses the
money it receives to [10] .... against poverty
all over the world and [11] .... human
rights. The organization is also often the first to
[12] .... aid in emergency situations.

Vocabulary bank 5

Crime and punishment

1 Match the compound nouns below to definitions 1–12.

- armed robbery ■ community service ■ death penalty
- gang violence ■ house arrest ■ internet fraud
- knife crime ■ life sentence ■ petty theft ■ prison term
- speeding fine ■ traffic offence

1 committing crimes using physical force in a group
2 being killed for a crime
3 being a prisoner in the place where you live
4 breaking the rules when you're driving
5 having to help others in a particular area
6 using a gun to steal something
7 carrying a sharp weapon to threaten people
8 having to pay money for driving too fast
9 a period of time in jail
10 cheating somebody online to get money or goods
11 having to stay in prison until death
12 stealing something minor

2 Complete the table with the words in exercise 1.

Crimes	Punishment
1	
2	
3	
4	
5	
6	

3 Match the compound nouns in exercise 1 to the headlines.

1 **Three months for vandals who destroyed museum**

2 **Murderer to be executed for his crimes**

3 **Car drivers to pay €500 for going over the limit**

4 *Serial offender to spend the rest of his days in jail*

5 **Illegal earnings sent to foreign bank accounts**

6 **Man tricked into posting bank details on website**

7 **Model sentenced to pick up rubbish for 104 hours**

8 **Teenager stabbed on crowded city street**

9 **Opposition leader told to stay at home**

10 **Bank clerk held at gunpoint while safe is emptied**

11 **Group of teenagers terrorize own neighbourhood**

12 **Youth grabs small change from supermarket till**

Law and order

1 Complete the table with the prepositions below.

■ for ■ from ■ of ■ to

1	2
admit	approve
have the right	rob somebody
sentence somebody	take account

3	4
be responsible	deter somebody
blame somebody	prohibit somebody
punish somebody	release somebody

2 Match the verbs and prepositions in exercise 1 to definitions 1–12.

1 to steal something
2 to say that something is somebody's fault
3 to let somebody come out of a place
4 to think that something is good
5 to cause something
6 to consider the facts when making a decision
7 to say that you have done something wrong
8 to give a punishment officially in court
9 to make somebody suffer because they have done something wrong
10 to be able to do something by law
11 to use authority to stop something being done
12 to make somebody decide not to do something

3 Complete the text with the correct prepositions.

Police have found the man they believe is responsible ¹........................ the car thefts in Ivybridge, Devon. They think that the suspect, 18-year-old Larry Anderson, has robbed at least ten of the villagers ²........................ their cars in the last three months. Anderson was caught breaking into an Audi last night. He admitted ³........................ the crime on the spot, although police told him he had the right ⁴........................ remain silent.

Many of the residents of the village blame the boy's parents ⁵........................ his crimes. Anderson's father was recently released ⁶........................ prison after serving a long sentence for armed robbery. His mother has been repeatedly punished ⁷........................ shoplifting. It is said that both parents approved ⁸........................ their son's life of crime and they never prohibited him ⁹........................ taking other people's property, even when he was a child.

Residents know that the court may take account ¹⁰........................ Anderson's situation, but they hope that the judge will sentence him ¹¹........................ a long term in prison, which will deter him ¹²........................ stealing in the future.

Types of advertising

1 Match the words below to definitions 1–12.

▪ banner ▪ billboard ▪ classified ad ▪ commercial
▪ endorsement ▪ flyer ▪ jingle ▪ logo ▪ pop-up ad
▪ slogan ▪ spam ▪ stealth marketing

1 a short piece of music used in an advert
2 a very large board used for advertising
3 a phrase that is easy to remember
4 a strategy in which people do not realize a product is being advertised
5 a statement by a famous person about a product
6 a long, narrow advertisement on a website
7 a small piece of paper used for advertising
8 an advertisement on the radio or on television
9 a small advertisement in a newspaper
10 unwanted advertising material sent by email
11 an advert on a website that opens in a new window
12 a design used by a company to identify it

2 Complete the text with the correct form of the words in exercise 1.

The first advertisements were pictures on large boards advertising the profession of a tradesman. These
[1] .... were hung outside houses in the Middle Ages. After the invention of printing, adverts were printed on [2] .... to be handed out in the street. With the emergence of newspapers, the first [3] .... appeared, listing houses and goods for sale. The nineteenth century saw the formation of companies and in 1876 a British drinks manufacturer registered the first [4] ....: a red triangle. The first celebrity [5] .... occurred around this time with a famous actress advertising the products of a soap manufacturer. The 1920s brought the invention of the radio and soon the first [6] .... appeared. These were often accompanied by a catchy [7] ...., which people associated with the product. In the 1950s television began and TV advertising followed soon afterwards. Some adverts included phrases, such as 'Put a tiger in your tank', a [8] .... used by a petrol company. Advertising spread to the internet in the 1990s and companies paid for [9] .... to appear down the side of web pages and [10] .... to flash up on the screen. At the same time, people started receiving [11] .... in their email accounts. The latest strategy is [12] .... which targets people without them realizing it. Who knows what advertisers will think up next?

3 SPEAKING Work in pairs. Which type of adverts do you come across on a typical day and where do you see them?

I see a banner as soon as I turn on my computer.

Consumerism

1 Complete the sentences with the nouns below.

▪ display ▪ experience ▪ influence ▪ market ▪ present
▪ promise ▪ purchase ▪ refund ▪ research ▪ risk

1 They'll **put** the new product **on the** .... soon.
2 TV can **have an** .... on children's behaviour.
3 There's a discount if you **make a** .... to the value of €50 or more.
4 I took the shoes back and they **gave** me a ....
5 You never **give** me a .... on my birthday.
6 They're **doing some** .... into new materials.
7 People who **have a bad** .... with a product don't buy it again.
8 I didn't **take a** .... – I tried it on first.
9 Adverts often **make a** .... they can't keep.
10 The new fashions are **put on** .... by the door.

2 Complete the table with the verb phrases in exercise 1.

do	give	have
....	....	....
	....	

make	put	take
....	....	....
....		

3 Rewrite the sentences so that the second sentence has a similar meaning to the first one. Use the phrases in exercise 2.

1 They'll show the new products in the shop window.
   They'll .... in the shop window.
2 Their most loyal customers receive a gift every year.
   Every year, they .... to their most loyal customers.
3 They tested it before they started selling it.
   They tested it before they ....
4 They're looking into colours.
   They're .... into colours.
5 Something bad happened in that restaurant.
   I .... in that restaurant.
6 We bought something in the sales.
   We .... in the sales.
7 I got my money back for the tickets.
   They .... for the tickets.
8 She's putting her life in danger by driving fast.
   She's .... by driving fast.
9 She said that she would call every day.
   She .... to call every day.
10 Weather often affects sales figures.
   Weather .... on sales figures.

Vocabulary bank 7

Food texture

1 Read the text. Find twelve adjectives that describe the texture of food.

My favourite starter is vichyssoise. This is a cold soup made of leeks, potatoes and onions. It isn't lumpy because the vegetables are puréed to make it smooth. There are more vegetables than liquid, so the soup isn't runny and it's nice and creamy because it's made with cream.

I prefer meat to fish and there's nothing better than a big juicy steak that melts in your mouth – I hate them when they're chewy. Steaks sometimes come with salad, but I like them best with a plate of hot crunchy chips – they don't taste so good if the chips are oily.

My favourite dessert is a piece of chocolate brownie with thick chocolate sauce. If the brownie isn't fresh, it can be crumbly, which isn't so good. The best brownies are soft and moist and this dessert really is the best way to finish off a meal.

2 Match the adjectives in exercise 1 to definitions 1–12.

1 making a sound when you bite it
2 containing a lot of juice and good to eat
3 having more liquid than is usual
4 that easily breaks into very small pieces
5 a liquid that doesn't flow very easily
6 a mixture without any lumps
7 a liquid containing pieces that are solid
8 slightly wet
9 changing shape easily when pressed
10 containing cream so that it is thick and smooth
11 needing to be chewed a lot before it can be swallowed
12 containing a lot of oil

3 Work in pairs. Think of more food items for each of the adjectives in exercise 1 and write a sentence about them.

Mashed potato can be lumpy if you don't make it properly.

Ways of speaking

1 Read what the people say. Match phrases a–h to verbs 1–8.

a 'Goal!'

b 'No, it isn't! You're wrong!'

c 'We're bored! Are we there yet?'

d 'What a great idea!'

e 'Get out!'

f 'I miss him!'

g 'Shhh ... it's a secret.'

h 'I d-d-don't kn-n-now.'

1 argue ....
2 cheer ....
3 exclaim ....
4 shout ....
5 sigh ....
6 stammer ....
7 whine ....
8 whisper ....

2 Match the verbs in exercise 1 to definitions 1–8.

1 say in a loud voice
2 say very quietly so that other people cannot hear
3 say with difficulty, repeating sounds or words
4 say in an annoying, complaining voice
5 say loudly to show support
6 say while letting out a long deep breath
7 say suddenly and loudly
8 say angrily when you don't agree

3 SPEAKING Work in pairs. Think of another phrase for each of the verbs in exercise 1.

'Stop!' he shouted.

Gender-neutral job titles

1 Label the photos with the words below.

■ actress ■ fireman ■ headmaster ■ policewoman
■ postman ■ salesman ■ spokesman ■ sportswoman
■ stewardess

1 ....

2 ....

3 ....

4 ....

5 ....

6 ....

7 ....

8 ....

9 ....

2 Match the gender-neutral words below to the jobs in exercise 1.

■ athlete ■ flight attendant ■ fire fighter ■ head teacher
■ actor ■ police officer ■ postal worker ■ shop assistant
■ spokesperson

3 Complete the sentences with the correct form of the gender-neutral job titles in exercise 2.

1 .... are investigating the crime.
2 The .... forgot her lines during the play.
3 We asked the .... what time the plane would arrive.
4 The student was sent to see the ....
5 They interviewed the .... after she won the race.
6 A .... made a statement on behalf of the company.
7 We asked a .... the price of the phone.
8 .... rescued five people from the building.
9 I asked the .... if he had any letters for me.

Conflict

1 Read the text and find ten phrasal verbs related to conflict.

Aung San Suu Kyi was born in Myanmar in 1945, but she and her mother went to live in India when she was fifteen. She didn't return to her homeland until 1988, when her mother was very ill. At the time the people of Myanmar were taking on the country's ruler because they wanted political reforms. On her return, Ms Suu Kyi became their leader and together, they stepped up the campaign. Like Martin Luther King, Ms Suu Kyi encouraged her supporters to engage in a non-violent campaign. However, the authorities fought back hard and in the end, the army gained power. They held elections in 1990, which Ms Suu Kyi's party won. But the army refused to give in to public opinion and they put Ms Suu Kyi under house arrest. In 1999, she rejected the offer to visit her sick husband in the UK, because she thought the government might throw her out of Myanmar. Ms Suu Kyi was under house arrest for fifteen years, but she didn't back down on her ideas. People abroad stood up for her throughout her arrest and, eventually, the government eased off the restrictions. When new elections were held in 2010 Ms Suu Kyi's party won again, but this time, the army had to face up to her popularity. Ms Suu Kyi is now a free woman and she is finally able to participate in the politics of her country.

2 Match the phrasal verbs in exercise 1 to definitions 1–10.

1 to admit that you have been defeated
2 to attack somebody who has attacked you
3 to take back an opinion that people are strongly opposed to
4 to support or defend something
5 to accept and deal with something difficult
6 to force somebody to leave a place
7 to fight against somebody
8 to increase the amount of something
9 to take part in something
10 to become or make something less strong

3 Think of a conflict that you know about. Write sentences about it using the phrasal verbs in exercise 2.

Students are taking on the government over cuts in education.

Vocabulary bank 9

Technology

1 Choose the word that cannot be used with the verbs.

1 attach
   a a document   b a file   c a folder   d a session

2 click on
   a a button   b a computer   c an image   d a link

3 delete
   a an account   b a button   c a comment
   d an email

4 download
   a a film   b a game   c an image   d a router

5 install
   a a comment   b a firewall   c a program
   d software

6 log into
   a an account   b a mistake   c a router   d a website

7 log out of
   a a computer   b a game   c a message
   d a session

8 post
   a a comment   b a message   c a program
   d a photo

9 share
   a an article   b a firewall   c a photo   d a video

10 update
   a an app   b your profile   c a mistake
   d your status

11 upload
   a an account   b a picture   c a song   d a video

12 undo
   a an action   b a change   c a post   d a picture

2 Complete the text with the verbs in exercise 1.

The first thing I do every morning is turn on my computer and check my emails. I ¹................ the ones that I don't need to keep and reply to those that need dealing with. When people ask me for documents, I open a window, ²................ the file and ³................ the document to an email. When I've dealt with my emails, I ⁴................ my favourite social networking website to see what my friends are up to. I ⁵................ my status and then I look at my wall. I often ⁶................ comments on my friends' walls but I sometimes spell something wrong. When that happens, I ⁷................ the post and start again. Whenever I take photos, I ⁸................ them onto my profile and ⁹................ them with my friends. I'm quite security-conscious about using the internet, so I always ¹⁰................ the site before I start work. I ¹¹................ quite a lot of games and videos, so last year, I decided to ¹²................ a better firewall on my computer.

3 SPEAKING Work in pairs. Which websites do you use most often? How do you use them?

I use a social networking site to chat with my friends. I log in to the site every morning ...

Poetry

1 Match the words below to definitions 1–12.

■ imagery ■ metaphor ■ personification ■ poem ■ prose
■ rhyme ■ rhythm ■ simile ■ stanza ■ symbol ■ theme
■ verse

1 a piece of writing arranged in short lines
2 a group of lines that form a unit of a poem
3 a regular repeated pattern of sound
4 a word that has the same sound as another
5 the subject of a piece of writing
6 an object that represents something
7 the practice of giving human qualities to an animal, object or thing
8 a phrase used in an imaginative way to show that one thing has the same qualities as another
9 a phrase that compares one thing to another using the words 'like' or 'as'.
10 language that produces pictures in the minds of the person reading
11 writing arranged in lines that have a definite rhythm and often finish with the same sound
12 ordinary language used in speech or writing

2 Complete the text with the correct form of the words in exercise 1.

John Keats is one of the most famous figures in English literature. Unlike authors like Charles Dickens whose major works were in ¹................ , Keats was a poet and so he wrote in ²................ . The ³................ To Autumn is probably one of his greatest works. It has three ⁴................ of eleven lines and each line has a regular ⁵................ . The ⁶................ scheme is variable, although the final words of the first and third lines and the second and fourth lines always have the same sound.
   The ⁷................ of To Autumn is the end of life and Keats uses the season of winter as a ⁸................ for death itself. He uses ⁹................ in nearly every line to fill the reader's mind with pictures of the four seasons. The most obvious example is the ¹⁰................ of autumn as a goddess who helps the trees grow and fills them with fruit. There are numerous ¹¹................ , for example the mention of lambs in spring to represent life, and at the end of the second verse, Keats uses a ¹²................ to compare autumn to a kind of farm labourer.

3 Match the words in exercise 1 to examples 1–6.

1 Her home was a prison.
2 The moon shone like a bright light.
3 The guitar was playing its own tune.
4 Tiger, tiger, burning bright
   In the forests of the night.
5 It was a bright, cold day in April and the clocks were striking thirteen.
6 A black bird flew above my head.

The arts

1 Complete the table with the people below.

▨ an actor ▨ an artist / a painter ▨ a biographer
▨ a composer ▨ a designer ▨ a musician ▨ a novelist
▨ a playwright ▨ a poet ▨ a scriptwriter ▨ a sculptor
▨ a singer

Literature	
1	writes biographies.
2	writes novels / fiction.
3	writes plays / comedies / tragedies.
4	writes poems / poetry.
5	writes scripts for films.
Performing arts	
6	stars / has a role in a film / play.
7	composes / writes music.
8	plays an instrument.
	gives a performance / a recital.
9	performs / sings a song / an aria.
Visual arts	
10	paints a picture / a painting / a portrait.
	draws / does a sketch.
11	creates / does a sculpture.
	sculpts a work.
	carves objects out of wood / stone.
	shapes figures out of clay.
12	designs dresses / furniture / posters.

2 Complete the headlines with the activities in exercise 1. Sometimes more than one answer is possible.

1 **Actor** .... **in London's West End**

2 **Poet** .... **for Olympic Games**

3 **Composer** .... **for film soundtrack**

4 *Musician* .... *in underground*

5 **Playwright** .... **about plane crash**

6 **Painter** .... **of Queen**

7 **Biographer** .... **of famous actor**

8 **Sculptor** .... **out of ice**

9 **Scriptwriter** .... **for *Avatar* sequel**

10 **Designer** .... **for millionaire's wife**

11 **Novelist** .... **set on planet Mars**

12 **Singer** .... **on balcony of hotel**

3 SPEAKING Work in pairs. Think of examples for the people in exercise 1. Tell a partner.

Alfred Ainger was a famous English biographer.

Organizing a festival

1 Match the verbs in A to the words in B to make collocations related to organizing a festival. Then match the collocations to the definitions.

A	B
attend	place
find	a venue
run	a performance
take	a stall
appeal	an event
hold	a catering service
provide	volunteers
recruit	to an audience
appear	on stage
get	security
headline	a good vantage point
manage	a festival

1 arrange a public occasion
2 search for a place to hold an event
3 perform in front of people
4 be the main performer at an event
5 interest people
6 find a place where you can see everything
7 carry out procedures that keep people safe
8 find people to do unpaid work
9 sell things from a table or a small shop
10 be present at a play or a concert
11 happen
12 sell food and drinks at an event

2 Complete the text with the collocations in exercise 1.

The organizers of a music festival have a lot to think about before they [1] .... First of all, they have to fix the date when they want the festival to [2] .... Then they have to [3] .... that suits the season they have chosen: indoor for the winter, outdoor for the summer. Next, they have to speak to the bands they want to [4] .... They need to book groups who [5] .... for the festival to be a success, but the big acts who [6] .... can sometimes be expensive. They also need to take into consideration how many people will [7] .... of the bands. In a crowd, it can be impossible to [8] .... to see the stage. In addition, they may need to contract a company to [9] ...., so that people do not enter without a ticket. They will need to contract another company to [10] .... with food and refreshments for the ticket holders. A cheaper option is to [11] .... from the organizers' families and friends. These people can [12] .... that offers sandwiches and soft drinks.

3 SPEAKING Work in pairs. Tell a partner about a festival that is held in your city or country.

I attended the performance of the Stone Roses in Heaton Park last month.

OXFORD
UNIVERSITY PRESS

Great Clarendon Street, Oxford, OX2 6DP, United Kingdom

Oxford University Press is a department of the University of Oxford.
It furthers the University's objective of excellence in research, scholarship,
and education by publishing worldwide. Oxford is a registered trade
mark of Oxford University Press in the UK and in certain other countries

© Oxford University Press 2013

The moral rights of the author have been asserted

First published in 2013

2019

18

ISBN: 978 0 19 401108 2

Printed in China

This book is printed on paper from certified and well-managed sources

ACKNOWLEDGEMENTS

The authors and the publisher would like to thank: Kath Stannett, Bess Bradfield, Jane
Hudson and Sarah Philpot for the material they contributed to this book.

*The authors and the publisher would also like to thank the many teachers who contributed
to the development of the course by commenting on the manuscript, taking part in lesson
observations, focus groups and online questionnaires.*

*The authors and the publisher are grateful to those who have given permission to reproduce
the following extracts and adaptations of copyright material:* p.88 Extract from *A Walk
in the Woods* by Bill Bryson, published by Doubleday. Reprinted by permission of
The Random House Group Limited and Bill Bryson. pp.14, 26, 40, 52, 66, 78, 92,
104, 118, 130 Entries taken from *Oxford Wordpower Dictionary 4th Edition*. © Oxford
University Press 2012. Reproduced by permission.

The publisher would like to thank the following for their permission to reproduce photographs:
Alamy Images pp.9 (Senior man/Discovod), 9 (Man with guitar/Golden Pixels LLC),
11 (Woman in gothic clothes/Sergey Orlov), 21 (London/Carolyn Clarke), 23 (Route
66 signs/Ruben Kincaid), 28 (kitchen/Chris Rose/PropertyStock), 30 (Chocolate/
Westend61 GmbH), 31 (Girl holding money/Corbis Bridge), 33 (Dance class/ZUMA
Wire Service), 34 (Woman running/Andres Rodriguez), 34 (Girls playing football/
moodboard), 35 (Teen boys talking/Buzzshotz), 36 (Obese teenagers/Aurora
Photos), 45 (The Critical Mass Bicycle Ride/Valerie Armstrong), 45 (supermarket/
Montgomery Martin), 46 (Student protest/Jim West), 46 (Student protest/aberCPC),
47 (Recycling Center sign/Ilene MacDonald), 50 (Well pumping water/Jonathan
Porter), 62 (Waitress/Golden Pixels LLC), 62 (Teenager driving vespa/Wave Royalty
Free/Design Pics Inc.), 63 (Ballot box/Rob Wilkinson), 64 (Teens/britstock images
ltd), 68 (Graffiti inspired car billboard/Richard Levine), 70 (Fairtrade/Jack Sullivan),
70 (Fairtrade cotton farmer/Simon Rawles), 70 (Fair trade chocolate/BSIP SA),
73 (Indoor market/Chris Howes/Wild Places Photography), 73 (Record shop/Alex
Segre), 74 (Christmas tree in Trafalgar Square/Justin Kase z12z), 74 (Halloween
party/MBI), 74 (Valentine's Day window display/Jeffrey Blackler), 80 (airport/MJ
Photography), 80 (souvenir shop/Andy Lane), 81 (teenagers/Bubbles Photolibrary),
81 (magazine rack/Realimage), 82 (Hand in water/Blackout Concepts), 82 (Cook
tasting food/Larry Lilac), 86 (Reading braille/Image Source), 87 (annoyed woman/
Piotr Marcinski), 97 (milking cows/Greenshoots Communications), 98 (Reuters
headquarters/Kevin Foy), 98 (McDonald's restaurant/Mark Richardson),
109 (Woman looking at Facebook website/CJG - Technology), 112 (Mobile phone/
Laurent Davoust), 112 (Digital camera/Helen Sessions), 112 (Apple iPod Nano/
Stefan Sollfors), 112 (Frustrated woman with computer manual/Corbis Flirt),
121 (Mozart chocolates/Sabine Lubenow), 124 (Tree illustration/John Takai),
125 (Students painting/Blend Images), 136 (Doctor with patient/Tetra Images),
137 (Job centre queue/Geoffrey Robinson), 140 (Chocolate brownies/MBI),
141 (Businessman giving a speech/Image Source), 141 (Police officer/Robert
Convery), 141 (Postman/John Angerson); Corbis pp.5 (Maori activist Tame Iti/
George Steinmetz), 6 (African leopard/Tom Brakefield), 6 (Polar bear/Paul Souders),
6 (Zebras at waterhole/Steve & Ann Toon/Robert Harding World Imagery), 7 (Honey
bee/Nigel Cattlin/Visuals Unlimited), 10 (Hispanic man with scooter/Hill Street
Studios/Blend Images), 10 (British Band The Who/Tony Frank/Sygma), 10 (Hippie
woman/Henry Diltz), 11 (Sex Pistols in concert/Neal Preston), 18 (first transatlantic
rowboat crossing/Philippe Eranian/Sygma), 20 (canoeing/High Sitton), 22 (planning
Route 66/Douglas Kirkland), 22 (Grand Canyon/Momatiuk-Eastcott), 23 (Grand
Canyon railroad/Tom Bean), 23 (Big Blue Whale on Route 66/Carol M. Highsmith),
24 (Mumbai rail station/Punit Paranjpe/Reuters), 28 (capsule hotel/Roger
Ressmeyer), 37 (Teen eating unhealthy food/Andy Richter/Aurora Photos), 38 (rock
climbing/Daniel Martinez/Somos Images), 42 (Solomon Island Cove/Stephen
Frink), 44 (Group picking up litter/Tim Pannell), 46 (Student rally/Jesse A.

Wanskasmith/First Light), 47 (Basketball court/Roy Morsch), 47 (Girl studying/
Image Source), 49 (boy at well/Annie Griffiths Belt), 54 (Gardening/Mika),
56 (Teenagers spraying graffiti/Nancy Honey/cultura), 62 (Teenage girl in car/Jose
Luis Pelaez Inc/Blend Images), 63 (Graduates/Laurence Mouton/PhotoAlto),
63 (Wedding couple/VStock LLC/Tetra Images), 70 (Boy carrying bananas/Bob Krist),
70 (Cocoa harvesting/Ann Johansson), 82 (Boy with binoculars/David Deas/DK
Stock), 83 (Listening to conch shell/Michele Constantini/PhotoAlto), 87 (Woman
using mobile phone in cinema/Daniel Koebe), 88 (grizzly bear/Paul Souders),
96 (Goat/PhotoAlto), 100 (Rosa Parks/Steve Schapiro), 100 (Martin Luther King Jr./
Bettmann), 101 (Rosa Parks riding the bus/Bettmann), 101 (Students from Little
Rock, Arkansas/Bettmann), 107 (Athens Touch Museum/John Kolesidis/Reuters),
120 (Pablo Picasso/Bettmann), 121 (Tourist souvenirs/Gaetan Bally/Keystone),
128 (Teenager at Hay-On-Wye Book Festival/Andrew Fox), 133 (costumes at Comic-
Con/Sandy Huffaker), 134 (Teen boy/Ocean), 137 (Aerial view of Portland/Craig
Tuttle/Design Pics), 137 (Man begging for money/Vstock LLC/Tetra Images),
137 (Refugees/Bettmann), 137 (Smoke stacks/Radius Images), 137 (Kilauea Volcano
erupting/Jim Sugar), 137 (Masai woman receiving vaccination/Hugh Sitton),
137 (Earthquake damage/Michael S. Yamashita), 137 (Floods/Gideon Mendel),
140 (Vichyssoise/Riou/SoFood), 140 (Grilled T-bone steak/Hall/photocuisine),
141 (Fire chief/Gaetano), 142 (John Keats/Lebrecht Music & Arts); Getty Images
pp.7 (Marmalade hoverfly/Visuals Unlimited, Inc./Robert Pickett), 7 (Busy street/
Lonely Planet), 8 (Exhausted jogger/PM Images), 9 (Woman walking in park/Paul
Piebinga), 10 (Hippies/Alija), 11 (Teen boy with mohawk/Steve West), 13 (Party/
Simon Winnall), 17 (rubbish at Everest base camp/Mary Plage/Oxford Scientific),
20 (tourists in the rain/Tim Hall/Photodisc), 24 (Alice Springs/Peter Walton
Photography/Photolibrary), 24 (neon diner/Pete Turner), 24 (hiking/Andrew
Geiger/Stockbyte), 28 (swimming pool/Jim Jurica/Vetta), 28 (yellow minimalist
kitchen/tulcarion/E+), 30 (Friends at the beach/Bounce), 31 (Happy woman in
convertible car/Digital Vision), 32 (classroom/Stacey Westott/Chicago Tribune/
MCT), 32 (meditating classroom/Kristian Sekulic/the Agency Collection),
34 (Woman practising tae kwon do/Hans Huber), 34 (Women playing volleyball/
Jean Luc Morales), 38 (tennis player/David Spurdens/www.ExtremeSportsPhoto.
com/Fuse), 48 (Crossing the race finish line/Yellow Dog Productions), 50 (Polar bear
crossing city street/Thomas Jackson), 68 (Times Square, New York/Photography by
Steve Kelley aka "mudpig"), 69 (Women looking at digital camera/PhotoAlto/James
Hardy), 71 (Ethical fashion show/Thomas Samson/Gamma-Rapho via Getty
Images), 72 (Teenagers shopping at mall/John Giustina), 73 (Woman looking at
vinyl records/Betsie Van Der Meer), 80 (Italian market/Sri Maiava Rusden/Digital
Vision), 82 (Man with blue cheese/Donna Day/Photodisc), 84 (Woman with guide
dog/altrendo images), 85 (Dolphins/David Olsen), 95 (Cartoonist Matt Groening
draws Bart Simpson/Robyn Beck/AFP), 96 (Beatrice Biira/David Livingston),
108 (Girl on sofa with floating globe of faces/John Lund), 110 (Two senior women/
David Sacks), 114 (Cyberspace illustration/Nanette Hoogslag), 121 (Wolfgang a.
Mozart/Time & Life Pictures), 124 (Doodle poodle/CSA/B&W Archive Collection),
127 (Portico Quartet perform on stage/C Brandon/Redferns via Getty Images),
133 (characters at Comic Con 2012/John Lamparski/WireImage), 134 (Happy teen/
Nathan Blaney), 134 (Teen boy wearing scarf/Troy Aossey), 134 (Woman with
plaited hair/Radius Images), 134 (Portrait of teenage girl/PT Images), 134 (Gothic
punk/Pascal Genest/Vetta), 134 (Teenage girl/Image Source), 134 (Smiling teen boy/
Siri Stafford), 134 (Teen girl portrait/Andreas Stamm), 137 (Polar bear/Daisy
Gilardini), 139 (Times Square, New York/Hisham Ibrahim), 141 (Hurdler/Milk &
Honey Creative); Guludo Beach Lodge p.16 (Amy Carter-James), p.17 (village
football team); iStockphoto pp.4 (Woman from Long Neck Padaung Tribe/Bartosz
Hadyniak), 9 (Italian man/Hilary Brodey), 36 (US flag/MistikaS), 51 (Blank
ringbinder/kyoshino), 58 (Man with writing on hands/Stephanie Phillips),
59 (Woman with long nose/Michele Piacquadio), 60 (Sorry note/Peter Burnett),
111 (Youth social network/Robert Churchill/Photomorphic), 112 (Samsung Galaxy
tablet/mozcann), 114 (Futuristic world map touchscreen/alexander kirch/
audioundwerbung), 124 (Stick figure skateboarding/Toby Bridson), 124 (Doodles
flower collection/Elena Kalistratova), 124 (Frame/Stacey Walker), 134 (Cheerful
student/Sean Locke), 141 (Victorian actors/Nuno Silva); Kobal Collection
p.123 (*Singing in the Rain*/MGM/Hubbell, Eddie); Marilyn Terrell p.122 (Matt Harding
dancing on USS Abraham Lincoln); One Week Job Productions Inc./Sean Aiken
pp.94 (dairy farming), 95 (cat tail picking); Oxford University Press pp.32 (Teacher
with students/AFLO RF), 34 (Playing tennis/Corbis), 70 (Coffee beans/Photodisc),
112 (Flat screen television/Tony Cordoza), 134 (Smiling girl/Photodisc), 134 (Man
with dreadlocks/Ciaran Griffin/Stockbyte), 135 (Maps/Ryan McVay/Photodisc),
137 (Lumber/Corbis), 141 (Flight attendant/Digital Vision), 141 (Supermarket/
Image Source); Rex Features pp.5 (Calabar woman/Justin Sutcliffe), 42 (Puil Island,
Carteret Atoll, Papua New Guinea/Sutton-Hibbert), 56 (Teenagers wearing hoodies/
John Powell), 57 (Alexander Rose/Albanpix Ltd), 61 (teacher & student/Monkey
Business Images), 73 (Louis Vuitton store), 73 (Roberto Cavalli clothes range at
H&M/Ray Tang), 73 (iTunes store), 84 (Police sniffer dog/Kevin Foy), 86 (Woman
signing/Garo/Phanie), 89 (Bill Bryson/Mike Lawn), 98 (Sony walkman cassette
player), 98 (Walt Disney/Everett Collection), 123 (Diversity dance group/Steven
Peskett), 126 (Sundance Film Festival/Rob Crandall), 141 (Headteacher Sir Michael
Wilshaw/Susannah Ireland); Robert A. Cantor p.122 (Matt Harding dancing at the
United States Capitol); Shutterstock pp.28 (inside tent/Jens Ottoson), 55 (Exercising
at gym/Aleksandr Markin), 88 (wood/Photoroller), 127 (wellies/Mojito.mak(dog)
gmail(dot)com); SuperStock pp.11 (gothic friends/Image Source), 19 (polar
explorer/age fotostock), 20 (man relaxing/Onoky), 84 (Avalanche dog/Juniors),
137 (Cracked mud/Radius).

Illustration by: Mark Duffin p.134.

Cover by: Nikali Larin/Image Zoo/Alamy.

*Although every effort has been made to trace and contact copyright holders before
publication, this has not been possible in some cases. We apologise for any apparent
infringement of copyright and, if notified, the publisher will be pleased to rectify any errors
or omissions at the earliest possible opportunity.*